THE

Who He Is

HOLY

What He Does

SPIRIT

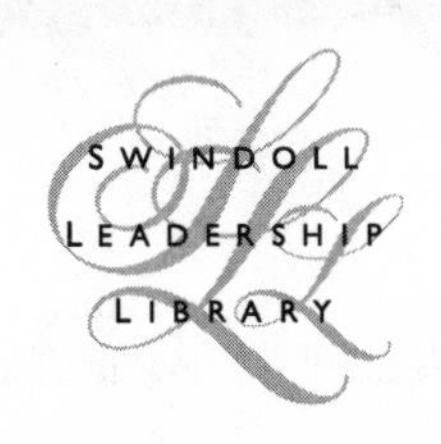

THE HOLY SPIRIT

WHO HE IS

WHAT HE DOES

ROBERT GROMACKI

WORD PUBLISHING
NASHVILLE
A Thomas Nelson Company

THE HOLY SPIRIT
Swindoll Leadership Library

Published by Word Publishing, a unit of Thomas Nelson, Inc.,
P. O. Box 141000, Nashville, Tennessee 37214.

Published in association with Dallas Theological Seminary (DTS):
General Editor: Charles R. Swindoll
Managing Editor: Roy B. Zuck

Library of Congress Cataloging in Publication Data:

Gromacki, Robert Glenn
The holy spirit / by Robert G. Gromacki.
p. cm.
Includes bibliographical references and indexes.

ISBN 0-8499-1370-5

1. Holy Spirit. I. Title.

BT121.2.G75 1999 98-51482
231'.3–dc21 CIP

Printed in the United States of America
99 00 01 02 03 04 05 06 BVG 9 8 7 6 5 4 3 2 1

To

my personal family

Gloria—my faithful and loving wife
Gary and Gail—our children
Kim and David—their spouses
Julie, Sarah, Gavin,
Jenna, Allison, and Jesse—our grandchildren

and to
my church family at
Grace Community Baptist Church,
Washington Court House, Ohio

with my love and gratitude for
allowing me to be a leader in your lives

CONTENTS

FOREWORD

One of my homiletics professors at Dallas Seminary was fond of saying, "When there's a mist in the pulpit, there's fog in the pews!" There remains a great deal of fog in the church today concerning the person and work of the Holy Spirit. Dr. Robert Gromacki cuts through that fog.

Writing in his usual clear and concise style, Gromacki lays out the major areas of study concerning the third person of the Godhead. He grounds the reader theologically, before addressing many of the practical issues. This is not dry textbook reading, however. Far from it. Stories and illustrations are sprinkled throughout, providing insight to keep the book moving along at a brisk pace.

Gromacki is eminently qualified to tackle this subject. He has been deeply engaged in local church ministry for over forty years. If that alone weren't enough, he has also served as professor of Bible and Greek at Cedarville College, Cedarville, Ohio, for forty years as well. He has faced the tough questions from inquiring church members and students who are wrestling with issues in the realm of pneumatology, the doctrine of the Holy Spirit.

By the end of this work you will be asking yourself, "Do I live my life in the power of the Holy Spirit?" Before that, you will learn the unique role the Spirit plays in the Trinity. You will find answers to current controversies. You will come face to face with three of the controversial issues surrounding the Spirit—tongues, prophecy, and healing. Because of the resourceful nature of this volume, you will come back to it again and again as you approach new areas of study regarding the Holy Spirit.

The Holy Spirit will define and refine your understanding. Clear definitions and penetrating illustrations will help you see and feel what the Holy Spirit is doing today.

Best of all, the author derives all his conclusions straight from the Scriptures. There's no fluff here. This book will move frequently from your shelf to your study desk. It's a reference tool we're pleased to add to this series. Thank you, Dr. Gromacki, for helping us understand the Holy Spirit, the One who guided your ministry for many years.

So, if you've wandered about in heavy fog lately trying to understand the role of the Holy Spirit, there's a clearing up ahead. Let Robert Gromacki lead the way!

—CHARLES R. SWINDOLL
General Editor

PREFACE

When Charles Swindoll asked me to participate in the Swindoll Leadership Library by contributing a volume on the Holy Spirit, I responded with both joy and fear—joy that I had even been asked and a fearful concern over my ability to complete the task.

After much prayer and thought I accepted the challenge. Since that early correspondence I have prayed and studied daily over this subject. In my forty years of ministry, I have preached and taught many times on topics relating to the doctrine of the Holy Spirit. As a professor of Bible and Greek at Cedarville College for forty years, I interacted often with students on this subject. As a pulpit supply, interim pastor, and recent pastor of Grace Community Baptist Church, Washington Court House, Ohio, for ten years, I have expounded the Scriptures that show the relationship of the Holy Spirit to our daily lives.

In many ways my experiences had prepared me to research and write this book. But yet I knew that this manuscript would be different. For example, to write on the fruit of the Spirit (Gal. 5:22–23), I had to ask these questions: Is the Holy Spirit producing these spiritual qualities in my life? Am I a loving person, a believer marked by joy, peace, longsuffering, gentleness, goodness, faith, meekness, and self-control?

On similar biblical topics I had to probe my soul. Am I walking in the

Spirit (Gal. 5:16)? Do I quench the Spirit (1 Thess. 5:19)? Am I filled with the Spirit (Eph. 5:18)? Do I pray in the Spirit (Eph. 6:18)? Am I being led by the Spirit (Rom. 8:14)? Am I a spiritual Christian, being taught through the Word of God by the indwelling Holy Spirit (1 Cor. 2:10–16)? Do I minister in my own strength or by the enabling of the Spirit (2:4)?

These questions had to move from the yesterdays to the todays and into the tomorrows of my life. Was I filled with the Spirit? Am I now filled? Do I want to be filled tomorrow?

I challenge you to examine your heart and mind as you read this book. As you learn about the biblical teaching on the Holy Spirit, may you also live these truths. Please join me in our spiritual pilgrimage through the pages of Scripture. May we glorify God the Father through our Lord Jesus Christ in the power of the Holy Spirit.

Special thanks are extended to Charles Swindoll, Roy B. Zuck, and the Word Publishing team for their encouragement and assistance throughout this project. I count it a privilege and honor to be a part of the team that put together this book series for Christian leaders.

With much love and gratitude I express my appreciation to my wife, Gloria. She deciphered my handwriting and typed the manuscript. She is my faithful companion and helpmeet. Together we have served the Lord for over forty years. I thank Him for giving her to me.

INTRODUCTION

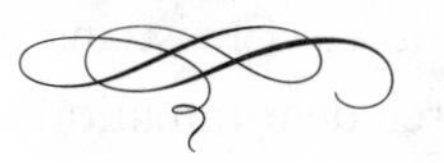

What in the world is happening? People are barking like dogs, roaring like lions, laughing uncontrollably, and slithering out of their chairs onto the floor. Others are touched on their heads and collapse in a faint, claiming they have been slain in the Spirit. The so-called Toronto and Pensacola revivals have produced curious notoriety among the secular media and have caused controversy within evangelicalism, both inside and outside the Pentecostal-charismatic camp. Books, articles, and videos either promote or criticize these strange phenomena. Are such dramatic displays of human behavior a sign of the times? Is this movement from God? Is this normal Spirit-filled Christianity? Arguments abound on both sides of the issue. How can we tell whether these unusual emotional and physical outbursts are genuine or false?

In this book we will investigate the Holy Scriptures to explore the ministry of the Holy Spirit. The Bible alone must be the authoritative basis of our faith and practice. Experiences must be analyzed and judged in the light of the Scriptures. Human experiences must neither set aside the teaching of the Word of God nor be imposed on the Word. Only from a proper understanding of pneumatology (the biblical doctrine of the person and ministry of the Holy Spirit) can we properly apply the truth to our lives. Genuine truth will always issue in correct testimony, but testimony alone could either circumvent or contradict divine truth. We must always be in submission to the inspired, inerrant, infallible Word of God. Our doctrinal beliefs and actions must bow to the authority of divinely revealed truth, not to the nonbiblical teaching of influential preachers nor to the alleged experiences of friends or celebrities.

Another area of confusion to Christians, especially to new converts, is the presence of many church denominations. Why are there so many different churches, denominations, and parachurch organizations? Should there not be only one? Jesus Christ predicted that He would build His church (Matt. 16:18), a singular entity, but yet in most cities of our nation there are churches of several denominations. The apostle Paul claimed that there is only one body, the true church (1 Cor. 12:13; Eph. 4:4). He challenged believers "to keep the unity of the Spirit in the bond of peace" (4:3), adding that there is only one body and only one Spirit (4:4). And yet a superficial observation of current Christendom seems to reveal many bodies and many spirits, at least many doctrines of the Holy Spirit. We even hear terms such as the Black church, the Hispanic church, the White church, and the Integrated church. Yet the Bible speaks of the body of Christ, the one spiritual organism that transcends race, time, and ecclesiastical distinctions.

To many people the mere mention of the Holy Spirit creates an aura of mystery. The old English designation, the Holy Ghost, which still remains within evangelical jargon, actually exacerbates the frustration of some believers. How do you get to know the Holy Ghost? Unfortunately the term *ghost* usually introduces thoughts of Casper the friendly ghost, scary spirits that permeate haunted houses, or the little "beggars" who knock on your door at Halloween, dressed in costumes. What do children in Sunday school classes imagine or think when they first hear about the Holy Ghost?

We evangelicals firmly believe in trinitarian monotheism, that is, one God existing eternally in three persons. We believe that God the Father, God the Son, and God the Holy Spirit are three distinct divine persons and yet we believe that they are coequally divine. We believe that there is an intrapersonal oneness of the three persons within the one divine being. However, we relate more easily to the Father and to the Son, probably because we see those same terms in our human family relationships. The designation the Holy Spirit, however, poses a problem. In this volume we will seek to understand the personhood of the Holy Spirit as declared in the Scriptures. He is real, a divine person whom we can know, relate to, and worship.

The church age has often been called the age of the Holy Spirit. The New Testament has far more explicit references to the person and ministry of the Holy Spirit than does the Old Testament. Over 250 New Testament passages include a clear reference to the Holy Spirit. These passages demonstrate that the Holy Spirit plays a vital part in the life of the true church, the spiritual body, of which Jesus Christ is the living Head. These passages reveal that Christ works in the life of each believer through the enabling of the Holy Spirit. The Holy Spirit is thus indispensable to the mission of the true church and to the purpose of each Christian. This book explores the work of the Spirit. If we are not rightly related to the Holy Spirit, then we are not experiencing the abundant life Jesus promised (John 10:10).

When does a genuine believer receive the indwelling ministry of the Holy Spirit? At conversion or in a subsequent experience? How do we know the Holy Spirit really lives in us? Can we lose the Holy Spirit? Does He leave us when we sin? Within Christendom much confusion exists over these areas. Churches have split and new denominations have been manufactured over the difficult opinions championed by various leaders. This book examines the biblical teaching on the indwelling and infilling ministries of the Holy Spirit.

The Bible classifies people in different categories. We are either saved or unredeemed. We are either lost or found. We are either in Adam or in Christ. We are either going to heaven or to hell. Most people are mainly concerned with these two major options, and rightly so. Eternal life or eternal condemnation are vital life choices. Paul, however, subdivided believers into two groups—"spiritual believers" and "carnal" believers (1 Cor. 2:14–3:4). Christians can choose to be yielded to the Holy Spirit or to be yielded to their sinful disposition. How can believers have victory over sin? How can believers grow into Christlikeness? This topic touches all of us. In this volume we will study those passages that can help us have a more effective Christian life, marked by the fruit of the Holy Spirit (Gal. 5:22–23).

The belief systems and practices of eastern religions and philosophies have penetrated our culture and churches. Transcendental meditation, the recitation of mantras, yoga, and spirit-channeling are popular in the western world, and have been made palatable to nominal churchgoers. In addition, there is a fascination with dreams, visions, and contacts with extraterrestrial beings. This attraction to metaphysical spirituality has provided fertile ground for attempts at tongues-speaking, prophesying, and speaking in so-called "words of wisdom." The twentieth century has witnessed three distinct movements wherein speaking in tongues, miracles, healings, and prophetic pronouncements have been alleged. Should Christians speak in tongues today? Should believers expect to be healed at all times? Is God revealing truths beyond the contents of the inspired sixty-six books? This volume also explores the gifts of the Holy Spirit mentioned in the Bible.

The first part of this book (chapters 1–3) looks at the personhood of the Holy Spirit, His deity, and symbols used to describe Him—to find out who He is. Then chapters 4–8 discuss the ministry of the Holy Spirit in the Old Testament era, in guiding the authors of Scripture, in the Gospel period, in the life of Jesus Christ, and in the Book of Acts. This will help us see what He did in the lives of biblical people and to relate those activities to our own experiences.

Chapters 9–13 focus on the work of the Holy Spirit in believers at the point of their conversion, including His various ministries such as indwelling, baptizing, and filling. We will perceive how He effects spirituality within us. We will look at the gifts of the Holy Spirit listed in the Word to help us ascertain our own personal gifts.

Chapter 14 examines Scriptures that set forth the future ministry of the Holy Spirit at the Rapture, during the Tribulation, and in the Millennium.

It is my hope and prayer that we will glorify God by growing into Christlikeness through the power of the Holy Spirit in us. May you read this book and the relevant Scriptures in constant dependence on the teaching ministry of the Holy Spirit.

CHAPTER ONE

The Personality of the Holy Spirit

Who or what is the Holy Spirit? Some view Him as the personification of holy power in the same sense as they view Satan as the personification of evil power. In both cases the Holy Spirit and Satan are not seen as personal beings. Others see the Spirit as the energy of God, an impersonal power or influence God uses to activate His will in the universe.

The influence of eastern religions and their belief in pantheism (the view that God is all and all is God) was seen in the Star Wars movie trilogy. The command to "feel the force" meant that Luke Skywalker was to sense his oneness with the eternal energy that permeates the universe and all of life. That energy, that sense of oneness with the divine, could be construed as a manifestation of the spirit that activates life.

The erroneous doctrine of modalism teaches that God is one being, manifesting Himself in three modes: the Father, the Son, and the Holy Spirit. This position denies the eternal existence of three separate persons within the one divine being. In monotheism which rejects the teaching of Trinitarianism, the Holy Spirit is seen as merely a mode or manifestation of God. Its advocates often use the illustration of water and its three form of liquid, vapor, and ice. However, water cannot *at the same time* be liquid, vapor, and ice and change from one form to the other. Furthermore

God does not exist sometimes as the Father, sometimes as the Son, and other times as the Holy Spirit. Nor does the Father change into the Son or the Son into the Spirit.

Unitarian monotheism, on the other hand, believes in one divine Being and in one eternal person, namely, God the Father. In that view, Jesus Christ is seen merely as a man with a strong God-consciousness, and the Holy Spirit is reduced to a title for God's activity in the world. The unitarian approach thus denies the personality of the Holy Spirit.

Evangelicals believe in Trinitarian monotheism. We believe in one God, eternally existing or subsisting in three persons, God the Father, God the Son, and God the Holy Spirit. We believe in the oneness of the three persons within the one divine Being. We also affirm that the Father is not the Son or the Spirit, that the Son is not the Father or the Spirit, and that the Spirit is not the Father or the Son. We affirm eternal and distinct personhood of the Father, the Son, and the Holy Spirit.

Sinclair Ferguson correctly observed, "For while his work has been recognized, the Spirit himself remains to many Christians an anonymous, faceless aspect of the divine being."[1] Some theologians have dubbed the Holy Spirit as the forgotten person or the unknown person of the Godhead. However, the Holy Spirit is a real, divine person, and we should desire to know Him better.

WHAT THE HOLY SPIRIT IS NOT

The Holy Spirit Is Not Like the Spirit of Man

In a Bible class at the church where I pastor, a perceptive student asked me whether the Holy Spirit was like the spirit which is within human beings. God, of course, formed the body of Adam from the dust of the earth, breathed into man the breath of life, and he became a living being (Gen. 2:7). Each person is thus a physical-psychical being. He is both material and immaterial. Christ distinguished between the body and the soul of man (Matt. 10:28). Paul spoke of people consisting of spirit, soul, and body (1 Thess. 5:23). In this life, the immaterial self is inseparably related to the material body; what affects one affects the other.

At death, the spirit-self separates from the lifeless body. The genuine believer goes to be with Christ, and the unsaved person goes to Hades to await the final judgment.

The Spirit of God, though, is not like the spirit of a person. Paul made this distinction: "For what man knows the things of a man except the spirit of the man which is in him? Even so no one knows the things of God except the Spirit of God" (1 Cor. 2:11). The words "which is in him," that is, in a person, are crucial. However, the same words "which is in him" are not repeated for the Spirit of God because the Holy Spirit is not *in* God. The Spirit knows the things of God because He is God. The Father, the Son, and the Holy Spirit all know the things of God because they are coequally God.

Besides being identified as the Spirit of God, the Holy Spirit is also identified as the Spirit of Christ (Rom. 8:9). This relationship is not the same as my saying "the spirit of Bob Gromacki." As a human, I am a spirit-being, made in the image of God, dwelling in a material body. Although God the Son took to Himself a human nature through the Incarnation, the Holy Spirit does not sustain the same relationship to Jesus Christ as my spirit sustains to me. While the Holy Spirit and Jesus Christ are two separate persons, my spirit and I are not.

The Holy Spirit Is Not a Physical Being

Jesus Christ taught that God is spirit in essence (John 4:24). Likewise, Paul affirmed that God is both immortal and invisible (1 Tim. 1:17). The very name of the Holy Spirit shows His immaterialistic nature. He is spirit, not corporeal. He has no shape or form.

The Old Testament records theophanies, the appearances of God in human form, and Christophanies, the appearances of the preincarnate Son in human form. God used these appearances to reveal Himself and His will to humans in ways they would understand. However, God does not have physical, human parts such as eyes, ears, or hands. Such wording was a means of the infinite God communicating with finite humankind.

Animals are creatures with a physical life. They act from created instinct, and when they die, their existence ends.

Humans are psychical-physical creatures, made in the image of God.

When a human dies, the spirit separates from the body. The person lives on because the life principle is centered in his or her spirit.

Angels are spirit beings who occupy limited space and can materialize themselves, often in human form. The angels never experience death as humans or animals do.

The Holy Spirit, however, is a spirit, a personal, eternal being. He is everywhere present; He has no physical properties.

The Holy Spirit Is Not a Thing

The designation "the Holy Spirit" translates the Greek *to hagion pneuma.* The word *pneuma* (usually translated "spirit" or "wind") is a grammatically neuter noun.

In Greek, nouns, pronouns, adjectives, and articles are either masculine, feminine, or neuter. These three groupings have nothing to do with personality or sexuality. For example, the Greek word for "house" is *oikos,* masculine in gender. All its modifiers are therefore masculine. However, since the house is a thing, an adjustment in translation is necessary to convey this fact. For example; if I say, "I see my house and am walking toward it," the pronoun for "it" is masculine in order to agree with "house." It would be ridiculous to say, "I see my house and am walking toward him."

Some who deny the personality of the Holy Spirit state that the term *pneuma* is neuter; thus they conclude that the Spirit must be an "it" or a "thing." Unfortunately the King James Version has this translation: "The Spirit itself beareth witness with our spirit that we are the children of God" (Rom. 8:16; also see 8:26). The Greek word rendered "itself" is the neuter pronoun *auto,* agreeing in gender with *to pneuma* ("the Spirit"), a neuter noun. A better translation, included in almost all modern versions, is "the Spirit Himself" (NASB, NIV, NKJV).

Christ used both masculine and neuter pronouns to describe the Holy Spirit. On the night before His crucifixion, He said to His disciples: "But when the Helper comes, whom I shall send to you from the Father, the Spirit of truth who proceeds from the Father, He will testify of me" (John 15:26). The title "Helper," usually translated as "Comforter," is the Greek *paraklētos,* a masculine noun. The relative pronoun "whom" (*hon*) is also masculine, agreeing with *paraklētos.* The relative pronoun "who" (*ho*) is neuter, agreeing with *pneuma* ("Spirit"). The pronoun "He" translates *ekeinos,* which is masculine in gender to agree with *paraklētos.*

Earlier, Christ promised the disciples, "And I will pray the Father, and He will give you another Helper [*allon paraklēton*], that He may abide with you forever" (14:16). The adjective "another" (*allon*) means "another of the same kind." Christ was a personal Comforter and Encourager to the Twelve; thus the Holy Spirit would also be a personal Helper. Christ contrasted Himself with another person, not with an impersonal influence or thing.

Christ also said to the apostles, "These things I have spoken to you while being present with you. But the Helper [*paraklētos,* masculine], the Holy Spirit [*to pneuma to hagion,* neuter], whom [*ho,* neuter] the Father will send in My name, He [*ekeinos,* masculine] will teach you all things, and bring to your remembrance all things that I said to you" (14:25–26). The mix of masculine and neuter nouns and pronouns again shows the personality of the Spirit. In addition, the teaching responsibilities of the Spirit also indicate He is a person just as Christ was a teaching person.

Christ later declared, "Nevertheless I tell you the truth. It is to your advantage that I go away; for if I do not go away, the Helper [*paraklētos,* masculine] will not come to you; but if I depart, I will send Him [*auton,* masculine] to you. And when He [*ekeinos,* masculine] has come, He will convict the world of sin, and of righteousness, and of judgment" (16:7–8). The usage of the masculine pronouns agrees with the masculine *paraklētos;* and the convicting ministry depicts the work of a real person.

Again the Lord Jesus stated, "However, when He [*ekeinos,* masculine], the Spirit [*to pneuma,* neuter] of truth, has come, He will guide you into all truth; for He will not speak on His own authority, but whatever He hears He will speak; and He will tell you things to come. He [*ekeinos,* masculine] will glorify me, for He will take of what is Mine and declare it to you" (16:13–14). The usage of *ekeinos* in these verses is significant because its nearest antecedent is *paraklēton* (16:7), whereas the neuter *pneuma* is found in the immediate context. Again the easy exchange of masculine and neuter pronouns argues for the personality of the Holy Spirit. The activities of the Spirit mentioned in these verses also point to a person rather than to a thing.

WHAT THE HOLY SPIRIT IS

We have seen that the Holy Spirit is neither like the human spirit nor physical nor an impersonal influence. We now turn to the positive evidence within the Scriptures that prove that the Holy Spirit is a true divine person, equal in personhood to God the Father and God the Son.

The Holy Spirit Has the Qualities of a Person

The marks of personality include an awareness of self-existence, an awareness of self-consciousness and of distinction from other persons and things, and a sense of moral awareness. The traits of personality also involve the capacities to think, to feel, to choose. As humans, we are moral, mental, emotional, volitional beings. Angels likewise have these marks of personality. From our understanding of the personality of humans and from an investigation of the Word of God, we can affirm unquestionably that the Holy Spirit is a person.

He thinks. The Holy Spirit has intelligence. He is omniscient, that is, He knows all things. Paul wrote, "Now He who searches the hearts [God the Father] knows what the mind of the Spirit is, because He [the Spirit] makes intercession for the saints according to the will of God" (Rom. 8:27). Thus the Spirit has a mind, an infinite mind.

In his exposition of the indispensable ministry of the Holy Spirit in divine revelation, inspiration, and illumination, Paul declared, "But God has revealed them to us through His Spirit. For the Spirit searches all things, yes, the deep things of God. For what man knows the things of a man except the spirit of the man which is in him? Even so no one knows the things of God except the Spirit of God" (1 Cor. 2:10–11). In order for Him to know the things of God completely, He must also be God, for only God can know God perfectly.

Obviously the Holy Spirit must have intelligence in order to teach (John 14:26), testify (15:26), convict (16:8), guide (16:13), reveal (16:13), and glorify Christ (16:14).

Isaiah identified the Holy Spirit as the one who would anoint, fill, and indwell the promised Messiah. He described Him in this way: "The Spirit of the LORD shall rest upon Him, the Spirit of wisdom and understanding, the Spirit of counsel and might, the Spirit of knowledge and of the fear of the LORD" (Isa. 11:2). These features show that the Holy Spirit has a mind, an infinite capacity to think.

He feels. Paul cautioned believers, "And do not grieve the Holy Spirit of God, by whom you were sealed for the day of redemption" (Eph. 4:30). Deliberate sin by a Christian hurts the indwelling Spirit emotionally. The Greek word *lypeō* ("grieve") is the same word used of the apostles' sorrow over the forthcoming crucifixion of Christ (Matt. 17:23), the sorrow of the rich young ruler after he left Christ in unbelief (19:22), the disciples' sorrow over the announcement that one of them would betray Christ (26:22), Christ's intense sorrow as He prayed in Gethsemane (26:37), Peter's sorrow over Christ's challenge of love and loyalty (John 21:17), the sorrow of the Corinthian church, which led to repentance (2 Cor. 2:2, 4; 7:8–9, 11), the sorrow of believers over the deaths of loved ones (1 Thess. 4:13), and the burden of heaviness produced by life's trials (1 Pet. 1:6).

The word "grief" (*lypē*), based on the verb "to grieve," is used of the sorrow of the disciples in Gethsemane (Luke 22:45), the sorrow of the apostles over the coming crucifixion and separation of Christ (John 16:20), the heavy burden on Paul's heart for the salvation of Israel (Rom. 9:2), the emotional hurt of Paul toward the rebellious Corinthians (2 Cor. 2:1, 3), Paul's concern over Epaphroditus's illness (Phil. 2:27), and the effect of divine chastisement on believers (Heb. 12:11).

Parents are grieved by their children's rebellion and disrespect. Husbands and wives grieve each other by verbal assaults and immoral acts. Emotional hurt seems far more severe when the ones whom we love the most violate our relationship. So it is with the Holy Spirit. All sin grieves the Spirit, but those deliberate sins committed against Him by believers whom He indwells hurt Him the most. Such grief shows the emotional aspect of His personality.

He decides. The Holy Spirit has a will, a volitional capacity. He can choose, He can decide. The Holy Spirit said to the prophets and teachers of the church at Antioch, "Now separate to me Barnabas and Saul for the work to which I have called them" (Acts 13:2). The Holy Spirit chose two out of the five. His will was for Paul and Barnabas to be the first missionaries into the gentile world.

On his second missionary journey Paul and his team were forbidden by the Holy Spirit to evangelize the Roman provinces of Asia and Bithynia (Acts 16:6–7). Again the Spirit revealed His will as to the geographical focus of the preached word.

All believers have received spiritual gifts or abilities from the Holy Spirit. He also determines which gift(s) will be imparted to each Christian: "But one and the same Spirit works all these things, distributing to each one individually as He wills" (1 Cor. 12:11). This distribution of gifts is as He wills, not as we wish.

The Holy Spirit thinks, feels, and decides because He is a person. Just as we manifest the traits of our human personality through our intelligence, emotions, and will, so the Holy Spirit reveals His divine personality through these same areas.

The Holy Spirit Acts Like a Person

We manifest who and what we are by what we do. Animals do what they do because they are animals. Birds do what they do because they are birds. Humans do what they do because they are human. Likewise, the Holy Spirit does what He does because He is a divine person.

He guides. Christ promised His disciples, "However, when He, the Spirit of truth, has come, He will guide you into all truth" (John 16:13). If moral, redemptive truth can be likened to the North Pole, the Holy Spirit is like a compass pointing us in that direction.

It has been my privilege to visit Israel on eight occasions. On five of those tours, I have served as tour pastor and as on-site Bible teacher. However, our tour group always employed the services of an official Israeli guide. These guides spoke English, Hebrew, and Arabic. They knew the land thoroughly. They knew where to go and how to get there. These guides are indispensable to the success of any Holy Land pilgrimage. On each tour we needed a person, not just a map or road signs, to lead us.

The verb *hodēgeō* ("to guide") occurs only five times in the New Testament. Christ used it twice of the blind leading the blind (Matt. 15:14; Luke 6:39). It is used of Christ, the Lamb, who will lead the redeemed to "living fountains of waters" (Rev. 7:17). When Philip encountered the Ethiopian eunuch and asked the ruler whether he understood what he was reading in

Isaiah, the eunuch responded, "How can I, unless someone guides me?" (Acts 8:31). The Holy Spirit can use yielded, knowledgeable believers to guide others into an understanding of the Word of God.

The verb "to guide" is related to a common noun *hodos* ("road" or "way"). Being guided involves destination, assistance, time, and determination to move forward in one's spiritual life.

He convicts. Speaking about the Holy Spirit, Jesus Christ said, "And when He has come, He will convict the world of sin, and of righteousness, and of judgment" (John 16:8). The verb *elenchō* ("to convict") is a legal term. In a courtroom the prosecuting attorney must present evidence to the jury and the judge that the accused defendant is guilty beyond a reasonable doubt. In the famous O. J. Simpson trial, Marcia Clark and Christopher Darden failed in their attempt to convince the jury of Simpson's guilt; therefore he was declared not guilty of all legal charges against him.

In the moral conviction of sin, righteousness, and judgment, the Holy Spirit does not attempt to convince a jury of a sinner's peers. Rather, He creates within the sinner an awareness of his own personal sin and guilt. He then persuades the sinner to confess his guilty status before the Judge of the universe. Only then can the sinner receive the gracious gift of salvation through Jesus Christ.

This process of moral and personal conviction can be done only by another moral person. It is life influencing life.

The same verb *elenchō* is used of one believer pointing out the sin of another believer (Matt. 18:15), the rebuke of Herod Antipas by John the Baptist (Luke 3:19), the exposure of a sinner's dark deeds by the light (John 3:20), the conviction of the unsaved by the declarations of church members (1 Cor. 14:24), the exposure of the unfruitful works of darkness by believers (Eph. 5:11, 13), the rebuke of sinning members and elders by the church leaders (1 Tim. 5:20), the rebuke of sinning Christians by God within divine chastisement (Heb. 12:5), the conviction of personal partiality by the law (James 2:9), and Christ's rebuke of believers in the church at Laodicea (Rev. 3:19).

Pastors have the responsibility to rebuke (2 Tim. 4:2; Titus 1:9, 13; 2:15). "Reproof" (*elenchos*, 2 Tim. 3:16) points out one of the features of the inspired Scriptures.

The Holy Spirit convicts people by the Scriptures through the witness of concerned believers. In our desire to lead others into the moral will of God, we must be sure they have truly violated God's moral law and not just our own pet peeves or biases.

He works. After Philip baptized the converted Ethiopian eunuch, "the Spirit of the Lord caught Philip away, so that the eunuch saw him no more; and he went on his way rejoicing. But Philip was found at Azotus" (Acts 8:39–40). Like a whirlwind, the Holy Spirit physically transported Philip from one geographic location to another. This unique miracle was the act of a divine person. In *The Wizard of Oz* a tornado whisked Dorothy from Kansas into the land of Oz, but that fictional adventure bears no resemblance to the real-life story of Philip.

On the island of Patmos, the apostle John, had an experience similar to that of Philip. When Jesus Christ called John into heaven (Rev. 4:1), he reported, "Immediately I was in the Spirit; and behold, a throne set in heaven, and one sat on the throne" (4:2). The Holy Spirit transported John from earth to the third heaven, and enabled the apostle to see part of the future as God sees it.

He prays. Paul wrote, "Likewise the Spirit also helps in our weaknesses. For we do not know what we should pray for as we ought, but the Spirit Himself makes intercession for us with groanings which cannot be uttered. Now He who searches the hearts knows what the mind of the Spirit is, because He makes intercession for the saints according to the will of God" (Rom. 8:26–27). We believers are not alone in our prayer burdens. As a pastor, I have often prayed for people with terminal illnesses. At those times I struggled. Should I ask God to perform a miracle of total healing, or should I ask God to relieve this person's pain by taking him or her home to heaven? Even though I often did not know which to pray for, God knew I wanted Him to be glorified. I wanted the best for the sick person and for his family. The Holy Spirit knew my heart, and I am sure He declared the intent of my heart to God the Father.

What a joy to know that the Holy Spirit helps us and intercedes for us. He knows the will of God far better than we do.

True prayer goes from our hearts through the mind of the Spirit to the Father. In the crevices between the huge stones in Jerusalem that form the Western Wall, also called the Wailing Wall, are prayers written on paper. These "paper prayers" are sometimes stolen by tourists as souvenirs. These devout Jews who place their written requests in the wall's crevices hope that this will help God remember their prayers. In contrast to this form of indirectly conveying requests to God, the prayer ministry of the Holy Spirit is direct and personal.

He searches. Paul wrote, "For the Spirit searches all things, yes, the deep things of God" (1 Cor. 2:10). The verb *eraunaō* ("to search") occurs six times in the New Testament. Christ challenged His critics to search the Scriptures concerning Him (John 5:39). The religious leaders who criticized Nicodemus for partially defending the ministry of Christ challenged him to "search and look, for no prophet has arisen out of Galilee" (7:52). Both God the Father and God the Son search out the hearts of men (Rom. 8:27; Rev. 2:23). The prophets searched the Old Testament to understand the correlation of the sufferings and the glory of the promised Messiah (1 Pet. 1:10–11).

In preparing to write this book, I had to research the topic both in the Scriptures and in relevant books. I compared, scrutinized, correlated, and wrote this material longhand on yellow pads. My wife then typed the manuscript into the computer system. No pencil or computer searched and completed the topic; I had to do it myself.

Searching involves mental analysis. Only persons can do it. Thus the Holy Spirit must be a person.

He forbids. In Acts 16:6–7 Luke recounted what happened to Paul and his team on the apostle's second missionary journey: "Now when they had gone through Phrygia and the region of Galatia, they were forbidden by the Holy Spirit to preach the word in Asia. After they had come to Mysia, they tried to go into Bithynia, but the Spirit did not permit them." Forbidding and permitting are choices of persons. The issue is life touching life, one person affecting another.

He speaks. When God spoke, He could be understood, by both people and angels (Heb. 1:1–2). Many Bible passages refer to the Father speaking and the Son speaking. Other passages also declare that the Holy Spirit spoke. We don't know whether the words of the Spirit were audible to everyone present or just to the intended recipient. Nor do we know if those words could have been tape-recorded if that technology had been available in those days.

When "the Spirit said to Philip, Go near and overtake this chariot" (Acts 8:29), Philip understood, obeyed, and thus evangelized the Ethiopian eunuch.

God gave a vision to Peter in the city of Joppa. "While Peter thought about the vision, the Spirit said to him, 'Behold, three men are seeking you. Arise therefore, go down and go with them, doubting nothing; for I have sent them' " (Acts 10:19–20). Peter obeyed the divine injunction.

The words of the Holy Spirit to the leader of the church at Antioch led to the appointment of the first missionary team. "As they ministered to the Lord and fasted, the Holy Spirit said, "Now separate to Me Barnabas and Saul for the work to which I have called them' " (13:2). How did the Spirit say those words to a group? We don't know, but apparently the leaders discerned the will of God and commissioned the pair.

The composition of Scripture is also related to the speech or words of the Holy Spirit. Before Matthias was selected to be an apostle to replace Judas, Peter announced, "Men and brethren, this Scripture had to be fulfilled, which the Holy Spirit spoke before by the mouth of David concerning Judas, who became a guide to those who arrested Jesus" (1:16). Paul used similar words: "The Holy Spirit spoke rightly through Isaiah the prophet to our fathers" (28:25). The text of Scripture is thus the voice of the Holy Spirit. Just as in verbal communication between individuals, so the Holy Spirit's words have meaning.

The words of Jesus Christ are also equated with the words of the Holy Spirit. Christ addressed Himself in seven letters to the seven churches of Asia (Revelation 2–3). Each letter also concludes: "He who has an ear, let him hear what the Spirit says to the churches" (2:7, 11, 17, 29; 3:6, 13, 22). These are shared words from two of the three persons of the Trinity.

He loves. We know that God the Father loves us (John 3:16) and that God the Son loves us (Eph. 5:25). God the Holy Spirit, being coequal with the Father and the Son, also loves us. Paul wrote, "Now I beg you, brethren, through the Lord Jesus Christ, and through the love of the Spirit, that you strive together with me in prayers to God for me" (Rom. 15:30).

Though this could mean either our love for the Spirit or His love for us, the latter seems more likely. After all, His purpose in us is to produce spiritual fruit, namely, love (Gal. 5:22–23). If He wants us to love others, then surely He also loves them and us.

The Holy Spirit Can Be Mistreated Like a Person

We can pollute the air we breathe, the water we drink, and the earth we farm. We can endanger animals, birds, and fish. Our sins, however, are greater when we violate other persons because they are created in the image of God (Gen. 9:6). Sin is a lack of conformity to the will and character of God. Ultimately all sin is against Him. All persons, both saved and unsaved, have sinned against God the Father, God the Son, and God the Holy Spirit.

He can be blasphemed. Once Jesus Christ encountered a blind, mute man whose physical problems were caused by demons (Matt. 12:22). Christ cast out the demons, and the man was then able to see and to speak. The multitude who witnessed this miracle questioned whether Christ could be the Son of David, the promised Messiah. The disturbed Pharisees rebutted the people's favorable inquiry with this declaration: "This fellow does not cast out demons except by Beelzebub, the ruler of the demons" (12:24). The Pharisees admitted the reality of the exorcism. The leaders affirmed that the man was indeed blind and mute, that he was indwelt by demons, that demons do exist as supernatural evil beings, and that Satan or Beelzebub is the ruler of the demons. The Pharisees, however, sinned when they claimed that Jesus Christ performed that miracle by the evil spirit of Satan rather than by the Holy Spirit.

Christ responded with this warning: "Therefore I say to you, every sin and blasphemy will be forgiven men, but the blasphemy against the Spirit will not be forgiven men" (12:31). Since only persons can be blasphemed, the Holy Spirit must be a person.

Christ admitted that the Holy Spirit had energized Him. "But if I cast out demons by the Spirit of God, surely the kingdom of God has come upon you" (12:28). The issue was clear: Was Jesus Christ controlled by the Holy Spirit or by Satan?

The blasphemy against the Holy Spirit was the Jewish leaders' unpardonable sin. Calling them "a brood of vipers" (12:34), Christ affirmed their condemnation: "Anyone who speaks a word against the Son of Man, it will be forgiven him; but whoever speaks against the Holy Spirit, it will not be forgiven him, either in this age or in the age to come" (12:32). "This age" refers to the age when Christ was on earth, preaching, healing, and offering the messianic kingdom to Israel. The phrase "the age to come" refers to the church age, the age that would occur after Christ's death and resurrection. These same Jewish leaders, blinded by their spiritual hardness, rejected the message of the apostles repeatedly (Acts 4:1–21; 5:1–40).

Some have said that to blaspheme against the Holy Spirit is to reject Jesus Christ as one's Savior. Of course, this was involved because only unbelievers made that accusation against Christ. However, this sin of blasphemy involved much more because the reason they rejected Christ's claims was specifically stated.

Remember what Jesus said: "Anyone who speaks a word against the Son of Man, it will be forgiven him" (Matt. 12:32). It is possible to malign Christ and to be later forgiven by Him. Paul himself confessed, "And I thank Christ Jesus our Lord who has enabled me, because He counted me faithful, putting me into the ministry, although I was formerly a blasphemer, a persecutor, and an insolent man; but I obtained mercy because I did it ignorantly in unbelief" (1 Tim. 1:12–13). In his unsaved life, Paul was a blasphemer and a Pharisee. However, he did not blaspheme the person of the Holy Spirit. He did not commit the same sin, either in word or essence, that the Pharisees in Jesus' day committed. He rejected the messiahship of Christ and persecuted the church, but apparently he never believed that Christ performed miracles by Satan.

In my book *The Modern Tongues Movement* I claimed that people today do not speak in tongues by the power of the Holy Spirit. I received several letters from enraged readers who charged me with the sin of blasphemy against the Holy Spirit. No one would like to receive letters like that, and I was no exception. I responded to those letters and encouraged the readers to examine carefully the historical situation in which the Pharisees blasphemed.

Blasphemy against the Holy Spirit is sin with eternal consequences. It is an affront to His person and His holiness. No genuine believer has committed or could commit such sin.

He can be lied to. In the early history of the Jerusalem church, Ananias and Sapphira sold some property, secretly kept some of the sale money, and gave the rest to the church under the care of the apostles (Acts 5:1–2). The couple deliberately gave the impression that they had given all of the proceeds to the church. Luke then recorded this incident: "But Peter said, 'Ananias, why has Satan filled your heart to lie to the Holy Spirit and keep back part of the price of the land for yourself?'" (5:3).

Through their planned deception the couple sinned against the apostles and the church body, but ultimately, they sinned against the Holy Spirit. Because the Spirit indwelt the believing couple, the apostles, and the Christians in the Jerusalem church, their lie was against the Holy Spirit. Ananias and Sapphira lied against both human persons and the divine person of the Holy Spirit.

Lying is a sin against people. We don't lie to inanimate objects or plants or animals. We lie to persons and persons lie to us. This lie by Ananias and Sapphira to the Holy Spirit thus demonstrates His personality.

For his sin, Ananias died immediately (5:5). Later, Peter confronted the wife Sapphira: "How is it that you have agreed to test the Spirit of the Lord?" (Acts 5:9). She then died instantly.

Because mistreating the Holy Spirit is a serious offense, fear came over the entire church. We too should not regard Him lightly.

He can be resisted. Stephen was one of the seven original deacons or servants who assisted the apostles in the Jerusalem church. He was "full of the Holy Spirit and wisdom" (Acts 6:3). He also had an active ministry for he, being "full of faith and power, did great wonders and signs among the people" (6:8). The religious leaders disputed with him, but "they were not able to resist the wisdom and the Spirit by which he spoke" (6:10).

In a public defense before his critics Stephen reviewed God's plan for Israel, her historical past, and her rejection of the prophetic messages. He concluded, "You stiff-necked and uncircumcised in heart and ears! You always resist the Holy Spirit; as your fathers did, so do you" (7:51). The Jewish people resisted the Spirit in that they rejected the Spirit-filled prophets who proclaimed the Spirit-inspired word of God. To reject the personal prophets was to reject the Holy Spirit. Such resistance is deliberate, sinful, and culpable.

He can be grieved. Paul gave this prohibition: "And do not grieve the Holy Spirit of God, by whom you were sealed for the day of redemption" (Eph. 4:30). Earlier we noted that this passage supports the emotional aspect of the Holy Spirit's personality. Since only a person can be grieved, the Holy Spirit is a person.

In this context, believers can grieve the Spirit by living like pagan Gentiles (4:17–19), by yielding to their sinful dispositions (4:22–24), by lying (4:25), by anger (4:26–27), by stealing (4:28), by using corrupt speech (4:29), by bitterness (4:31), by an unforgiving spirit (4:32), and by sexual immorality (5:3–5).

He can be quenched. Paul commanded, "Do not quench the Spirit" (1 Thess. 5:19). This concept of quenching, based on the metaphor of fire, is used eight times in the New Testament. The foolish virgins lamented that their lamps had gone out (Matt. 25:8). In His tenderness Christ would not quench any smoking flax, meaning that He would not stamp out the smallest amount of flickering faith and commitment (12:20). Christ described hell as a place where the fire would not be quenched (Mark 9:44, 46, 48). Believers can use the shield of faith "to quench all the fiery darts of the wicked one" (Eph. 6:16). Heroes of faith, like Shadrach, Meshech, and Abednego, were able to quench the violence of fire when they survived in the fiery furnace (Heb. 11:34; see Dan. 3:23–28).

Like a fire dwelling within each believer, the Holy Spirit wants to express Himself through our actions and attitudes. When we Christians prevent the Holy Spirit from doing what He wants to do in our lives, we quench Him.

He can be insulted. Persons can verbally reproach or insult other individuals. The verb *hybrizō* ("to insult") stresses the shameful treatment of persons (Matt. 22:6; Luke 11:45; 18:32; Acts 14:5; 1 Thess. 2:2). Both Christ and Paul were treated this way (Luke 18:32; 1 Thess. 2:2). The unsaved are often spiteful in their insults of others (Rom. 1:30). Paul confessed in his unsaved life that he was an insolent man, injuring others with his verbal insults (1 Tim. 1:13).

The Book of Hebrews contains a dire warning: "Of how much worse punishment, do you suppose, will he be thought worthy who has trampled the Son of God underfoot, counted the blood of the covenant by which he was sanctified a common thing, and insulted the Spirit of grace?" (Heb. 10:29). Interpreters debate the meaning of this verse. Is the person who commits this terrible sin a believer or an unbeliever? I personally think the person is a believer. This verb *enybrizō* found only here in the New Testament, is based on the verb *hybrizō* ("to insult") and the prefix *en* ("in"). That prefix seems to indicate that the believer has insulted the Holy Spirit who dwells within him. That concept makes the sin more heinous than one committed by an unsaved person. Regardless, the verbal insult against the gracious Holy Spirit shows that He is indeed a person, not an influence or a thing.

The Holy Spirit Relates to Other Persons

We had a family dog named Frisky. Actually his AKC registered name was Baron von Friska, but we treated him like a mongrel rather than as a purebred poodle. He lived with us for over fifteen years. We gave him to our children, Gary and Gail, as their pet, but he soon became my dog. I usually fed him, washed him, and took him out for walks. Frisky and I became friends. However, Frisky had a stronger attraction for Mishy, the toy poodle who lived across the street, than for me. Frisky would rather romp with Mishy than walk beside me.

Dogs relate to dogs. Cats relate to cats. Birds relate to birds. So naturally, persons relate to persons. My closeness to Frisky did not compare at all to my relationships with my family and friends.

In a similar fashion the personality of the Holy Spirit can be seen in His relationships to other persons.

To the Father and to the Son. In several passages the Father, the Son, and the Holy Spirit are mentioned together. They are seen as three distinct persons, relating to each other in divine works.

After His resurrection but before He ascended, Jesus Christ commissioned the apostles, "All authority has been given to Me in heaven and on earth. Go therefore and make disciples of all the nations, baptizing them in the name of the Father and of the Son and of the Holy Spirit, teaching them to observe all things that I have commanded you; and lo, I am with you always, even to the end of the age" (Matt. 28:18–20). The baptismal authorization is significant. The Father, the Son, and the Holy Spirit are joined together under a singular name (not "names"). Genuine believers should be baptized in the name of the triune God. God is one in being and thus He has one name. At the same time, there are three separate personal distinctions or persons within the one divine Being. If the Father and the Son are persons, then the Holy Spirit must also be a person. If the Spirit were merely an impersonal power, the sense of the baptismal formula would be ridiculous.

Speaking about the security of our salvation, Paul taught, "Now He who establishes us with you in Christ and has anointed us is God, who also has sealed us and given us the Spirit in our hearts as a guarantee" (2 Cor. 1:21–22). The mention of Christ, God, and the Spirit shows the distinction of persons and their function in our position of spiritual justification.

Probably the most common biblical benediction quoted in our church services is that given by Paul in 2 Corinthians 13:14: "The grace of the Lord Jesus Christ, and the love of God, and the communion of the Holy Spirit be with you all." For this blessing to make sense theologically, the Holy Spirit must be a person, coequal to God (the Father) and the Lord Jesus Christ. The three spiritual entities, namely, grace, love, and communion, have their source in the three divine persons.

At conversion believing sinners become children of God and sons of God. Paul explained: "And because you are sons, God has sent forth the Spirit of His Son into your hearts, crying out, "Abba, Father!'" (Gal. 4:6). The mention of God (Father), the Son, and the Spirit in this verse again reveals three separate persons.

Peter spoke of eternal redemption in these words: "Elect according to the foreknowledge of God the Father, in sanctification of the Spirit, for obedience and sprinkling of the blood of Jesus Christ" (1 Pet. 1:2). The Father elected us, the Spirit sanctified us, and Christ redeemed us. Those three actions are done by three divine persons. So the Spirit must be seen as a person in the same sense that the Father and Jesus Christ are persons.

Jude identified the three persons of the Trinity in this exhortation:

"But you, beloved, building yourselves up on your most holy faith, praying in the Holy Spirit, keep yourselves in the love of God, looking for the mercy of our Lord Jesus Christ unto eternal life" (Jude 20–21).

To Jesus Christ. In the Upper Room Discourse (John 13–17), Jesus often distinguished the Holy Spirit from Himself. (14:16–17, 26; 15:26; 16:7–11, 13–15). Christ declared that the Holy Spirit would help believers, indwell them, teach them, assist them in their witness, and guide them. The Savior also pointed out that the Spirit would convict the world and that He would glorify Christ.

Christ regarded the Spirit as a person who could minister in the place of Christ, doing what Jesus had previously done. The Lord Jesus did not give the impression that the Spirit was a mere divine influence or power, an impersonal entity.

To the apostles, elders, and church members. At a council convened in Jerusalem the apostles and the church elders in the presence of the congregation debated the relationship of physical circumcision to divine justification. They concluded that both Jews and Gentiles are saved by grace alone through faith alone in Christ alone. They affirmed that the rite of circumcision was unnecessary and should not be imposed on uncircumcised Gentile believers.

The council then composed an authoritative letter to the gentile believers. The authors concluded, "For it seemed good to the Holy Spirit, and to us, to lay upon you no greater burden than these necessary things" (Acts 15:28). They themselves ("us") and the Holy Spirit were both persons.

IMPLICATIONS FOR US

First, we must not be afraid of the Holy Spirit. He is a warm, loving, divine person. He is not a dark, mysterious, ethereal thing. We need to see Him for who He is, not just for what He can do in our lives. How can we do this? A helpful way is to read the Scriptures each day with a pen and paper at hand. Whenever you come to a passage where the Holy Spirit is mentioned, list it. Then think about the personal qualities of the Spirit which can be gleaned from the passage. Write them down. Then when you pray, thank God for these personal traits of the Holy Spirit.

Second, we must worship God every day in spirit and in truth. Love Him with all your heart, soul, strength, and mind. Love God as the triune God. Focus on all three persons, not just on the Father or the Son.

Third, we must bond with the Holy Spirit. Realize He lives within you. Thank Him for being your Teacher and Encourager. Be conscious that He is the Paraclete.

Fourth, we must be careful not to sin against Him. We must remember that our sinful actions and attitudes grieve His holy person.

CHAPTER TWO

The Deity of the Holy Spirit

Conceivably, the Holy Spirit could be a person without being God. Angels and humans are personal beings without being divine. However, if the Holy Spirit is God, then He also must be a person because God is a personal being. Deity implies the possession of personality.

Evangelicals relate the deity of the Holy Spirit to both the deity of God the Father and the deity of God the Son. As we argue for the oneness of the divine Being (monotheism), we also hold to the Trinity of the Godhead (Trinitarianism). We maintain that the Father, the Son, and the Holy Spirit are three distinct divine persons who have an intrapersonal oneness as the one Being, God.

We can only know the true essence of God through the Scriptures, in which God has chosen to reveal Himself. As Millard Erickson observed, "The deity of the Holy Spirit is not as easily established as is that of the Father and the Son. It might well be said that the deity of the Father is simply assumed in Scripture, that of the Son is affirmed and argued, while that of the Holy Spirit must be inferred from various indirect statements found in Scripture."[1]

An examination of all of the Scriptures where the Holy Spirit is mentioned will show that He is indeed God, coequal to the Father and to the Son in deity.

HIS NAMES

Names often reveal what we are, that is, our character and conduct. Sometimes, they indicate how others perceive us. Do you remember the names of the seven dwarfs? Doc, Sleepy, Dopey, Grumpy, Sneezy, Happy, and Bashful. Those names reflect their character.

The Scriptures use many names to describe the Holy Spirit. Each title reveals something about His essence.

Names That Relate Him to the Father and the Son

The Holy Spirit is related to God the Father in these titles: the Spirit of God (Gen. 1:2; 1 Cor. 3:16); the Spirit of the Lord God (Isa. 61:1); the Spirit of the Lord (Luke 4:18); the Spirit of our God (1 Cor. 6:11); the Spirit of the living God (2 Cor. 3:3); the Spirit of the LORD (Yahweh) (Judg. 3:10); His Spirit (Num. 11:29); Your Spirit (Ps. 139:7); the Spirit of your Father (Matt. 10:20); My Spirit (Gen. 6:3); and the Spirit of Him who raised Jesus from the dead (Rom. 8:11).

The Holy Spirit is related to God the Son through these titles: the Spirit of Jesus Christ (Phil. 1:19); the Spirit of Christ (1 Pet. 1:11); the Spirit of Jesus (Acts 16:7, NASB); the Spirit of His Son (Gal. 4:6); and the Spirit of the Lord (Acts 8:39).

These names definitely show a relationship between two distinct persons. They also imply the possession of deity in those special relationships.

Names That Relate Him to the Divine Attributes

Holy. His most familiar name is the Holy Spirit. That title is indelibly inscribed within the formula of Christian baptism: "baptizing them in the name of the Father and of the Son and of the Holy Spirit" (Matt. 28:19). What He does manifests who and what He is. Since God is holy (Lev. 11:44; 1 Pet. 1:16), He is the eternal objective standard of personal holiness. Sin therefore is a lack of conformity to the will and essence of the infinitely holy God. This title for this divine person, the Holy Spirit, certainly denotes His deity. He is also designated as the Holy One (1 John 2:20) and the Spirit of holiness (Rom. 1:4).

Eternal. Being eternal, God has no beginning nor ending. The Holy Spirit is called the eternal Spirit, manifesting that divine attribute (Heb. 9:14).

Glory. The glory of God is the manifestation of all He is. Only God has glory in that infinite sense. The Holy Spirit bears the name, the Spirit of glory (1 Pet. 4:14).

Life. God has self-sufficient life. He is not dependent on anyone or anything outside of Himself for the sustenance of His Being. He was, is, and always shall be. He exists, and immutably so. The Holy Spirit is called the Spirit of life (Rom. 8:2). Christ is life (John 14:6), and so is the Spirit. Both can impart and sustain life in others without diminishing themselves.

Truth. God is truth, always acting and speaking in truth (John 17:17). There is no duplicity in Him. Likewise, the Holy Spirit is named the Spirit of truth (John 14:17, 16:13). In the life of each child of God, the Holy Spirit teaches the truth revealed in the Word of truth, namely, the Scriptures, and guides believers into all truth.

Grace. God is gracious in and of Himself. He bestows His grace on undeserving sinners. The Lord Jesus Christ is full of grace (John 1:14), and so is the Holy Spirit, for He is identified as the Spirit of grace (Heb. 10:29). He dispenses the grace of God as He works out the redemptive purpose of God in each converted sinner.

Wisdom. God alone is wise (1 Tim. 1:17). Paul praised God for His wisdom: "Oh, the depth of the riches both of the wisdom and knowledge of God! How unsearchable are His judgments and His ways past finding out!" (Rom. 11:33). God knows everything, actual and possible, and yet He has never learned anything. He is infinitely omniscient. With this understanding about the nature of God, Paul identified the Holy Spirit as the Spirit of wisdom and revelation (Eph. 1:17).

At the baptism of Jesus, God anointed His Son with the Holy Spirit. Christ then began His public ministry of preaching, teaching, and healing. Isaiah predicted this key messianic event: "The Spirit of the LORD shall rest upon Him, the Spirit of wisdom and understanding, the Spirit of counsel and might, the Spirit of knowledge and of the fear of the LORD" (Isa. 11:2). The role of the Holy Spirit in the life of Christ is inseparably linked to the concepts of wisdom and knowledge.

Other significant names. On the day of His ascension Christ equated the promise of the Father with the Holy Spirit (Acts 1:4). The Savior had earlier taught that the Father would send the Spirit once Christ had ascended into the presence of the Father (John 14:16–17, 26).

Christ also gave to the Holy Spirit the name *paraklētos* ("Comforter" or "Helper," John 14:16, 26). Christ comforted, helped, and encouraged the apostles when He was on earth with them and the Holy Spirit would perform the same ministry for the disciples after Jesus had ascended. In that sense the Spirit would be "another" (Greek, *allos,* "of the same kind") Comforter. To be another of the same kind, the Spirit would have to be as divine as Jesus Christ.

Each believer has received the Holy Spirit, namely, the Spirit of adoption (Rom. 8:15). The indwelling presence of the Spirit, made possible through spiritual regeneration, enables each Christian to call God his or her Father.

HIS ATTRIBUTES

The attributes of God are those qualities or characteristics that belong only to Him eternally and infinitely. They constitute who He is. God did not acquire them nor can He lose them. He is immutable; therefore He can be neither more nor less than what He is.

The creatures of God can possess and manifest some of these attributes in a limited manner. We humans can know many things, but we can never know all things. We have the capacity to know because we have been made in the image of God, but we will never know as God knows. We will never become divine.

God the Father, God the Son, and God the Holy Spirit each possess all of the divine attributes coequally, eternally, and infinitely. What is true of one divine person is also true for the other two persons. The Scriptures indicate that the Holy Spirit has those attributes which only the true God possesses.

He Knows All Things

Isaiah asked, "Who has directed the Spirit of the Lord, or as His counselor has taught Him? With whom did He take counsel, and who instructed Him, and taught Him in the path of justice? Who taught Him knowledge, and showed Him the way of understanding?" (Isa. 40:13–14). The apostle Paul used this passage to exalt the omniscience of God (Rom. 11:33–35). Do these passages refer to the triune God without referring to any specific person in the Trinity? The Pauline passage implies that conclusion, but Isaiah focused on the Spirit of the Lord. The prophet's point was that no one could teach the Spirit because He already knows all things.

No creature, by sense perception, rationalization, or imagination, could ever know the things God has prepared in His creative-redemptive plan. For us to know, God must reveal them. God has done exactly that through the ministry of the Holy Spirit. As Paul explained, "But God has revealed them to us through His Spirit. For the Spirit searches all things, yes, the deep things of God. For what man knows the things of a man except the spirit of the man which is in him? Even so no one knows the things of God except the Spirit of God" (1 Cor. 2:10–11). The Spirit knows exactly what God the Father knows. The Holy Spirit, therefore, must be God, because only God can know as God knows. There is no sense of learning within the eternal knowledge of the Spirit.

Jesus Christ declared, "However, when He, the Spirit of truth, has come, He will guide you into all truth; for He will not speak on His own authority, but whatever He hears, He will speak; and He will tell you things to come" (John 16:13). God is always true. The Spirit, whose essence is truth, speaks truth and guides us into truth. There are no errors in His ministry because of any misinformation or faulty reasoning.

Christ added, "He will glorify Me, for He will take of what is Mine and declare it to you. All things that the Father has are Mine. Therefore I said that He will take of Mine and declare it to you" (16:14–15). The Father, the Son, and the Spirit share this truth. What belongs to one belongs to the others. Any one of the divine persons can reveal the mind of God because each One knows His mind fully. The Father knows all things (Jer. 17:10), the Son knows all things (Rev. 2:23), and the Spirit knows all things (1 Cor. 2:11).

He Is Everywhere Present

All creatures can be in only one place at a time. People and animals are localized, finite beings. God, however, can be present everywhere. He can be present in heaven and on earth at the same time. He can be present in Africa, Asia, and North America simultaneously. He can be both here and there. He is omnipresent.

While God is present everywhere, He can also localize or manifest Himself in specific places. Christ did not restrict the omnipresence of the Father when He instructed His disciples to pray, "Our Father in heaven" (Matt. 6:9). God localized His presence in the cloud and in the pillar of fire, that guided the Israelites in the wilderness. He also localized His presence in the cloud of glory that filled the temple of Solomon, but even the wise king confessed, "But will God indeed dwell with men on the earth? Behold, heaven and the heaven of heavens cannot contain You. How much less this temple which I have built!" (2 Chron. 6:18).

The omnipresence and the local presence of God constitute a divine mystery. It can be true only of God, and this truth can be known only through divine revelation in the Scriptures. The Bible definitely teaches that the Holy Spirit is everywhere present in the totality of His divine personhood.

David wrote, "Where can I go from Your Spirit? Or where can I flee from Your presence? If I ascend into heaven, You are there; if I make my bed in hell, behold, You are there. If I take the wings of the morning, and dwell in the uttermost parts of the sea, even there Your hand shall lead me, and Your right hand shall hold me" (Ps. 139:7–10). No human, either before or after death, can escape the omnipresence of the Spirit. To the child of God, this truth is actually a blessing, not a threat. How wonderful to know that wherever we go, God is there, the God of all grace and comfort.

Another proof for the omnipresence of the Holy Spirit can be seen in His ministry in redemption. To enter the kingdom of God, a person must be born again of the Spirit of God (John 3:3–8). The Spirit can give birth to believing sinners in different places at the same time. He can also simultaneously indwell all believers at the same time (1 Cor. 6:19–20). These ministries are possible only because the Spirit can be everywhere present.

He Is All-Powerful

To Abraham, God said of Himself, "Is anything too hard for the LORD?" (Gen. 18:14). When the angel Gabriel informed Mary of Jesus' forthcoming virginal conception and birth, he assured her, "For with God nothing will be impossible" (Luke 1:37). Only God is omnipotent. He can do anything consistent with His essence and will. The Bible affirms that the Holy Spirit has this divine attribute.

Elihu said to Job, "The Spirit of God has made me, and the breath of the Almighty gives me life" (Job 33:4). Elihu attributed his human existence and providential preservation of his life to the creative activity of the Holy Spirit. All human life is derived from parents and eventually from Adam and Eve. God is the source of all life, and the Spirit of God is involved in the giving of that life.

Paul claimed that he performed miracles "by the power of the Spirit of God" (Rom. 15:19). These signs and wonders were the authenticating marks of his apostleship (2 Cor. 12:12). Commissioned directly by the resurrected Christ, Paul carried out his missionary ministry by the enabling of the Holy Spirit. It was God who testified to the witness of the apostles (Heb. 2:4); thus the Holy Spirit manifested His deity through the miracles performed by the apostles.

He Is Eternal

Only God is eternal, having no beginning and no ending. Both angels and humans have their beginning in time, but they will continue to live forever in their creative existence.

The Holy Spirit is as eternal as the Father and the Son. The writer to the Hebrews asked: "How much more shall the blood of Christ, who through the eternal Spirit offered Himself without spot to God, cleanse your conscience from dead works to serve the living God?" (Heb. 9:14). Jesus Christ, full of the Holy Spirit, offered Himself as the redemptive sacrifice for our sins through the ministry of the Spirit. The Spirit is here identified as the eternal Spirit.

He Is Called God

Acts 5. A lie violates the truth, and is also a sin against the God of truth. The ninth commandment codified for Israel the divine prohibition of bearing false witness (Exod. 20:16). Paul instructed believers to tell the truth and not to lie (Eph. 4:25). In all ages, lying is wrong because it ultimately is a sin against God.

In the early life of the Jerusalem church, believers often sold their possessions and brought the sale proceeds to the apostles. The church leadership used the funds to assist those in financial need (Acts 4:34–37). Two church members, Ananias and Sapphira, sold some real estate but secretly kept back some of the sale money for themselves. They then brought the remaining money to the apostles and indicated that the amount was the total sale price (5:1–2).

Peter then criticized Ananias: "Ananias, why has Satan filled your heart to lie to the Holy Spirit and keep back part of the price of the land for yourself? While it remained, was it not your own? And after it was sold, was it not in your own control? Why have you conceived this thing in your heart? You have not lied to men but to God" (5:3–4). Ananias then died under severe divine chastisement (5:5).

Peter equated three phrases: lying to the Holy Spirit (5:4), lying to God (5:3), and testing the Spirit (5:9). The apostle may have made a distinction between the Holy Spirit and God the Father, but the more plausible interpretation is that He named the Holy Spirit as God. In other words, a lie against the Holy Spirit is a lie against God because the Holy Spirit is God.

1 Corinthians 3. Every believer is indwelt by the Holy Spirit. When believers come together as a local church, that corporate body is also indwelt by the Spirit. Paul thus warned the Corinthian assembly: "Do you [plural] not know that you [plural] are the temple of God and that the Spirit of God dwells in you [plural]? If anyone [singular] defiles the temple of God, God will destroy him. For the temple of God is holy, which temple you [plural] are" (1 Cor. 3:16–17). Believers, individually and corporately, constitute the temple of God. God dwells in them individually and as a corporate assembly because the Spirit of God is in them. Paul thus equated God with the Holy Spirit.

Believers should not violate their own personal lives with sin nor should they defile the local church. God will discipline believers for both effects of their sins.

HIS WORK

God manifests who He is by what He does. His works are divine because He is divine. His works are supernatural, unable to be duplicated by humans. The Holy Spirit thus has manifested His deity by what He has done.

In Creation

The first two verses of the Bible read, "In the beginning God created the heavens and the earth. The earth was without form, and void; and darkness was on the face of the deep. And the Spirit of God was hovering over the face of the waters" (Gen. 1:1–2). Other translations give the sense that the Spirit was brooding or moving over the waters. To be sure, the Holy Spirit was present and actively involved in the creation event and process. The Hebrew word *ʾĕlōhîm* ("God") implies the triune God, the one God in three eternal persons. Some interpreters claim that the plural ending *-îm* for the name of God is a plural of majesty. However, the singular name *ʾĕl* ("God") is majestic in and of itself. It needs no amplification.

Later, God decreed, "Let Us make man in Our image, according to Our likeness; let them have dominion over the fish of the sea, over the birds of the air, and over the cattle, over all the earth and over every creeping thing that creeps on the earth. So God created man in His own image; in the image of God He created him; male and female He created them" (1:26–27). The two phrases, "in Our image " and " in His own image," show the Triunity of God. God is one being, thus man was created in His [singular] image. God exists in three persons, and so the creation of man is in "Our [plural] image."

The Father, the Son, and the Holy Spirit were all involved in the divine work of creation. As Paul explained, "Yet for us there is one God, the Father, of whom are all things, and we for Him; and one Lord Jesus Christ, through whom are all things, and through whom we live" (1 Cor. 8:6). Creation came out of (Greek, *ek)* God the Father; He was its source. Creation came through (Greek, *dia)* God the Son; He was its channel or means. John likewise wrote, "All things were made through [*dia*] Him, and without Him nothing was made that was made" (John 1:3).

The two New Testament verses in the preceding paragraph do not mention the Holy Spirit's part in creation. The Book of Genesis, however, indicates that the Spirit was providentially controlling the created order for the divine purpose. Job confessed, "By His Spirit He adorned the heavens" (Job 26:13). The Holy Spirit was apparently active in creation's order, design, and control.

His sustaining ministry in creation was affirmed by the psalmist: "You send forth Your Spirit, they are created; and You renew the face of the earth" (Ps. 104:30). The Spirit is both life-giving and life-sustaining.

The name for the Spirit, in both Hebrew and Greek, can also refer to the "wind" or "breath." In the days of creation God spoke, and life came into existence out of nothing. The Holy Spirit may have actualized the divine intent and spoken word. At the creation of man, we read, "And the LORD God formed man of the dust of the ground, and breathed into his nostrils the breath of life; and man became a living being" (Gen. 2:7). The Holy Spirit could well have been involved in the outbreathing and the inbreathing of this divine work of creation. God created a lifeless materialistic form and then caused that body to become a living person, a spirit-body person or a physical-psychical person. The Spirit was active in that expression of divine power.

In the Incarnation

Paul identified the manifestation of God in the flesh—the Incarnation—as "the mystery of godliness" (1 Tim. 3:16). John claimed that God the Son, the eternal Word, "became flesh and dwelt among us" (John 1:14). The Incarnation was achieved by the conception and birth of Jesus Christ through the virgin Mary. Mary was a virgin both when she conceived and when she gave birth (Isa. 7:14). Parthenogenesis is a biological impossibility within the human race, and yet it occurred within the life of Mary. In the creative-redemptive purpose of God this divine work in Mary was accomplished through the ministry of the Holy Spirit.

God sent Gabriel to Mary to tell her she would become the mother of the promised Messiah. The angel announced, "Do not be afraid, Mary, for you have found favor with God. And behold, you will conceive in your

(Acts 1:16). How did the Holy Spirit speak? He spoke through what David said. How do we know what David said? We can read what he wrote in the Psalms (for example, Ps. 41:9).

Paul also affirmed this equation of divine and human words. He stated: "The Holy Spirit spoke rightly through Isaiah the prophet to our fathers, saying . . ." (Acts 28:25–26). How do we know what the Holy Spirit spoke through Isaiah? How do we know what Isaiah said? We can read these words in what Isaiah wrote (Isa. 6:9–10).

The Holy Spirit superintended the process of the production of the Scriptures. "Knowing this first, that no prophecy of Scripture is of any private interpretation, for prophecy never came by the will of man, but holy men of God spoke as they were moved by the Holy Spirit" (2 Pet. 1:20–21). No person, unaided by God, can determine the divinely intended meaning of the Scriptures. And no writer of a biblical book determined by his own initiative and intelligence to write. The sixty-six books did not originate within the impulse or imagination of mere man. Rather, God providentially set them apart for the task of writing and prepared them through their genetic inheritance, family background, educational opportunities, and life experiences. This divine action, executed by the Holy Spirit, changed these men into "holy men of God." The Holy Spirit then guided them in what they spoke and wrote. The Spirit burdened their hearts and minds. The Spirit "moved" them just as a wind would move ancient sailing vessels. The divinely prepared and enabled men then wrote exactly what God wanted them to write, adding nothing and leaving out nothing.

The net result of this divine work of the Holy Spirit is the written Word of God. The Bible is a divine-human book, the revealed truth of God written in human vocabulary and grammar, apart from any human error. The Bible is inerrant, without error in all matters, including theology, history, geography, and science.

The Holy Spirit superintended the lives of the biblical writers much as He guided Mary at Jesus' conception. Mary was able to pass on her human nature to Jesus, but she was not able to pass on her sinfulness. Similarly, the biblical writers could pass on their human style of writing to the written text, but they were prevented from passing on errors at the critical moment their pens hit the paper and words appeared (1 Cor. 2:9–13).

Apart from the superintending work of the Holy Spirit the authors of Scripture were ordinary men—shepherds, farmers, kings, fishermen, physicians, politicians, and tax collectors. They wrote narrative history, poetry, proverbs, and letters to individuals and groups. Under normal circumstances, they could have easily incorporated errors into their writings. The composition of Scripture, however, was no ordinary event.

These forty writers of the sixty-six books were holy men of God, set apart and controlled by the Holy Spirit. They were used by God and they used what was personally their own. Throughout the process of divine revelation, inspiration, and illumination, they were prevented from passing on errors, either intentional or unintentional, into the texts of the original writings.

In Redemption

From the belly of the sea creature Jonah cried out, "Salvation is of the LORD" (Jonah 2:9). The name Jesus, based on the Hebrew Joshua, means "Jehovah saves" or "Jehovah is salvation" (Matt. 1:21). Spiritual redemption, from beginning to end, is the exclusive work of God. Only God deserves the glory for all He has done, all He is doing, and all He will do for us (Eph. 1:3–14).

His active role in this redemptive work also reveals the deity of the Holy Spirit.[2] The works of the Father and of the Son would be incomplete without the work of the Holy Spirit. Redemption, therefore, is the work of the triune God.

All believers are born of God into His family (John 1:13). That act of spiritual regeneration is directly attributed to the Holy Spirit. Jesus said to Nicodemus, "Most assuredly, I say to you, unless one is born of water and the Spirit, he cannot enter the kingdom of God" (John 3:5; see also 3:6–8). To be born of God and to be born of the Spirit is synonymous; thus the Holy Spirit must be God.

Paul described the essence of salvation in this way: "But when the kindness and the love of God our Savior toward man appeared, not by works of righteousness which we have done, but according to His mercy He saved us, through the washing of regeneration and renewing of the Holy

Spirit, whom He poured out on us abundantly through Jesus Christ our Savior, that having been justified by His grace we should become heirs according to the hope of eternal life" (Titus 3:4–7). All three divine persons are inseparably involved in the total work of our salvation. The Father, the Son, and the Holy Spirit all have distinctive roles in the execution of the plan of redemption, but it is the work of the one God, to whom we give glory and whom we worship.

HIS ASSOCIATION WITH THE FATHER AND THE SON

As stated earlier, we evangelicals believe in one God, eternally existing in three persons: Father, Son, and Holy Spirit.

How can God be both one and three? How can monotheism and Trinitarianism be harmonized? How can the finite God be explained by finite individuals? Can the thing made define the essence of its maker? Zophar correctly quizzed Job, "Can you search out the deep things of God? Can you find out the limits of the Almighty?" (Job 11:7).

The oneness of God is taught throughout the Scriptures. Moses declared, "Hear, O Israel: The LORD our God, the LORD is one! You shall love the LORD your God with all your heart, with all your soul, and with all your strength" (Deut. 6:4–5). Jesus Christ reaffirmed this belief (Mark 12:29–31). If there were more than one God, then an individual could love one of them to the exclusion of the others, or he could split his devotion at any one time. However, he could never give many gods his total worship at the same time.

Paul rejected the reality of false gods and idols when he affirmed God's oneness (1 Cor. 8:4–6; 1 Tim. 2:5), and James did the same (James 2:19). There is no indication that the concept of monotheism changed or evolved from the Old Testament to the New Testament. Paul, Peter, and other Christians claimed to worship the same God adored by Adam, Abraham, David, and other Old Testament saints.

Since God is one in His basic essence and being, how can He also be three? It must be pointed out that *one* and *three* are not being used in the same sense. The word *one* applies only to the nature of the divine Being; there is only one God. The word *three* refers to the three persons or personal distinctions within the divine oneness. It is therefore just as wrong to state that God is one person as to claim that there are three gods.

In Personal Distinction

In the divine program of progressive revelation, the Old Testament stressed the monotheistic nature of God whereas the New Testament emphasized the Trinitarian concept. The Old Testament, however, implied the existence of more than one person within the divine oneness.

Plural indications. First, the Hebrew name for God (*ʾĕlōhîm*) has a plural ending (*-îm*) added to the singular noun (*ʾēl*).

Second, plural pronouns were ascribed to God. God said, "Let us make man in Our image" (Gen. 1:26). The plural cannot refer to both God and a nondivine being. It can refer to only the three persons within the one God.

Third, both singular and plural pronouns are used together to describe the one action of the one God. When He created man, God said, "Let Us make man in Our image, according to Our likeness. . . . so God created man in His own image; in the image of God He created him; male and female He created them" (1:26–27).

God commissioned the prophet Isaiah with the question, "Whom shall I send, and who will go for Us?" (Isa. 6:8). Since God is one, He could say "I." Because of the plurality of the persons, He could also say "Us."

Fourth, in the Shema of Israel—the foundational confession that God is one—the choice of the adjective "one" (*ʾeḥād*) is significant (Deut. 6:4). The adjective can be used in two different ways: as one person or one people. The corporate usage (one people) implies that there is more than one person within the singular group. This usage was common in the Old Testament (Gen. 2:24; Exod. 24:3; 26:11; Judg. 6:16; Ezek. 37:19). These usages reveal a plurality in unity, not a single undiversified sameness.

Indications of three persons. The number of persons within the oneness of the divine Being cannot be determined from the above study. Conceivably, there could be two, three, four, or more. It can only be safely stated that the above passages indicate more than one person within the Godhead.

However, the first suggestion of three persons is seen in the priestly blessing God directed Aaron to pronounce on Israel: "The LORD bless you and keep you; the LORD make His face shine upon you, and be gracious to you; the LORD lift up His countenance upon you, and give you peace" (Num. 6:24–26). Here is a triple blessing with a triple mention of God's name. It was not given once, twice, or four times; rather, it was stated three times.

The second suggestion of three persons is found in the worship and praise of the angelic seraphim: "Holy, holy, holy is the LORD of hosts; the whole earth is full of His glory" (Isa. 6:3). This triple invocation coupled with the later plural pronoun "Us" argue for three persons.

Mention of three names. Isaiah revealed a distinction of three persons. God said through the prophet: "Come near to Me, hear this: I have not spoken in secret from the beginning; from the time that it was, I was there. And now the Lord GOD, and His Spirit have sent Me" (Isa. 48:16). Here is the mention of one person, the speaker ("I," "me"), another person ("Lord God"), and a third person ("His Spirit").

In a prediction, Isaiah recorded the words of the promised Messiah: "The Spirit of the Lord GOD is upon Me, because the LORD has anointed Me to preach good tidings to the poor; He has sent Me to heal the brokenhearted, to proclaim liberty to the captives, and the opening of the prison to those who are bound; to proclaim the acceptable year of the LORD, and the day of vengeance of our God; to comfort all who mourn" (61:1–2). Jesus Christ applied this prophecy to Himself when He taught in the synagogue at Nazareth (Luke 4:16–21). This significant passage mentions one person, the speaker ("Me"), a second person ("the Spirit"), and a third person ("Lord God," "LORD," "our God").

In themselves these two passages from Isaiah do not establish beyond a shadow of doubt that these three persons can all be called divine. But they do indicate the presence of three distinct persons at the same event. Their explicit identification and equation of deity was made later in the New Testament.

God the Father, Jesus Christ, and the Holy Spirit. The New Testament clarified the prior allusions of the Old Testament to the plurality of divine persons in the Godhead. At Jesus' baptism by John the Baptist in the Jordan River, all three persons were active and identified. "When He had been baptized, Jesus came up immediately from the water; and behold, the heavens were opened to Him, and He saw the Spirit of God descending like a dove and alighting upon Him. And suddenly a voice came from heaven, saying, 'This is my beloved Son, in whom I am well pleased'" (Matt. 3:16–17). The three persons were Jesus ("He," "Son"), "the Spirit," and "God," who spoke from heaven and referred to Himself as "I." This event does not demonstrate that all three persons are coequally divine, but it does show that three separate persons were at the same event at the same time.

At His temptation by Satan, Jesus was led by the Holy Spirit into the wilderness (4:1). As the divine-human Son of God, He knew that it was wrong for Him or anyone to tempt the Lord God by presumptuous acts (4:7). He also knew that true worship must always be directed toward the Lord God (4:10). In this event there is another distinction in the mention of the three persons, although this Scripture does not attribute deity to all three persons.

On the night before His crucifixion, Jesus Christ made a distinction among the three persons: "And I will pray the Father, and He will give you another Helper, that He may abide with you forever; the Spirit of truth" (John 14:16–17). He later repeated the distinction: "But the Helper, the Holy Spirit, whom the Father will send in My name, He will teach you all things, and bring to your remembrance all things that I said to you" (14:26; see also 15:26). He referred to the Father, the Holy Spirit, and Himself together as separate persons in heaven.

Christ distinguished the three persons of deity when He gave the missionary commission to the apostles: "Go therefore and make disciples of all the nations, baptizing them in the name of the Father and of the Son and of the Holy Spirit" (Matt. 28:19). God is one, so the name is singular. Since there are three persons within the divine being, they are distinguished as Father, Son, and Holy Spirit.

The Trinity is involved in the administration of spiritual gifts to believers within the body of Christ, the true church. "There are diversities of gifts, but the same Spirit. There are differences of ministries, but the same Lord. And there are diversities of activities, but it is the same God who works all in all" (1 Cor. 12:4–6). Here the Holy Spirit, the Lord Jesus Christ, and God the Father are each mentioned.

Paul ended an epistle with this glorious benediction: "The grace of the Lord Jesus Christ, and the love of God, and the communion of the Holy Spirit be with you all. Amen" (2 Cor. 13:14). The names of these three distinct persons are presented in this sequence: the Lord Jesus Christ, God the Father, and the Holy Spirit.

Peter explained the activity of the three persons in the program of redemption in this doctrinal exposition: "Elect according to the foreknowledge of God the Father, in sanctification of the Spirit, for obedience and sprinkling of the blood of Jesus Christ" (1 Pet. 1:2). Here the order of the three names is God the Father, the Holy Spirit, and Jesus Christ.

In an exhortation to believers to safeguard their spiritual experience, Jude wrote, "But you, beloved, building yourselves up on your most holy faith, praying in the Holy Spirit, keep yourselves in the love of God, looking for the mercy of our Lord Jesus Christ unto eternal life" (Jude 20–21). The order of the names here is the Holy Spirit, God the Father, and the Lord Jesus Christ.

These passages show that there is not a set order in which the names of the three persons appear. This observation is consistent with the equality of the three persons within the divine oneness. Evangelicals identify the Trinity as the Father, the Son, and the Holy Spirit. We use that order because of the familiar baptismal formula (Matt. 28:19) and because of the roles of the three persons in redemption in which the Father sent the Son, and both the Father and the Son sent the Holy Spirit.

In Personal Equality

Writers often identify the three persons of the Trinity as the First Person (the Father), the Second Person (the Son), and the Third Person (the Holy Spirit). Those nonbiblical designations may convey the impression that the Father is superior to both the Son and the Spirit and that the Son is superior to the Spirit. That perception, based on the name designations, is false.

There is no personal superiority or inferiority among the three persons of the Trinity. They are coequal in every way: eternal, infinite, omnipotent, omniscient, omnipresent divine persons.

Biblical statements. All three persons are named God. In Paul's greetings in his epistles, he wrote, "Grace to you and peace from God our Father and the Lord Jesus Christ" (Rom. 1:7; see also 1 Cor. 1:3; 2 Cor. 1:2; Gal. 1:3; Eph. 1:2; Phil. 1:2; Col. 1:2; 1 Thess. 1:1; 2 Thess. 1:2; 1 Tim. 1:2; 2 Tim. 1:2; Titus 1:4; Philem. 3).

According to the Book of Hebrews, God the Father said, "But to the Son He says: Your throne, O God, is forever and ever; a scepter of righteousness is the scepter of Your kingdom" (Heb. 1:8). Here God the Father called God the Son "God." Paul also called Jesus Christ God in Romans 9:5: "Of whom are the fathers and from whom, according to the flesh, Christ came, who is over all, the eternally blessed God. Amen."

As seen previously, Peter identified the Holy Spirit as God when he confronted Ananias: "Why has Satan filled your heart to lie to the Holy Spirit? . . . You have not lied to men but to God" (Acts 5:3–4). The couple, Ananias and Sapphira, conspired to test the Spirit of the Lord (5:9). According to Christ, such testing is a sin against the Lord God (Matt. 4:7).

The Bible repudiates polytheism, including the existence of three separate gods. These passages, therefore, must teach a Trinity in unity, a plurality of three persons within the divine oneness. Only then could the one divine being be called God while simultaneously three separate persons are also called God.

Creeds. The doctrine of Trinitarian monotheism, of which the deity of the Holy Spirit is a vital part, is a biblical mystery, a truth that could be revealed only by God Himself. No human, by a detailed study of nature or his own personality, would have concluded that God is Trinitarian in essence. The problem of understanding the nature of God is further compounded when we try to communicate the definition or description of God to others. What words, out of a finite human vocabulary, could sufficiently explain the infinite God? Many words tend to change in their meanings with the passing generation. Still other words can mean different things to various people.

The early church had to face this problem when it attempted to put into creedal statement its belief in the biblical teaching of the Trinity. The Athanasian Creed, formulated in the fourth century, stated, "We worship one God in Trinity, and Trinity in Unity, neither confounding the Persons, nor dividing the Substance." The church fathers used three important words to stress their belief in monotheism: *one, unity,* and *substance.* Likewise, they used these words to denote their belief in Trinitarianism: *Trinity* and *persons.* They were careful to point out that God could not be divided into three parts ("dividing the substance"). They also declared their belief in three persons who had an intrapersonal oneness within the one divine Being. They did not want to confound the persons, that is, they wanted to make it clear that the Father is neither the Son nor the Holy Spirit, that the Son is neither the Father nor the Spirit, and that the Holy Spirit is neither the Father nor the Son.

The Nicene Creed, formed about A.D. 325, stated, "I believe in one God . . . and in one Lord Jesus Christ, the . . . Son of God, begotten of the Father . . . light of light, very God of very God, begotten, not made, being of one substance with the Father . . . and . . . in the Holy Ghost." The Nicene-Constantinople Creed, formed in A.D. 381, reaffirmed this position. These creeds stood for centuries as the standard of doctrinal orthodoxy.

After the Protestant Reformation broke out over Europe in the sixteenth century, various church groups set forth their own doctrinal confessions. The Augsburg Confession, composed in A.D. 1530, reflected the belief system of Martin Luther and the Lutheran Church: "There is one Divine essence which is called and is God, eternal, without body, indivisible, of infinite power, wisdom, goodness, the Creator and Preserver of all things, visible and invisible, and yet there are three Persons of the same essence and power, who also are coeternal, the Father, the Son, and the Holy Ghost."

The Westminster Confession of the Presbyterian Church, composed in A.D. 1647, was also adopted by the Reformed Church in the Canon of the Synod of Dort. It affirmed, "There is but one living and true God. In the unity of the Godhead there are three Persons, of one substance, power, and eternity—God the Father, God the Son, and God the Holy Ghost. The Father is one, neither begotten nor proceeding; the Son is eternally begotten of the Father; the Holy Ghost eternally proceeding from the Father and the Son."

All these creeds affirmed Trinitarian monotheism. In the exposition of that belief, more content was given to explain the deity of Jesus Christ because of His incarnation and the Hypostatic Union. The confession of the deity of the Holy Spirit was generally given without much explanation to complete the statement on the Trinity.

Today a person must affirm his belief in Trinitarian monotheism along with other foundational doctrines in order to be known as orthodox, evangelical, or fundamentalist. If a person denies the Trinity, the deity of Jesus Christ, or the deity of the Holy Spirit, he is classified as a liberal, an apostate, or a cult member. Major religious groups, such as the Jehovah's Witnesses and the Mormons, deny the deity of the Holy Spirit.

As a faculty member at Cedarville College, I affirm annually its doctrinal statement with my written signature. One section states: "We believe in one God—eternal, omnipotent, omniscient, and omnipresent existing as three Persons—Father, Son, and Holy Spirit, one in nature, attributes, power, and glory." Another section reads: "We believe that the Holy Spirit is a divine Person, equal with God the Father and God the Son." No person can teach at Cedarville College if he denies the Trinity or the deity of the Holy Spirit.

Although it is difficult to use the right words to communicate the biblical teaching of the Trinity, we must attempt to do so. The difference between orthodoxy and heresy is often found in outright denials. Many times, however, the difference can be detected in what is not said, a deliberate silence on a key doctrinal point. Other differences can be seen in an understatement, an overstatement, or even a misstatement. Our choice of words should be purposeful and biblically driven. We should be cautious not to state more or less than what the Scriptures teach.

Loraine Boettner, a respected theologian, carefully expressed the biblical teaching on the Trinity in these words: "The Father, Son, and Holy Spirit can be distinguished, but they cannot be separated; for they each possess the same identical numerical substance or essence. They do not merely exist alongside of each other, as did Washington, Jefferson, and Franklin, but they permeate and interpenetrate each other, are in and through each other."[3] Boettner further stated, "What the one knows, the others know; what the one desires, the others desire; and what the one wills, the others will. Independence and self-existence are not attributes of the individual persons, but of the Triune God."[4]

Procession. Church councils and theologians have attempted to define the eternal relationships of the three divine Persons as to their roles or functions. They affirmed the eternal generation of the Son by the Father (Ps. 2:7; Acts 13:33) while denying that Christ was made or created. They also affirmed the eternal procession of the Holy Spirit from the Father and the Son. They used the terms *generation* and *procession* to designate the functional differences. The Creed of Constantinople (A.D. 381), stated that the Holy Spirit proceeded from the Father. At the Synod of Toledo in A.D. 589, the word *filoque* ("and Son") was added to show that the procession of the Spirit came from both the Father and the Son. At that time, the western half of Christendom, namely the Roman Catholic Church, accepted the view that the Spirit proceeds from both the Father and the Son. The eastern half, the Greek Orthodox Church, claimed that the procession was from only the Father.

The term *procession* comes from a promise made by Christ: "But when the Helper comes, whom I shall send to you from the Father, the Spirit of truth who proceeds from the Father, He will testify of Me" (John 15:26). The verb *ekporeuetai* ("proceeds") literally means "to go out of." Christ taught that the Father would give the Spirit in answer to the Savior's prayer (14:16–17), that the Father would send the Spirit in the name of Christ (14:26), that He would send the Spirit from the presence of the Father (15:26), and that He would send the Spirit once Jesus departed from the earth (16:7).

A distinction is to be noted between the "ontological" Trinity and the "economic" Trinity. The ontological Trinity deals with God as He is. The Father, the Son, the Holy Spirit are ontologically equal in person, sharing the same divine essence. Jesus Christ could thus affirm, "I and my Father are one" (10:30). They were one in essence, not one in person. Christ also declared, "He who has seen me has seen the Father" (14:9). Christ was not the Father, nor was the Father the Son. But all that the Father is in essence, the Son is in essence. God in His triune being is invisible, but God the Son through the incarnation "declared Him" (1:18), that is revealed Him. The visible, divine-human Son of God literally "exegeted" (*exēgēsato;* "declared") the essence of the divine Being. What is God like? The answer is to look at the incarnate Son, Jesus Christ.

The economic Trinity refers to God as He acts. Christ set forth this principle of function: "Most assuredly, I say to you, a servant is not greater than his master; nor is he who is sent greater than he who sent him" (13:16). With that principle in mind, Christ later said, "My Father is greater than I" (14:28). This greatness is an economic greatness, not an ontological greatness. The Father sent the Son; therefore the Father is greater than the Son. The Father and the Son sent the Holy Spirit; therefore the Father and the Son are economically greater than the Spirit.

Paul set forth the order of authoritative function: "But I want you to know that the head of every man is Christ, the head of woman is man, and the head of Christ is God" (1 Cor. 11:3). The man and the woman are coequally human. In ontological personhood, neither is superior or inferior to the other. In the family and in the church, however, the man has a headship role; thus the wife is to submit to her husband (Eph. 5:22; Col. 3:18; Titus 2:4–5). The headship of the husband over the wife must manifest the headship of God the Father over Jesus Christ. In that functional relationship the Father sent the Son, and the Son came in obedience to the will of the Father (Phil. 2:8; Heb. 10:7).

Thus the procession or sending of the Holy Spirit by the Father and the Son is similar in principle to the sending of the Son by the Father. The Spirit has come to do the will of the Father and the Son. The subordination of the Holy Spirit refers to His role within the economic Trinitarian concept, the way God acts. The Holy Spirit, ontologically, is very God of very God, coequal to the Father and the Son in eternal attributes and essence.

IMPLICATIONS FOR US

First, we must acknowledge the full eternal deity of the Holy Spirit. We must affirm His coequality with the Father and the Son. Thus we must view His divine personhood and ministry seriously. Because He is God, we must bow before Him in humble respect and obedience.

Second, we must learn to verbalize the doctrine of the Trinity accurately. We must not be sloppy in our choice of words or in our expression of the relationship of the three persons within the one divine Being. Since we affirm Trinitarian monotheism, we should be able to defend that teaching from the Scriptures. May I suggest that you do more reading on pneumatology, the doctrine of the Holy Spirit. Consult the selected bibliography at the end of this book. Add some of these books to your church library or personal library. Also read sections on Christology, the doctrine of Christ, and on theology proper, the doctrine of God. Think of the deity of the Holy Spirit in relation to the deity of Christ and of the Father.

Third, we must be alert to error concerning the doctrine of the Trinity, and especially the teaching of the Holy Spirit. Paul cautioned, "Test all things; hold fast what is good" (1 Thess. 5:21). And John warned, "Beloved, do not believe every spirit, but test the spirits, whether they are of God; because many false prophets have gone out into the world. By this you know the Spirit of God: Every spirit that confesses that Jesus Christ has come in the flesh is of God" (1 John 4:1–2). We should avoid being naive or gullible, carefully analyzing what we read, hear, or watch. We should double-check all references to the Holy Spirit by the clear teaching of the inspired Word of God.

Fourth, let's learn about proper biblical subordination from the person of the Holy Spirit. From His doing the will of the Father and the Son, we, too, can learn to be submissive in our homes, our churches, and society.

CHAPTER THREE

The Symbols of the Holy Spirit

Illustrations are often windows through which we can see and understand spiritual truths. We are prone to perceive the supernatural from our natural point of view. We like to reduce the abstract to the concrete. We want to know the unknown from the known. We gaze at the eternal through our temporal sight.

God recognized this human limitation when He directed the human authors of Scripture to describe spiritual truths in terms people could understand. These contemporary symbols were used to illustrate many doctrinal areas, including the doctrine of the Holy Spirit.

THEIR SIGNIFICANCE

Jesus Christ often made a direct correlation between life situations and spiritual lessons. For example, He asked, "What man is there among you who has one sheep and if it falls into a pit on the Sabbath, will not lay hold of it and lift it out? Of how much more value then is a man than a sheep. Therefore it is lawful to do good on the Sabbath" (Matt. 12:11–12).

In His public ministry to an audience of both receptive and critical listeners, Jesus spoke in parables. The Greek word *parabolē* ("parable") literally means "cast beside." Christ placed redemptive truth beside natural occurrences to clarify His teaching. Thus He equated responses to the spoken gospel to various types of soil and the preacher to a sower of seed (13:3–23). He related the eternal separation of the saved from the unsaved to the separation of the wheat from the tares in a harvest (13:24–32, 36–43), to the separation of good fish from bad fish (13:47–51), and to the separation of sheep from goats (Matt. 25:31).

Christ also used metaphors to explain His person and ministry. He equated Himself to the shepherd of the sheep (John 10:11), to the door of the sheepfold (10:9), and to light (8:12). He saw Himself as the vine and His disciples as the branches (15:5).[1]

The authors of the New Testament books used events, persons, and objects mentioned in the Old Testament to point out an illustrative fulfillment in the redemptive work of Jesus Christ. Theologians call this study typology. The type is found in the Old Testament, and its fulfillment, known as the antitype, is seen in the New Testament. For example, Paul wrote, "For indeed Christ, our Passover, was sacrificed for us" (1 Cor. 5:7). Christ's redemptive sacrifice on the cross was equated with the experience of the Israelites under the bondage of Egypt in the time of Moses. God told each Jewish household to kill a lamb and to sprinkle its blood on the doorposts and lintels of their houses. God then explained that He would pass over the Jewish families and that He would judge the Egyptian households with the deaths of the firstborn males (Exod. 12:12–13). In fulfillment all believers are under the protective blood of Christ's death; thus they will not experience eternal judgment. Other well-accepted types are the elevated serpent of brass (John 3:14–15) and the ripped veil of the Jerusalem temple (Heb. 10:19–20).

Most types, metaphors, analogies, and symbols focus on the work of redemption, centered in Jesus Christ and His death on the cross. However, God also guided the biblical authors to use some symbols to describe the person and ministry of the Holy Spirit.

THEIR DESCRIPTION

He Surrounds Like Clothing

In His postresurrection ministry, Jesus Christ informed His apostles: "I am going to send you what the Father has promised; but stay in the city

[Jerusalem] until you have been clothed with power from on high" (Luke 24:49, NIV). The verb *endyō* ("endued") is normally used of putting on clothing. Some major translations (NASB, NIV, RSV) use that metaphor, translating the phrase, "until you have been clothed with power from on high." Christ later identified the power (*dynamis*) as the Holy Spirit when the Savior instructed His apostles shortly before His ascension: "But you shall receive power when the Holy Spirit has come upon you; and you shall be witnesses to Me in Jerusalem, and in all Judea and Samaria, and to the end of the earth" (Acts 1:8). There is no power or enablement apart from the Holy Spirit. This enduement with the Holy Spirit occured once and for all on the Day of Pentecost (Acts 2). It was a nonrepeatable event in the history of Christendom and in the lives of the apostles.

Endyō is used of putting on various types of clothing: the daily wardrobe (Matt. 6:25), a wedding garment (22:11), Christ's clothing (27:31), the camel-hair garment of John the Baptist (Mark 1:6), the purple robe placed on the scourged Christ (15:17), the best robe placed on the prodigal son (Luke 15:22), and the royal apparel of Herod Agrippa I (Acts 12:21).

This verb is also used to depict spiritual clothing. As spiritual soldiers, believers should put on the armor of light (Rom. 13:12), the whole armor of God (Eph. 6:11), the breastplate of righteousness (6:14), and the breastplate of faith (1 Thess. 5:8). In their spiritual position, all believers have "put on" Christ (Gal. 3:27) and the new man (Col. 3:10). In spiritual practice, believers should "put on" the Lord Jesus Christ to win over the lusts of sin (Rom. 13:14), "put on" the new man (Eph. 4:24), and "put on" the qualities of holiness (Col. 3:12).

The verb is also employed of putting on the immortal, incorruptible body (1 Cor. 15:53–54; 2 Cor. 5:3). On the island of Patmos, John saw the glorified Christ clothed (*endyō*) with a garment down to His feet (Rev. 1:13). The seven angels who bore the seven bowls of divine judgment were clothed in pure bright linen (15:6), and the heavenly armies that will return with Christ to the earth will be clothed in fine linen, white and clean (19:14).

Clothing identifies. It reveals status (a king), a vocation (an NFL player), membership in the military (a Marine), and religious preference (a Buddhist monk). When the apostles were clothed with the Holy Spirit, they were identified as Christ's authenticated spokesmen who were to evangelize the world. In modern jargon, they were "dressed for success."

One symbol of the power of the Holy Spirit in the life of Elijah was his mantle. He once took his mantle, rolled it up, and struck the waters of the Jordan River (2 Kings 2:8). The waters divided, and both Elisha and he walked to the other side on dry ground. Later God took Elijah into heaven. Elisha witnessed this remarkable event, tore up his own clothes, and took the mantle of Elijah that had been left behind. Elisha then struck the Jordan River with the mantle and walked through the parted waters.

The Holy Spirit became the "clothing" of the twelve chosen apostles. He identified, enabled, and protected them. They could not have an effective ministry without being properly dressed. Their spiritual ministry required spiritual "attire," namely, the Holy Spirit Himself. In like manner, we, too, must also be surrounded by the powerful clothing of the Spirit as we seek to serve our God.

He Guarantees Like a Deposit

In three key passages dealing with the security of our salvation, Paul equated the Holy Spirit with a deposit guaranteed by God. He wrote, "Now He who establishes us with you in Christ and has anointed us is God, who also has sealed us and given us the Spirit in our hearts as a guarantee" (2 Cor. 1:21–22). Later, to the same church, he added, "Now He who has prepared us for this very thing is God, who also has given us the Spirit as a guarantee" (5:5).

In his doxology to the triune God for the plan of redemption, Paul set forth this ministry of the Holy Spirit: "In Him you also trusted, after you heard the word of truth, the gospel of your salvation; in whom also, having believed, you were sealed with the Holy Spirit of promise, who is the guarantee of our inheritance until the redemption of the purchased possession, to the praise of His glory" (Eph. 1:13–14).

In the New Testament the Greek word *arrabōn* ("guarantee") is found in only these three passages. It has also been translated as "deposit" (NIV), "pledge" (NASB), and "earnest" (KJV). It originally referred to earnest-money deposited by a purchaser. It was a guarantee that the rest of the purchase price would be paid in the future. The word also referred in ancient culture to a gift a man would give to a woman as an expression of his love for her. In modern Greek usage the word *arrabōn* refers to the engagement ring as the pledge of love and of the intention to marry.

There is one event in Old Testament history where the *arrabōn* ("pledge") played an important part. Judah, now widowed, wanted to have sexual relations with a woman he believed to be a prostitute (Gen. 38:15). The woman actually was Tamar, his daughter-in-law, whose husband Er had died many years before. In response to his request Tamar asked, " 'What will you give me, that you may come in to me?' " And he said, 'I will send a young goat from the flock.' So she said, 'Will you give me a pledge [*arrabōn* in the Septuagint] till you send it?' Then he said, 'What pledge shall I give you?' So she said, 'Your signet and cord, and your staff that is in your hand.' Then he gave them to her, and went in to her, and she conceived by him" (38:16–18). Later Judah sent a goat to her and retrieved his pledge (38:20). Tamar later gave birth to twins, and one of them, Perez, was a part of the genealogical ancestry of the Messiah, Jesus Christ (Matt. 1:3).

How then does the Holy Spirit compare to the *arrabōn?* First, God is the giver of the pledge (2 Cor. 1:22). Second, it is a gift (1:22). We believing sinners do not receive the Holy Spirit by our efforts. Third, God gives the Spirit as a guarantee only to "us," namely, believers (1:22). The unsaved do not possess the Spirit (Rom. 8:9). Fourth, the Holy Spirit is Himself the guarantee, the pledge, the earnest, the deposit (2 Cor. 1:22). Fifth, God has placed the guarantee of the Spirit in our hearts (1:22). This act is the fulfillment of the promises made by God in the New Covenant (Ezek. 36:26–27).

Sixth, the presence of the Holy Spirit in our lives is the divine guarantee that we will have immortal, incorruptible bodies in eternity, totally free from the effects of sin (2 Cor. 5:5). Seventh, the Holy Spirit is the guarantee of our spiritual inheritance (Eph. 1:14). Although the believer has already been blessed with bountiful spiritual gifts, he does not yet have the experience of the full enjoyment of all that Christ has graciously provided. The presence and witness of the Holy Spirit is God's pledge to us that we will one day have all that belongs to us because we are in Christ. Eighth, the Holy Spirit will remain as the guarantee until the return of

Christ and the rapture of the church, namely, the "redemption of the purchased possession" (Eph. 1:14). The Greek word *peripoiēseōs* ("purchased possession") is a noun based on the verb *peripoieō* ("to purchase"). Paul used this term to describe Christ's purchase of the church of God with His blood (Acts 20:28). Ninth, our understanding of the blessed truth that the Holy Spirit is God's guarantee to us should cause us to praise the glory of His grace (Eph. 1:14). God is truth; therefore He would never lie about the secure position of our personal salvation.

He Descends Like a Dove

Dove awards are given each year to Christian musicians for their successful accomplishments. Many believers wear dove jewelry to manifest their Christian identity. At the church where I pastor, pictures of doves are often projected onto the wall behind the pulpit platform.

The symbol of the dove for the person and ministry of the Holy Spirit is based on the baptism of Jesus Christ, an event recorded in all four Gospels. "When He had been baptized, Jesus came up immediately from the water; and behold, the heavens were opened to Him, and He saw the Spirit of God descending like a dove and alighting upon Him. And suddenly a voice came from heaven, saying, 'This is My beloved Son, in whom I am well pleased' " (Matt. 3:16–17). Luke added that Jesus was praying when the Spirit descended on Him (Luke 3:21), and John mentioned that the Spirit remained on Christ (John 1:32). The representation of the Spirit as a dove is indicated only in this event in the life of Christ. It is never connected to His ministry in the lives of the prophets or the apostles.

What is the significance of this symbolism? First, it was a visible confirmation of the fact that the invisible Holy Spirit had indeed come upon Jesus Christ. Concerning Christ, the forerunner John the Baptist declared, " 'I did not know Him, but that He should be revealed to Israel, therefore I came baptizing with water.' And John bore witness, saying, 'I saw the Spirit descending from heaven like a dove, and He remained upon Him. I did not know Him, but He who sent me to baptize with water said to me, "Upon whom you see the Spirit descending, and remaining on Him, this is He who baptizes with the Holy Spirit." And I have seen and testified that this is the Son of God' " (John 1:31–34). John needed to see, and he did.

Second, the heavenly descent of the dove revealed that the Holy Spirit had proceeded out of God. It depicted His divine essence.

Third, the dove is a symbol of peace, gentleness, and beauty. These qualities—attributes of the divine essence—marked both Jesus Christ and the Holy Spirit. Christ, as our compassionate High Priest, is both holy and harmless (Heb. 7:26). The Savior charged His followers to be harmless as doves (Matt. 10:16). The impact of the Spirit on a life is like that of a dove, not like that of an eagle, hawk, or vulture.

He Burns Like a Fire

Our God is a "consuming fire" (Heb. 12:29). God appeared to Moses in the midst of a burning bush (Exod. 3:2). God led the redeemed Israelites through the wilderness by day in a pillar of cloud and by night in a pillar of fire (13:21). Fire has often been associated with the presence of the Lord (13:21), the refining tests of the Lord (Mal. 3:2–3), the approval of the Lord (1 Kings 18:38), the guidance and protection of the Lord (Mal. 3:2–3; 1 Pet. 1:7), the Word of God (Jer. 5:14), and the judgment of the Lord (Lev. 10:2).

Some interpreters have tried to equate the baptism of the Holy Spirit with the baptism of fire (Matt. 3:11). They see the fire as a good fire designed to purify believers of sin. However, in Matthew 3:11, John the Baptist used the symbol of fire to refer to eternal punishment. John charged his listeners to flee from the coming wrath, and he told the Jews not to trust in their racial heritage. He declared that trees, that is people, who did not produce the good fruit of repentance, would be cut down and cast into the fire (3:7–10). John then set forth the ministry of the coming Messiah: "He will baptize you with the Holy Spirit and fire. His winnowing fan is in His hand and He will thoroughly clean out His threshing floor, and gather His wheat into the barn; but He will burn up the chaff with unquenchable fire" (3:11–12). The wheat represents the saved, and the chaff depict the unsaved. The triple mention of fire must be interpreted consistently as the same type of fire, namely, the fire of judgment for unbelieving sinners. John the Baptist spoke to a divided audience, composed of critical unbelievers like the Pharisees and the Sadducees, and genuine converts who had been baptized by him in water.

Christ later informed the apostles that they would be baptized in the

Holy Spirit (Acts 1:5), but He made no mention of a baptism in fire because the apostles were believers. When the apostles were baptized in the Holy Spirit and filled by the Spirit on the Day of Pentecost, some interpreters have assumed that the Twelve were also baptized in the fire of the Holy Spirit. They base that conclusion upon this statement: "Then there appeared to them divided tongues, as of fire, and one sat upon each of them" (2:3). Earlier, the Spirit as the sound of a rushing mighty wind filled the room where the apostles were sitting (2:2). At that point, the apostles were literally surrounded or baptized in the Holy Spirit. The phenomenon of the fiery tongues showed that the Spirit had indeed come on each of the apostles. Subsequently all were filled with the Spirit (2:4). Thus the Spirit was around them, on them, and in them. These phenomena dramatized the coming of the Holy Spirit, even as Jesus Christ had prayed and promised. Their experience of having tongues of fire on them was not repeated in the experiences of any future believers.

When the apostle John was caught up into heaven, he saw the throne of God the Father, and he observed, "And from the throne proceeded lightnings, thunderings, and voices. Seven lamps of fire were burning before the throne, which are the seven Spirits of God" (Rev. 4:5). These seven spirits are interpreted either as seven angelic spirits or as the Holy Spirit described in symbolic perfection. Christ is later depicted as "a lamb, as though it had been slain, having seven horns and seven eyes, which are the seven Spirits of God sent out into all the earth" (5:6). In an opening blessing, John stated that grace and peace came "from Him who is and who was and who is to come [God the Father], and from the seven Spirits [God the Holy Spirit] who are before His throne and from Jesus Christ" (1:4–5). Grace and peace proceed from God, not from people or angels. It is more plausible to believe that the "seven Spirits" refer to the Holy Spirit because the symbolic phrase is used between the names of the Father and of the Son.

Isaiah predicted the time "when the Lord [will have] washed away the filth of the daughters of Zion, and purged the blood of Jerusalem from her midst, by the spirit of judgment and by the spirit of burning" (Isa. 4:4). God will judge and refine Israel during the seven-year time period prior to the coming of Jesus Christ to the earth to establish His millennial kingdom.

He Anoints Like Oil

There is no explicit statement in the Bible that equates the Holy Spirit with oil. However, there is some symbolical significance in the ways oil was used.

The high priest and the priests were anointed with oil when they were inducted into their priestly offices (Exod. 40:12–16). It was predicted that God would anoint the Messiah with the Spirit of God (Isa. 61:1). That prophecy was fulfilled at the baptism of Jesus Christ when God anointed Him with the Holy Spirit and with power (Acts 10:38). No actual oil was poured on Jesus, but He did begin His official prophetic and priestly ministries after the Spirit came on Him.

Samuel anointed with oil both Saul and David to become kings (1 Sam. 10:1; 16:13). God anointed Christ with "the oil of gladness" when the Father established the eternal throne and kingdom of the Son (Heb. 1:8–10; see Ps. 45:7).

As members of the true church, believers constitute "a royal priesthood" (1 Pet. 2:9). Through the sacrifice of Christ, we are able to go into the heavenly Holy of Holies, the actual presence of God (Heb. 10:19–22). Israel *had* a priesthood, but we *are* a priesthood. When Christ reigns on the earth, believers will also reign with Him as priests (Rev. 1:6; 5:10). When a person is saved, God anoints him or her with the Holy Spirit (2 Cor. 1:21; 1 John 2:27).

He Secures Like a Seal

God seals a person at the moment of salvation (2 Cor. 1:22). Paul explained, "In Him you also trusted, after you heard the word of truth, the gospel of your salvation; in whom also, having believed, you were sealed with the Holy Spirit of promise" (Eph. 1:13). Paul later warned believers, "And do not grieve the Holy Spirit of God, by whom you were sealed for the day of redemption" (4:30). These three passages are the only places where the Holy Spirit is equated to a seal.

The concept of sealing was common in biblical times. It signified security, ownership, authority, and permanence. These characteristics can also be seen in our spiritual sealing.

First, God is the One who sealed us (2 Cor. 1:22). There is no authority or protector greater than Him. Second, God seals only believers (1:22). Third, He sealed us completely in a moment of time (1:22). Sealing is not a process: It is a nonrepeatable event.

Fourth, a person is sealed when he believes in Christ (Eph. 1:13). Logically, the sealing occurs after one believes, but chronologically it happened at the moment of salvation. Fifth, the Holy Spirit is Himself the seal (Eph. 1:13). Elsewhere Paul explained, "Nevertheless the solid foundation of God stands, having this seal: 'The Lord knows those who are His,' and, 'Let everyone who names the name of Christ depart from iniquity'" (2 Tim. 2:19). How does the Lord know who is His? He knows by the presence of the Holy Spirit in our lives. Sixth, the seal of the Spirit is God's promise that we will have full redemption in eternity (Eph. 1:14).

Seventh, believers can grieve the Spirit by their sins, but they cannot break the divine seal (4:30). Eighth, the seal points to the day of redemption, the day when Christ returns to take us to be with Him (4:30).[2]

He Serves like a Servant

There is a striking analogy between the ministry of the Holy Spirit in the church age and the ministry of Abraham's servant, Eliezer of Damascus (Gen. 15:2). Some interpreters have identified this comparison as a type, but the Bible does not say it is. However, there are enough similarities in their respective ministries to warrant serious consideration.

First, Abraham sent Eliezer from Canaan, the Promised Land, to Mesopotamia on a mission (24:1–10). God the Father sent the Holy Spirit from heaven to earth on a mission (John 14:26).

Second, the mission of Eliezer was to secure a virgin bride for Isaac, Abraham's son (Gen. 24:3–4). The mission of the Holy Spirit is to secure the bride, the true church, for Jesus Christ (1 Cor. 12:13; 2 Cor. 11:2).

Third, Eliezer gave gifts to Rebekah (Gen. 24:22). The Holy Spirit gives spiritual gifts to the members of the body of Christ (1 Cor. 12:4, 7–11).

Fourth, Eliezer glorified Isaac as he explained his mission to Rebekah and her family (Gen. 24:34–49). The Holy Spirit glorifies Christ (John 16:14).

Fifth, Eliezer completed his task as he escorted Rebekah and presented her to Isaac (Gen. 24:57–67). The Holy Spirit will finish His task as He brings people to Christ and completes the bride of Christ.

This servant motif is definitely true of the Holy Spirit.

He Produces Fruit Like a Vine

Christ identified Himself as the true Vine, the believers as the branches, and God the Father as the Vinedresser (John 15:1, 5). The fruit of the vine is Christlikeness. Although the Holy Spirit is not called a vine, He is a producer of fruit. The analogy could refer to a grapevine or to a fruit-bearing tree.

Paul wrote, "But the fruit of the Spirit is love, joy, peace, longsuffering, kindness, goodness, faithfulness, gentleness, self-control" (Gal. 5:22–23). These moral qualities can be produced within believers only by the Spirit's power. These spiritual virtues accurately describe the essence of Christlikeness. As the Spirit was upon Christ and filled Him, these nine aspects of spiritual fruit can be seen in the life of the Savior. Indwelt by the living Christ and the Spirit, we, too, can manifest moral excellence before others.

He Refreshes Like Water

I love the melody and the opening words of that classic western song: "All day I face / the barren waste / without the taste / of water / cool, clear water." We can all identify with the dry mouths of those cowboys out on the prairie. There is nothing so refreshing on a hot summer day as a drink of cool, clear water. Soft drinks and other man-made beverages cannot compare with the pure water created by God.

In a significant passage Christ equated the Holy Spirit with the cool, clear water springing up out of a deep artesian well. The Savior said to the multitude who attended the Jewish Feast of Tabernacles, "If anyone thirsts, let him come to Me and drink. He who believes in Me, as the Scripture has said, out of his heart will flow rivers of living water" (John 7:37–38). John then gave the following explanation: "But this He spoke concerning the Spirit, whom those believing in Him would receive; for the Holy Spirit was not yet given, because Jesus was not yet glorified" (7:39).

The Feast of Tabernacles commemorated the time when the Israelites lived in tents or tabernacles as they wandered through the wilderness for forty years. Two major events occurred during this religious national celebration. The first was the lighting of a large menorah or lampstand in the temple court. This action symbolized the provision of light in the pillar of fire that guided them at night. The second event was a priest-led procession to the Pool of Siloam, where they filled many pitchers with water. They then went back to the temple court where they poured out the water. This action symbolized the time when the Israelites drank water that came out of the rock.

Paul equated the rock with Christ: "And [they] all drank the same spiritual drink. For they drank of that spiritual Rock that followed them, and that Rock was Christ" (1 Cor. 10:4). God instructed Moses to smite the rock in Horeb (Exod. 17:5–7). When he did, water came out of the rock, and the people drank. The smiting of the rock pictures the crucifixion of Christ, who was smitten for us.

On a later occasion, God charged Moses to speak to the rock so that water would come out (Num. 20:7–9). Moses, however, in anger smote the rock twice (20:10–11). Water came out, and the people drank, but God criticized Moses for striking the rock instead of speaking to it. He informed Moses that he would not be the leader who would take the people into Canaan (20:12). The chastisement of God was severe because Moses' sin had violated the divine intention of the type. Christ, the Rock, had to be smitten only once to produce the water of everlasting life. Henceforth, people can receive forgiveness by speaking to Him in faith.

Christ thus equated the "rivers of living water" with the Holy Spirit (John 7:37–39). At the time Christ spoke at the Feast of Tabernacles, He had not yet died. He, the Rock, had not yet been smitten. After His crucifixion the Holy Spirit could then indwell and refresh the lives of believers.

There may be another allusion to the Spirit as water in Christ's invitation to the Samaritan woman at the well in Sychar: "Whoever drinks of this water will thirst again, but whoever drinks of the water that I shall give him will never thirst. But the water that I shall give him will become in him a fountain of water springing up into everlasting life" (4:13–14). There is a contrast between habitual drinking of normal water with a once-for-all drink of spiritual water. There is another comparison between constant, daily thirst and a permanently satisfied thirst.

On one of my trips to Israel, I went to Sychar (modern Nablus), situated between Mount Ebal and Mount Gerizim. It is the Old Testament town of Shechem. Located within a religious compound is a deep well, known as Jacob's Well. The priest lowered a bucket into the artesian well and drew it back to the top. I tasted the refreshing, cool water. However, later in the day I was thirsty again. But years before when I was a teenager, I drank of Christ, and He satisfied me forever.

Isaiah predicted a spiritual refreshing of Israel that would occur in the messianic kingdom: "For I will pour water on him who is thirsty, and floods on the dry ground; I will pour My Spirit on your descendants, and My blessing on your offspring" (Isa. 44:3). Here Isaiah spoke of water as an illustration of the Spirit of God.

Like water, the indwelling presence of the Holy Spirit brings life, freshness, and vitality to the believer. Each Christian has within himself a spiritual artesian well that will never run dry.

He Moves Like a Wind

Winds can be either destructive or refreshing. My family and I witnessed the terrifying tornado that ravaged the Ohio towns of Xenia, Wilberforce, and Cedarville in April 1974. We went into our basement and huddled under a Ping-Pong table. Fortunately, the tornado passed a few hundred yards north of our house. The winds within it were estimated at three hundred miles per hour. There was extensive property damage and severe loss of lives. Tornadoes, hurricanes, and typhoons have wreaked havoc in every generation.

At the same time, there is nothing like a cool breeze on a hot, humid summer day to revive a soul. My wife has often spoken of the joy of feeling a warm Chinook wind in the middle of winter in the Pacific Northwest.

The word *pneuma* can be translated as "Spirit," "spirit," "wind," or "breath." The imagery of the Holy Spirit as wind is found in the Scriptures. He is like a productive wind, not a destructive one. As God, He is always the source of good and perfect gifts (James 1:17). His ministry renews us (Titus 3:5).

Jesus said to Nicodemus: "The wind [*pneuma*] blows where it wishes, and you hear the sound of it, but cannot tell where it comes from and where it goes. So is everyone who is born of the Spirit [*pneuma*]" (John 3:8). Wind is invisible. You can't see it, but you can feel it and see its effects, such as the moving of leaves or the bending of branches. Wind is unpredictable. It can swirl, change directions, start and stop quickly.

Likewise, the Holy Spirit sovereignly moves on people in convicting them of sin and regenerating them. Through faith, people can be born again in a church service, in a car, at home, or at a country retreat. In an audience, many will hear the gospel, but the Spirit will selectively give spiritual birth to some while passing by others. That sovereign activity reminds us of pictures where we see one house spared and houses on either side destroyed by a tornado. It is impossible to explain, but it is so.

The activity of the Holy Spirit in regeneration thus can't be programmed by humans. We cannot know in advance whom the Spirit will regenerate. Also we can't restrict the sovereign work of the Spirit to our prescribed programs of evangelism.

Luke described the advent of the Holy Spirit on the Day of Pentecost in this way: "And suddenly there came a sound from heaven, as of a rushing mighty wind [*pnoē*], and it filled the whole house where they were sitting" (Acts 2:2). The wind filled the room and literally enveloped the apostles. They were in the wind. Thus, they were in the Holy Spirit, baptized in the Holy Spirit, even as Jesus had promised ten days earlier (1:5). They heard the sound and were surrounded by it. They did not see the invisible Spirit, but they sensed His presence and control. The effects of His coming were later detected by the appearance of the fiery tongues, by their speaking in foreign languages they had not learned, by the listening of the multitude, and by the conversion of three thousand people (2:3–41).

On the night Christ first appeared to the apostles after His resurrection He declared, "'Peace to you! As the Father has sent Me, I also send you.' And when He had said this, He breathed [*enephysēsen*] on them, and said to them, 'Receive the Holy Spirit'" (John 20:21–22). The verb *emphysaō* ("to breathe") is found only here in the New Testament. In the Septuagint this verb is used of God breathing the breath of life into Adam (Gen. 2:7). The word is also used of the breathing of life into the dry bones, a vision that depicted the regeneration and reestablishment of the nation of Israel in the end times (Ezek. 37:9). The outbreathing of Christ placed the Holy Spirit in the lives of the apostles. They could then receive the postresurrection teaching of Christ and fulfill the missionary commission.

Peter described the movement of the Spirit on the authors of inspired Scripture: "For prophecy never came by the will of man, but holy men of God spoke as they were moved by the Holy Spirit" (2 Pet. 1:21). The Holy Spirit "moved" (*pherō*) men as ancient sailing ships were moved by the tradewinds. Sails without wind have no power to generate movement. Likewise, the sanctified authors could not produce Scripture on their own. Their enablement came through the divine wind, namely, the Holy Spirit.

IMPLICATIONS FOR US

First, we must relate the ministry of the Holy Spirit to our daily activities. As the Bible used the symbols of life to describe the Spirit, so we should think consciously of Him whenever we engage in the pursuits of life. Whenever we make a down payment on a purchase, we should thank God for the *arrabōn* of the Spirit. Whenever we break a seal on a package or a registered letter, we should thank God for our sealing until the day of redemption.

Second, we should ask God for forgiveness whenever we think the Christian life is stale and boring. The indwelling Spirit is the source of freshness, vitality, and fruit-bearing. We should focus on personally submitting to Him and not on legalistic conformity to liturgy or the faulty expectations of others.

Third, we must recognize that the ministry of the Holy Spirit is indispensable. Without Him, we can do nothing for the glory of God. In our evangelistic efforts, we need to trust His sovereign work in people's lives, not in our own charisma or expertise.

Fourth, we must learn how to serve even as the Spirit serves. If we are indeed controlled by the Spirit, we will be neither arrogant nor passive. Rather, we will be actively glorifying Christ as we serve others.

CHAPTER FOUR

The Ministry of the Holy Spirit in the Old Testament

The Old Testament includes about one hundred references to the Holy Spirit. Sometimes it is difficult to determine whether the mention of the word "Spirit" refers to the person of the Holy Spirit or to God's own spiritual essence. The emphasis in the Old Testament is on the oneness of God in contrast to polytheism. However, the New Testament declares that the Holy Spirit was active in the ancient history of Israel (Acts 7:51; 2 Pet. 1:21).

THE HOLY SPIRIT IN CREATION

The Bible begins, "In the beginning God created the heavens and the earth" (Gen. 1:1). John claimed that the created order came through Christ (John 1:3). Paul asserted that all things were created by Christ and for Him (Col. 1:16). Paul also stated that God the Father was the Source of all created things (1 Cor. 8:6). Though the New Testament nowhere speaks of the actual ministry of the Holy Spirit in creation, He, however, was actively involved in the Creation event. Moses wrote, "The earth was without form, and void; and darkness was on the face of the deep. And the Spirit of God was hovering over the face of the waters" (Gen. 1:2). Sinclair Ferguson commented, "What is of interest is that the activity of the divine *rûaḥ* ['Spirit'] is precisely that of extending God's presence into creation in such a way as to order and complete what has been planned in the mind of God."[1] Whenever the Holy Spirit is involved in any activity, there is control, order, purpose, and beauty (1 Cor. 14:40). The Spirit of God hovered over the created matter of the universe like a dove covering her newly laid eggs. He providentially superintended the waters that surrounded the earth until the triune God finalized the creative design in six days.

The psalmist declared, "By the word of the LORD the heavens were made, and all the host of them by the breath of His mouth" (Ps. 33:6). Is the breath (*rûaḥ)* of God's mouth an anthropomorphism or a reference to the Holy Spirit? When God breathed out His inspired Word, the Scriptures, He did it by the activity of the Holy Spirit (2 Tim. 3:15–16; 2 Pet. 1:21). It is plausible to believe that the Holy Spirit actively energized the spoken decree of God in creation.

Another psalm has the superscription, "Praise to the God of creation" (Ps. 104), and one of its verses reads, "You send forth Your Spirit, they are created; And You renew the face of the earth" (v. 30). The Spirit is connected to the earth, both in creation and renewal. Preserving, animating, and refreshing the creation are all aspects of the ministry of the Spirit.

The Book of Job has three references to creation and to the Spirit of God. Job asserted, "By His Spirit He adorned the heavens" (Job 26:13). Job also attributed his life principle to God when he said, "As long as my breath is in me, and the breath of God in my nostrils" (27:3). Elihu later gave a similar confession: "The Spirit of God has made me, and the breath of the Almighty gives me life" (33:4). These passages group together the concepts of God, Spirit, life, breath, heavens, and personal existence.

God is both transcendent (supreme over the universe) and immanent (near His creation). His transcendence denies the concept of pantheism, the false theory that all is God, and yet He is actively involved in the time-space universe. His immanence denies the concept of deism, the false theory that He withdrew completely from superintending the created world. Since God is triune, the Holy Spirit must have manifested both His transcendence and immanence at the Creation.

THE HOLY SPIRIT IN PEOPLE

God has administered His creative-redemptive program in various ways in different ages. He has guided and is presently moving the affairs of men and nations toward the goal of the establishment of His kingdom on the earth.

In past ages the Holy Spirit ministered in the lives of people. Some Christians have thought that the Spirit began His ministry on earth only in this church age. It is true that the Spirit of God began a different ministry with His descent on the Day of Pentecost (Acts 2), but as the omnipresent God, He worked in the lives of selected people.

From Creation to the Exodus

The Book of Genesis covers the period from Adam to Joseph. It includes both the beginnings of the human race (Gen. 1–11) and of the Hebrew people (Genesis 12–50).

Restraining sin. There is no mention of any ministry of the Holy Spirit in the lives of Adam, Eve, Abel, Seth, Enoch, or Noah. Abel, Enoch, and Noah are cited, however, as examples of true faith (Heb. 11:4–7), and Jude identified Enoch as a prophet (Jude 14).

The only mention of the ministry of the Spirit in this early era is in relationship to the wickedness of sinners. God said, "My Spirit shall not strive with man forever, for he is indeed flesh; yet his days shall be one hundred and twenty years" (Gen. 6:3). The pre-Flood period ended with only eight righteous persons, Noah and his family, living in the midst of a sin-dominated world. The situation was extremely grave: "Then the LORD saw that the wickedness of man was great in the earth, and that every intent of the thoughts of his heart was only evil continually. And the LORD was sorry that He had made man on the earth, and He was grieved in His heart" (6:5–6).

God declared that His Spirit would not strive or "contend" (NIV) with man endlessly. He gave that world 120 years in which to repent. The Hebrew word rendered "contend" means "to judge, or to render a judicial decision against one." As Merrill Unger commented, "The meaning is to be taken in the sense of the Holy Spirit bringing a judicial charge of guilt against the pre-Flood sinners through the ministry of God's servants warning them of their lawlessness."[2] The Holy Spirit convicted that world through the godly lives and proclamation of men such as Enoch and Noah. His convicting work on them and their opportunity to repent ceased, however, when the Flood destroyed the wicked.

Joseph. There is no mention of the ministry of the Holy Spirit in the lives of the Hebrew patriarchs, Abraham, Isaac, and Jacob. These men were godly examples of genuine faith (Heb. 11:8–21). The New Testament speaks often of Abraham, declaring him to be the father of the faithful (Gal. 3:7). The Scriptures never speak of any activity of the Spirit in his life, although it was certainly possible.

After Joseph interpreted the two dreams of Pharaoh and set forth a plan for food conservation, the ruler of Egypt asked concerning Joseph, "Can we find such a one as this, a man in whom is the Spirit of God?" (Gen. 41:38). Pharaoh then appointed Joseph as the administrator of the land of Egypt. How much understanding about God and the Spirit of God did Pharaoh have? We do not know. The Egyptian ruler did recognize that God had revealed the meaning of the dreams, even as Joseph had confessed (41:25–37).

From the Exodus to the Kingdom

This era included the Exodus of the Israelites out of Egypt, their wilderness wanderings, their entrance into Canaan, their conquest of the Canaanites, and their subsequent direction by the judges appointed by God (Exodus–Ruth). This time period covered about four hundred years (1446–1050 B.C.).

Moses. Moses was the great liberator and lawgiver of Israel. He stood as the voice of God before the Egyptian pharaoh and performed miracles that demonstrated His divine authentication. However, John Walvoord correctly observed that "a clear reference to miracles as being generally accomplished by the work of the Holy Spirit is not found in the Old Testament."[3] In Exodus through Deuteronomy Moses nowhere mentioned that he performed miracles by the power of the Holy Spirit. He attributed the miracles and the divine plagues directly to the God of Israel.

When God instructed Moses to appoint seventy elders to administer the affairs of the people, He said, "Then I will come down and talk with you there. I will take of the Spirit that is upon you and will put the same upon them; and they shall bear the burden of the people with you, that you may not bear it yourself alone" (Num. 11:17). The Bible nowhere mentions the occasion when God initially placed the Spirit of God on Moses. One logical possibility would be the time when God consecrated Moses at the burning bush (Exodus 3). It is plausible to believe that Moses was always controlled by the Spirit as he spoke to Pharaoh, led the Israelites out of Egypt, passed through the Red Sea, and guided the people through the wilderness.

God spoke to Moses face to face, and then Moses communicated those words to the people (19:9; Num. 12:8). Moses became a pattern for all future prophets within Israel (Deut. 18:15–22). Christ said that Moses, who wrote the first five books of the Bible, wrote about Him (John 5:45–47). The books Moses wrote were divinely inspired, the breathed-out Word of God (2 Tim. 3:16). Peter asserted that holy men of God spoke and wrote as they were moved by the Holy Spirit: Thus Moses had to be moved by the Spirit to write (2 Pet. 1:21). Peter also claimed that the Spirit of Christ was in the prophets when they wrote about the sufferings and glory of the promised Messiah (1 Pet. 1:10–11). The Holy Spirit thus must have been in Moses when he wrote about Christ.

Joshua. Just before Moses died, God instructed him to appoint Joshua as his successor: "Take Joshua the son of Nun with you, a man in whom is the Spirit, and lay your hand on him; set him before Eleazar the priest and before all the congregation, and inaugurate him in their sight" (Num. 27:18–19). The Holy Spirit had indwelt Joshua before Moses placed hands on him. The time of that initial indwelling is not stated in the Scriptures.

After the death of Moses, the Israelites submitted to the new leadership of Joshua, because they perceived that he was "full of the spirit of wisdom" (Deut. 34:9).

As a writer of inspired Scripture, namely, the Book of Joshua, Joshua would have been moved by the Holy Spirit also (2 Tim. 3:16; 2 Pet. 1:21).

Seventy elders. God directed Moses to select seventy elders who would assist Moses in the administration of national affairs (Num. 11:16–17).

When he selected the seventy and gathered them around the tabernacle, "the LORD came down in the cloud, and spoke to him, and took of the Spirit that was upon him, and placed the same upon the seventy elders; and it happened, when the Spirit rested upon them, that they prophesied, although they never did so again" (11:25). The Spirit also rested upon Eldad and Medad, two of the seventy, who remained in the camp. They likewise prophesied, to the consternation of Joshua, but Moses approved of this prophesying (11:26–30).

Both Moses and the seventy elders needed the enabling of the Holy Spirit to direct the affairs of the people. They could not do it of their own ingenuity.

Tabernacle workers. The gifted artisans who made the garments for the priests were "filled with the spirit of wisdom" by God (Exod. 28:3).

The general contractor for the construction of the tabernacle was Bezalel. God said concerning him, "And I have filled him with the Spirit of God, in wisdom, in understanding, in knowledge, and in all manner of workmanship, to design artistic works, to work in gold, in silver, in bronze, in cutting jewels for setting, in carving wood, and to work in all manner of workmanship" (31:2–5; see also 35:30–35). Both Bezalel and his assistant Aholiab had divinely given ability to work and to teach others how to build according to God's commands. God probably did not make craftsmen out of noncraftsmen. Rather, He used those whom He had providentially prepared in secular pursuits. He was the giver of their natural abilities. The Holy Spirit then gave them special wisdom and guidance to build the tabernacle exactly as God wanted it, adding nothing and leaving out nothing.

Othniel. Othniel, Caleb's nephew, became the first judge in Israel after the death of Joshua. The Israelites, under the domination of Mesopotamia, cried out in repentance for divine deliverance. Then "the Spirit of the LORD came upon him [Othniel], and he judged Israel. He went out to war, and the LORD delivered Cushan-Rishathaim king of Mesopotamia into his hand" (Judg. 3:10). The Holy Spirit gave Othniel military skill and victory. He also enabled him to judge Israel for the next forty years.

Deborah. Deborah was a prophetess who judged Israel (Judg. 4:4). Along with Barak, she led Israel to victory over Jabin, king of Canaan, and his general Sisera. Later Barak and she composed a song of praise that has been included in Scripture (5:1–31). Although there is no specific mention of the activity of the Holy Spirit in her life, it is reasonable to conclude that He directed her accomplishments.

Gideon. Gideon delivered the children of Israel from seven years of oppression by the Midianites (Judg. 6:1). Just before he gathered his army together, "the Spirit of the LORD came upon Gideon" (6:34). God then instructed Gideon about His unique strategy to win the war—by reducing his forces to three hundred men, by surrounding the camp of the Midianite army at night, by blowing trumpets, by breaking clay pitchers, by raising torches, and by shouting (7:7, 19–22). Gideon went on to judge Israel for forty years (8:28). For his valor, he was enshrined as a hero of faith (Heb. 11:32).

Jephthah. Jephthah was a mighty man of valor, but he was also the son of a harlot (Judg. 11:1). Driven from the house of his father, he was later recalled by the elders of Gilead to lead an insurrection against the nation of Ammon. Prior to the engagement of war, "the Spirit of the LORD came upon Jephthah" (11:29). With this divine enablement, he led Israel to victory. He then judged Israel for six years (12:7). He, too, has been cited as an example of faith (Heb. 11:32).

Samson. The most notorious and intriguing judge was Samson. I still remember the movie *Samson and Delilah* that I saw as a young boy. Produced by Cecil DeMille, the film starred Victor Mature as Samson and Hedy Lamarr as Delilah. The drama fascinated me with the beauty of Delilah, the strength of Samson, and his loss of power when Delilah cut his hair.

The Angel of the Lord informed Samson's parents that he would be a unique son, a Nazarite who would deliver the Israelites from their forty years of oppression under the Philistines (Judg. 13:3–5). Early in his life "the Spirit of the LORD began to move upon him" (13:25). Once he killed a young lion with his own hands when "the Spirit of the LORD came mightily upon him" (14:6). Later, he killed thirty Philistines in one encounter when again "the Spirit of the LORD came upon him mightily" (14:19). Subsequently, when "the Spirit of the LORD came mightily upon him" again, he broke two new ropes that had bound him and used the jawbone of a donkey as a weapon to kill three thousand Philistines (15:13–15).

When Delilah cut Samson's hair, he lost his unusual physical strength. His superhuman strength was not caused by the length of his hair; rather, "the LORD had departed from him" (16:20). There is no specific mention of the Holy Spirit leaving him on this occasion, but apparently the Spirit sovereignly left Samson just as He had come on him. God later returned unusual strength to Samson and he destroyed the temple of Dagon, and killed thousands of Philistines and himself (16:26–30).

Samson had judged Israel for twenty years (16:31), and he, too, is included among the heroes of faith (Heb. 11:32). The ministry of the Holy Spirit to Samson was directly related to his obedience to the Nazarite vow. The Spirit's enabling was manifested only in his unusual physical strength. Unfortunately, the temporary filling of the Spirit did not produce consistent spiritual excellence in him.

From the Kingdom to the New Testament Era

This period covered over one thousand years. The time from the first king, Saul, to the end of Old Testament history was about six hundred and fifty years (1050–400 B.C.). The intertestamental era covered the next four hundred years.

Saul. When Samuel anointed Saul with oil, the judge-prophet announced that Saul would become the first king of Israel and that the Spirit of the Lord would come on Saul (1 Sam. 10:1, 6). Later the Spirit of the Lord did come on Saul, and he prophesied among the prophets (10:10). The Holy Spirit thus authenticated the divine choice of Saul to become king. The Spirit also prepared Saul for the task and enabled him to rule. Later "the Spirit of God came upon Saul" when he exercised decisive leadership (11:6).

Saul, however, violated his office as king and sinned against God. He intruded into the priestly office, forbidden to him, when he personally offered the sacrifice of a burnt offering (13:9). He then made a rash vow that could have led to his killing of Jonathan, his son (14:24–46). He then disobeyed the command of God when he spared the king of Amalek and the best of the Amalekite flocks (15:1–33). God judged Saul for these three major sins. God said that kingdom rulership would be removed from Saul and his family forever.

After Samuel anointed David to be the next king, "the Spirit of the LORD departed from Saul" (16:14). Saul no longer had the enablement of the Holy Spirit to rule as king. Saul should have stepped aside and allowed David to take his place, but instead he rebelled against the will of God and sought to kill David.

In his rebellion Saul sent messengers to seize David at Naioth. When the emissaries saw Samuel and the prophets, "the Spirit of God came upon the messengers of Saul, and they also prophesied" (19:20). Later Saul himself traveled to Naioth. "Then the Spirit of God was upon him also, and he went on and prophesied until he came to Naioth in Ramah. And he also stripped off his clothes and prophesied before Samuel in like manner, and lay down naked all that day and all that night" (19:23–24). These two events revealed God's sovereign control over David's enemies. The Holy Spirit temporarily came on Saul and his messengers to change their attitude of persecution to an action of prophesying. They did what they did not expect to do. This divine action also came on men who were not spiritually right before God. Saul eventually died in battle, a frustrated and depressed soul.

David. God chose David, the son of Jesse, to be the successor of Saul. When Samuel anointed David with oil, "the Spirit of the LORD came upon David from that day forward" (1 Sam. 16:13). Although David was the divinely authenticated king, he could not publicly rule until Saul was dead.

The Holy Spirit enabled David to rule as king for forty years. God established the Davidic Covenant with him: "And your house and your kingdom shall be established forever before you. Your throne shall be established forever" (2 Sam. 7:16). The promised Messiah would be from the house of David.

In spite of all the blessings God bestowed on him, David sinned against the Lord. He committed adultery with Bathsheba, caused her husband, Uriah, to be killed in battle, and tried to cover up his infidelity (2 Samuel 11).

Through Nathan the prophet, God confronted David with his sin. Convicted, David confessed his sin and repented (12:13). Under the Mosaic Law, David deserved to die, but God graciously spared his life. However, the sin of David resulted in the deaths of four of his sons; the seven-day-old child born to Bathsheba, Amnon, Absalom, and Adonijah.

In his psalm of confession David pleaded with God, "Do not cast me away from Your presence, and do not take Your Holy Spirit from me. Restore to me the joy of Your salvation, and uphold me by Your generous Spirit. Then I will teach transgressors Your ways, and sinners shall be converted to You" (Ps. 51:11–13). David knew what had happened to Saul. He did not want to be removed from the office of king. He knew that the Spirit of God came on him when Samuel anointed him, and he was aware that the Spirit had left Saul. His plea was a legitimate Old Testament prayer, prayed by a Spirit-anointed king in a difficult situation. This prayer pertained only to David. No other believer in his day would have prayed that prayer. Nor is it a valid prayer for believers in the church age. Whenever we sin, we need not fear that the Holy Spirit will be taken from us.

David asked for a restoration of the "joy" of divine salvation, not for salvation itself. In fact, when he prayed, the Holy Spirit was still on him. Otherwise he would have asked for the return of the Spirit. God had not taken the Spirit away from David as He had removed the Spirit from Saul. David knew that and pleaded that the Spirit would remain on him.

God answered the prayer of David. Late in his life, it is recorded, "Now these are the last words of David. Thus says David the son of Jesse; thus says the man raised up on high, the anointed of the God of Jacob, and the sweet psalmist of Israel: The Spirit of the LORD spoke by me, and His word was on my tongue" (2 Sam. 23:1–2). David composed inspired psalms after his great sin with Bathsheba. David knew that the Holy Spirit controlled both his tongue and his pen (Acts 1:16). David, too, is also listed as an example of faith (Heb. 11:32).

Solomon. The Bible is silent about any ministry of the Holy Spirit in the life of Solomon. However, since he penned several books within the inspired canon, it is logical to assume that the Holy Spirit was involved in the divine gift of wisdom to him. The Spirit superintended him as he wrote in the same way that He guided other biblical authors (2 Pet. 1:21).

Huram. Huram was the chief artisan who superintended the construction of Solomon's temple. Solomon specifically requested him (1 Kings 7:13). The Bible stated that Huram "was filled with wisdom and understanding and skill in working with all kinds of bronze work" (7:14). Although there is no mention of the Holy Spirit as the source of his ability, his expertise sounds similar to that of the Spirit-filled craftsmen who built the tabernacle (Exod. 28:3). God was pleased with the temple of Solomon and filled it with the glory of His presence (1 Kings 8:10–11).

Elijah. Both Obadiah and the sons of the prophets believed that the Spirit of the Lord could supernaturally move Elijah from one location to another (1 Kings 18:12; 2 Kings 2:16). Elisha knew that the Spirit had enabled Elijah to prophesy and to perform miracles (2:9).

An angel informed Zacharias that his son, John the Baptist, would go before the Messiah "in the spirit and power of Elijah" (Luke 1:17). Since John was filled with the Holy Spirit from his mother's womb, it is safe to conclude that Elijah must have been filled with the Holy Spirit during his ministry (1:15).

Azariah. Asa was a godly king ruling over the southern kingdom of Judah. One day "the Spirit of God came upon Azariah the son of Oded" (2 Chron. 15:1–2), and he gave Asa a Spirit-guided message, which Asa obeyed. Then revival broke out in the land, much idolatry was destroyed, and the nation experienced peace (15:8–19).

Micah. The word of the Lord came to Micah in the days of Jotham, Ahaz, and Hezekiah, kings of Judah (Mic. 1:1). He predicted the destruction of the Northern Kingdom of Israel and its capital city of Samaria by the Assyrians. He also prophesied about the coming desolation of Judah and Jerusalem by the Babylonians. False prophets and lying priests attempted to discredit him, but Micah confidently responded, "But truly I am full of power by the Spirit of the LORD and of justice and might, to declare to Jacob his transgression and to Israel his sin" (3:8).

Jeremiah later declared the same message of divine judgment on Jerusalem. He asserted, "For truly the LORD has sent me to you to speak all these words in your hearing" (Jer. 26:15). Some of the princes, priests, and false prophets wanted to kill Jeremiah. Some elders defended Jeremiah by referring to Micah who likewise predicted the fall of Jerusalem (26:17–19).

Micah, as with Jeremiah later, knew that the Holy Spirit was upon him and that he had faithfully declared the divine message.

Zechariah. Joash began to rule over Judah when he was only seven years old (2 Chron. 24:1). He "did what was right in the sight of the LORD all the days of Jehoiada the priest" (24:2). Under the spiritual and political guidance of Jehoiada, Joash repaired the temple and encouraged true worship of God. When Jehoiada died, Joash began to follow poor advice and tolerated the rise of idolatry as the nation refused to repent.

In this period of moral decline "the Spirit of God came upon Zechariah the son of Jehoiada the priest" (24:20). He rebuked the people and the leaders for their transgressions. The people conspired against Zechariah and stoned him to death in the temple court under the command of King Joash (24:21). Christ referred to this murder when He declared that all the righteous blood shed in past ages would be required of His generation since they would crucify Him (Matt. 23:35–36).

Ezekiel. Ezekiel was both a priest and a prophet. He ministered as an exile in Babylon (2 Kings 24:10–16; Ezek. 1:1–3). He recorded his divine commission: "And He said to me, 'Son of man, stand on your feet, and I will speak to you.' Then the Spirit entered me when He spoke to me, and set me on my feet, and I heard Him who spoke to me. And He said to me: 'Son of man, I am sending you to the children of Israel, to a rebellious nation that has rebelled against Me; they and their fathers have transgressed against Me to this very day' " (2:1–3). The Holy Spirit enabled Ezekiel to receive and understand divine revelation. The Spirit also enabled Ezekiel to proclaim the Word of God to the exiles of Israel (2:7). Ezekiel was doubtless a believer before the Spirit entered him. The entrance of the Holy Spirit thus set Ezekiel apart for a special divine task.

The Spirit of God also moved Ezekiel from one geographical location to another (3:12, 14; 11:1, 24). The Spirit also moved him through time so that he could see the future, including the regathering of Israel as seen in the valley of dry bones (37:1) and the millennial temple (43:5).

Ezekiel acknowledged that the Holy Spirit compelled him to speak: "Then the Spirit of the LORD fell upon me, and said to me, 'Speak!' " (11:5). Once when the Spirit entered him, God said: "But when I speak with you, I will open your mouth, and you shall say to them, 'Thus says the Lord GOD' " (3:27). Apparently the Spirit entered and departed Ezekiel as He willed. The Holy Spirit enabled the prophet to express God's words to the people.

Daniel. Daniel, like Ezekiel, was forced to go to Babylon as a captive (Dan. 1:1–4). The Babylonians selected him for special political and cultural education because he was part of an elite group: "Young men in whom there was no blemish, but good-looking, gifted in all wisdom, possessing knowledge and quick to understand" (1:4).

Subsequently God revealed to Daniel the content and meaning of a dream King Nebuchadnezzar had (2:19–49). The king later recognized that "the Spirit of the Holy God" was in Daniel (4:8–9).

Another king, Belshazzar, brought Daniel into the palace to interpret the handwriting on the wall. He confessed, "I have heard of you, that the Spirit of God is in you, and that light and understanding and excellent wisdom are found in you" (5:14). Daniel explained the vision with a prediction that literally came to pass (5:26–31).

Another king, Darius, elevated Daniel to a high administrative office because he recognized that "an excellent spirit" was in Daniel (6:3).

The Holy Spirit enabled Daniel to receive divine revelation, to interpret dreams and visions given to pagan rulers, and to administer public policy justly.

THE HOLY SPIRIT IN PREDICTIONS

The Holy Spirit moved the authors of the Old Testament books to speak and to write (2 Pet. 1:21). Some prophets only spoke (for example, Elijah and Elisha), whereas others both spoke and wrote. Some of the biblical authors had both the gift and the office of prophet (for example, Jonah), whereas others had only the gift (for example, David).

However, they all had the right to bear the name of prophet. Christ said Daniel, the political statesman, was a prophet (Matt. 24:15), and Peter said David, the king, was a prophet (Acts 2:30).

The entire Old Testament testifies to the person and redemptive work of Jesus Christ (John 5:39). Peter thus observed, "Of this salvation the prophets have inquired and searched carefully, who prophesied of the grace that would come to you, searching what, or what manner of time, the Spirit of Christ who was in them was indicating when He testified beforehand the sufferings of Christ and the glories that would follow" (1 Pet. 1:10–11). The Holy Spirit was in each prophet when he spoke and wrote about the Messiah, His death and resurrection, and His return to the earth in glory. The prophets did not fully understand all they spoke and wrote. They revealed what the Messiah would do when He came, but apparently they did not realize that He would come twice—first to suffer and second to reign. Even the apostles did not initially perceive this truth (Matt. 16:21–23).

The Spirit of God guided the prophets in making predictions of His future ministry—in relation to the Messiah and to Israel, His covenant people.

About the Messiah

Isaiah is the only prophet who predicted the ministry of the Holy Spirit in the life of the Messiah. He wrote: "There shall come forth a Rod from the stem of Jesse, and a Branch shall grow out of his roots. The Spirit of the LORD shall rest upon Him, the Spirit of wisdom and understanding, the Spirit of counsel and might, the Spirit of knowledge and of the fear of the Lord" (Isa. 11:1–2). Jesse was the father of David. The descriptive titles "Rod" and "Branch" refer to the Messiah who would descend from David's family.

In describing the ministry of the Messiah, Isaiah said He would judge in righteousness, He would destroy the wicked, He would remove the curse on the world of animals, He would fill the earth with divine knowledge, and He would be believed on by both Jews and Gentiles (11:3–10).

Isaiah later quoted the actual confession of the Messiah: "The Spirit of the Lord GOD is upon Me, because the LORD has anointed Me to preach good tidings to the poor; He has sent Me to heal the brokenhearted, to proclaim liberty to the captives, and the opening of the prison to those who are bound; to proclaim the acceptable year of the LORD, and the day of vengeance of our God; to comfort all who mourn" (61:1–2). In the synagogue at Nazareth, Jesus Christ read these two verses, with the exception of the closing words about "the day of vengeance" (Luke 4:16–19). He then declared, "Today this Scripture is fulfilled in your hearing" (4:21). After God the Father anointed Jesus with the Holy Spirit at His baptism, Christ began His public messianic ministry. He did not read the closing words because He will fulfill that action at His second coming to the earth.

Isaiah also recorded this testimony from God the Son: "Come near to Me, hear this: I have not spoken in secret from the beginning; from the time that it was, I was there. And now the Lord GOD and His Spirit have sent Me" (Isa. 48:16). Christ, who was with the Father in the beginning (John 1:1), here claimed that both the Father and the Spirit had sent Him. Isaiah's other predictions about the Messiah confirmed the fact that the Savior was to be Immanuel, "God with us" (Isa. 7:14; 9:6).

About Israel

Rebuilding the temple. The temple of Solomon was destroyed by the Babylonians in 586 B.C. Cyrus, the Persian king who conquered the Babylonian Empire, permitted a Jewish delegation to return to Jerusalem to rebuild the temple in 536 B.C. Under the leadership of Zerubbabel, the people laid the foundation of the temple, but they ceased their work when opposition arose (Ezra 1–4). God then raised up Haggai and Zechariah to encourage the people to finish the task (5–6). Zechariah gave this message of optimism: "This is the word of the LORD to Zerubbabel: 'Not by might nor by power, but by My Spirit,' says the LORD of hosts" (Zech. 4:6). Later he added, "The hands of Zerubbabel have laid the foundation of this temple; his hands shall also finish it. Then you will know that the LORD of hosts has sent Me to you" (4:9). The people returned to the work and finished the temple in 516 B.C.

Cleansing of Israel. In the seven years before the return of Christ to the earth God will spiritually refine Israel and prepare her to accept the Messiah. That time period is known as the seventieth week of Daniel's prophecy (Dan. 9:24–27). Jeremiah named it "the time of Jacob's trouble" (Jer. 30:7). Christ called it the "great tribulation" (Matt. 24:21). The prophets called it the Day of the Lord.

Isaiah set forth the divine purification of Israel in the future: "When the Lord has washed away the filth of the daughters of Zion, and purged the blood of Jerusalem from her midst, by the spirit of judgment and by the spirit of burning" (Isa. 4:4). If this "spirit" refers to the person or ministry of the Holy Spirit, then He will produce chastisement, conviction, and repentance.

Protection against enemies. Satan, the demonic world, and the human forces led by the Antichrist will attempt to destroy ethnic Israel during that seven-year time period before the return of Christ to the earth. God, however, will overcome their anti-Semitism. Isaiah wrote, "When the enemy comes in like a flood, the Spirit of the LORD will lift up a standard against him. The Redeemer will come to Zion, and to those who turn from transgression in Jacob, says the LORD" (Isa. 59:19–20). The Holy Spirit thus will actively protect Israel until the Redeemer, Jesus Christ, destroys the forces of the Antichrist at Armageddon.

Outpouring of the Holy Spirit. Several prophets predicted that God will pour out His Spirit on Israel in the last days. This outpouring will produce both national repentance and divine revelation. It will occur just before the Messiah returns to establish His kingdom on the earth.

Isaiah announced that the Spirit would be poured on Israel from on high (Isa. 32:15). His coming will end national mourning and usher in peace, prosperity, and righteousness.

God assured Israel, "Yet hear now, O Jacob My servant, and Israel whom I have chosen. Thus says the LORD who made you and formed you from the womb, who will help you: 'Fear not, O Jacob My servant, and you, Jeshurun, whom I have chosen. For I will pour water on him who is thirsty, and floods on the dry ground; I will pour My Spirit on your descendants, and My blessing on your offspring' " (44:1–3). In faithfulness to His covenant, God will remove fear from Israel and replace it with assurance. This outpouring seems to be restricted to Israel, her descendants, and offspring.

Ezekiel predicted that God will bring Israel back to the Promised Land, that He will have mercy on the nation, and that He will become their God through personal knowledge (Ezek. 39:25–28). God then said, " 'And I will not hide My face from them anymore; for I shall have poured out My Spirit on the house of Israel,' says the Lord God" (39:29). This outpouring of the Spirit will precede Israel's national conversion and her enjoyment of the land in the kingdom.

Joel has given the most significant prediction on the outpouring of the Spirit: "And it shall come to pass afterward that I will pour out My Spirit on all flesh; your sons and your daughters shall prophecy, your old men shall dream dreams, your young men shall see visions. And also on My menservants and on My maidservants I will pour out My Spirit in those days" (Joel 2:28–29). Some claim that the phrase "all flesh" refers to both Jews and Gentiles. However, the context restricts the meaning of "all flesh" to all types of people within Israel: sons, daughters, old men, young men, male servants, and female servants. The usage of the pronoun "Your" points to Israel's national family, not to the entire world.

When the outpouring happens, God will also produce heavenly and earthly wonders or miracles: blood, fire, pillars of smoke, the sun turned into darkness, and the moon turned into blood (2:30–31).

The occasion for the outpouring is the regathering of Jews back into their land, the destruction of the anti-Semitic nations in the Valley of Jehoshaphat, and the return of the Lord Jesus Christ to the earth (3:1–17).

The divine intent behind Joel's prophecy finds its ultimate fulfillment in Israel, after the church age is over and just before Christ returns to save Israel from her national sins and enemies. Some commentators believe the prophecy of Joel was fulfilled on the Day of Pentecost, because Peter quoted the passage in his message (Acts 2:15–21). They equate the outpouring of the Spirit with the promise of Christ to baptize the apostles in the Holy Spirit (1:5), and they equate the signs and wonders with the sound of the rushing mighty wind, the tongues of fire, and the speaking in tongues (2:1–4).

Although there are some similarities between the two accounts, there are enough differences to demonstrate that the prophecy of Joel will be fulfilled when Christ returns to the earth and that it was not realized on the Day of Pentecost, the beginning of the church age. First, Peter began, "But this is what was spoken by the prophet Joel" (Acts 2:16). Peter did not use the formula for fulfillment which he had used earlier in 1:16. The normal verbs used to show the fulfillment of Old Testament predictions were *pleroō* ("fulfill," Matt. 1:22) and *gegraptai* ("it is written," 2:5).

Second, the wonders predicted by Joel did not occur on the Day of Pentecost: blood, fire, vapor of smoke, the darkening of the sun, and the moon becoming blood.

Third, though the twelve apostles spoke in foreign languages and dialects (Acts 2:4–11), "all flesh" were not moved by the Spirit to prophesy, to see visions, and to dream dreams (2:17–18).

Fourth, Peter used the prophecy of Joel to show that Jesus Christ will be the one who will pour out the Spirit on Israel in the latter days. By use of

Old Testament predictions, historical events, personal eyewitness testimony, and logic, Peter proved that Christ was raised from the dead, that He ascended to the right hand of God the Father, that He poured out the Spirit on the Day of Pentecost, and that He is the Lord and Christ (2:22–36).

Fifth, Peter closed his quotation of Joel with an evangelistic verse: "And it shall come to pass that whoever calls on the name of the Lord shall be saved" (2:21). The apostle thus challenged his listeners to repent, and about three thousand believed and were saved (2:37–41).

Zechariah predicted an invasion of wicked nations against Israel in the end time (Zech. 12:9). In that day, God will act. "And I will pour on the house of David and on the inhabitants of Jerusalem the Spirit of grace and supplication; then they will look on Me whom they pierced. Yes, they will mourn for Him as one mourns for his only son, and grieve for Him as one grieves for a firstborn" (12:10). This outpouring of the Holy Spirit will be on the nation of Israel only. It will result in national mourning and repentance, for it will cause them to see the crucified, resurrected, and returning Christ. It will lead to the conversion of Israel, thus preparing the nation for entering the messianic kingdom.

Regeneration and the New Covenant. Ezekiel predicted that God will bring back the scattered Israelites into their own land (Ezek. 36:24). At that time, God will purify them morally and spiritually and will give them a new heart and a new spirit (36:25–26). God also announced, "I will put My Spirit within you and cause you to walk in My statutes, and you will keep My judgments and do them. Then you shall dwell in the land that I gave to your fathers; you shall be My people, and I will be your God" (36:27–28). Israel must undergo spiritual regeneration to enjoy the blessings of her covenant relationship to God. Israel will be brought back to the Promised Land in unbelief in the last days. National conversion will occur just before the messianic, millennial kingdom is established.

Christ used that logic when He told Nicodemus that he had to be born again before he could see or enter the kingdom of God (John 3:3–7). When Nicodemus expressed his ignorance of this truth, Christ responded, "Are you the teacher of Israel, and do not know these things?" (3:10). Christ used the demonstrative pronoun *tauta* ("these things") to refer to the truth of regeneration mentioned in the New Covenant promised to Israel in the

Old Testament (Jer. 31:31–37; Ezek. 36:22–32).

Outside of the Promised Land Israel is like lifeless bones (37:11). In his vision of the valley of dry bones, Ezekiel saw that God put flesh on the bones and breathed life into the united body when He brought Israel back into the land. God then said: "'I will put My Spirit in you, and you shall live, and I will place you in your own land. Then you shall know that I, the LORD, have spoken it and performed it,' says the LORD" (37:14).

According to the Old Testament, God has not permanently and completely set aside ethnic, national Israel from His creative-redemptive program for the ages. In this present age God is still regenerating Jews and uniting them with believing Gentiles in the true church, the body of Christ (Romans 9–11). After this age ends with the coming of Christ to rapture the church into His presence, God will prepare and regenerate Israel through the ministry of the Holy Spirit (11:26–27).

IMPLICATIONS FOR US

First, we must recognize that the filling of the Spirit in our lives does not remove our human finiteness. The Spirit was in the prophets when they spoke and wrote, but they did not fully understand everything. In the same sense we know in part and we speak in part (1 Cor. 13:9). We must read and study the Scriptures continually, but we must not claim divine omniscience in our interpretations and understanding.

Second, we must understand that the filling of the Spirit does not remove the possibility of moral and spiritual failure. Leaders such as Samson, Saul, and David sinned even though the Spirit was in their lives. Their triumphs were quickly superseded by their tragedies. They acted irresponsibly and selfishly even though the Spirit enabled them to rule. As church leaders, we must daily take heed to ourselves and to the doctrine lest we fail and lead others to fail (1 Tim. 4:16).

Third, we must humbly accept God's sovereign will to choose and use whomever He pleases. God chose David, but He bypassed the other sons of Jesse. He gifted some to be Spirit-guided builders of the tabernacle, but not all. We must rejoice in God's activity in the lives of others without becoming envious, jealous, or bitter.

Fourth, we must not pattern our relationship to the Holy Spirit today after the experiences of Old Testament characters. The Spirit of God came on chosen people and departed from them as He would. We need not fear that the Holy Spirit will leave us if we sin. As the adopted sons and daughters of God, we are sealed until the day of redemption (Rom. 8:14–16; Eph. 1:13–14; 4:30). We never need pray the prayer of David, "And do not take Your Holy Spirit from me" (Ps. 51:11).

Fifth, though we are godly people, filled with the Holy Spirit, people may still reject us and our ministry to them. Moses, Joshua, and the prophets were hurt by fellow Israelites. Christ told the apostles to expect hatred, persecution, ostracism, and possible martyrdom in the world. In every generation, the majority has repudiated the spiritual leadership of the minority.

Sixth, we must have a spiritual concern for Israel, the covenant nation of God. We must never be anti-Semitic. We must thank God for giving us the Messiah-Redeemer, Jesus Christ, through the ethnic ancestry of Israel. We must be thankful for the Scriptures, authored for the most part by Jews. We must realize that the church has not replaced Israel in the divine plan of the ages. We must recognize that God has a glorious future for Israel after He pours out the Holy Spirit on her.

CHAPTER FIVE

The Ministry of the Holy Spirit in Inspiration

Romantics can identify a brilliant sunset or an unusual cloud formation as inspiring. Some athletes, performing at the Olympic Games, claimed that they were inspired to better achievements. A hymnal is entitled *Inspiring Hymns.* The words related to the concept of inspiration have various usages in our culture. We use them and understand them in their contexts, but they have nothing to do with the biblical idea of inspiration.

Inspiration has a distinctive biblical meaning and function. John F. Walvoord defines it this way: "God so supernaturally directed the writers of Scripture that without excluding their human intelligence, their individuality, their literary style, their personal feelings, or any other human factor, His own complete and coherent message to man was recorded in perfect accuracy, the very words of Scripture bearing the authority of divine authorship."[1] Inspiration thus deals with the divine origin of the Scriptures, the sixty-six books we accept as the basis of authority for our faith and practice.

The International Council on Biblical Inerrancy, founded in 1977, held a summit meeting in Chicago in 1978. At that conference, the ICBI issued a statement on biblical inerrancy which stated: "We affirm that inspiration was the work in which God by His Spirit, through human writers, gave us His Word. The origin of Scripture is divine. The mode of divine inspiration remains largely a mystery to us. We deny that inspiration can be reduced to human insight, or to heightened states of consciousness of any kind."[2] The ICBI statement affirmed that the divine origin of Scripture came through the ministry of the Holy Spirit in the lives of biblical authors.

Inspiration deals with the text of Scripture. It technically refers to the divine-human product, the actual written words, not to the authors or to the effect produced within the readers. The Holy Spirit definitely prepared the lives of the human authors and guided them as they wrote, but He technically did not inspire them. It is therefore correct to say that the Book of Romans is inspired, but it would be incorrect to say that Paul was inspired when he wrote the Book of Romans.

We evangelicals believe that the written Bible is just as authoritative and just as much the Word of God as the oral pronouncements of God Himself. To us, "the Bible says" and "God says" are the same.

We believe God's authority extends equally to all sixty-six books of the Bible. The Old and New Testaments are equally inspired. The genealogies are just as inspired as key evangelistic verses (such as John 3:16). This concept is called *plenary inspiration.*

We believe that the divine inspiration and authority extends to every word of each sentence in every paragraph of each book. This concept is called *verbal inspiration.* Choices of words (for example, singular or plural) and the grammatical relationship of those words thus were inspired. The ICBI expressed this concept in this way: "We affirm that the whole of Scripture and all its parts, down to the very words of the original, were given by divine inspiration. We deny that the inspiration of Scripture can rightly be affirmed of the whole without the parts, or of some parts but not the whole."[3]

We believe that the Bible is inerrant truth, no matter in what area it speaks: theology, ethics, history, science, or geography. Jesus prayed, "Sanctify them by Your truth. Your word is truth" (John 17:17). Some theologians believe in limited inerrancy. They accept inerrancy for issues of salvation and moral living, but reject it in areas which they say are nonessential, such as history and geography. However, since all Scripture has been breathed out by God, all Scripture must be truth, because God is truth and He always speaks truth.

Christ affirmed that the Scriptures cannot be broken (John 10:35). To Him, they are absolute divine truth, inerrant and infallible.

The Holy Spirit was active in the process of divine revelation and inspiration. The mind of the triune God was revealed through the Spirit to the biblical spokesmen. The Spirit also guided the authors as they wrote, sovereignly controlling them so that they wrote exactly what God wanted them to write, adding nothing and leaving out nothing.

THE TESTIMONY OF THE OLD TESTAMENT

The biblical authors claimed divine origin for what they spoke and wrote. They sometimes prefaced their pronouncements by writing, "The Word of the LORD came to me, saying" (example, Ezek. 12:1; Jon. 1:1). Other times, they asserted, "Thus says the LORD" (Amos 1:3; Hag. 1:5). Other arresting formulas were also used: "Hear the word of the LORD" (Hos. 4:1); and "The burden of the word of the LORD to Israel by Malachi" (Mal. 1:1).

These prophetic spokesmen, however, seldom attributed the divine revelation to the Holy Spirit. Since they were strongly monotheistic, they spoke only of God as the source of their words. Some biblical writers, however, asserted that the Holy Spirit was in their lives when they spoke and wrote.

Moses

God instructed Moses to write (Exod. 17:14; 34:27). At Sinai he orally told the people all the words of the Lord, and then he wrote down those words (24:3–4). Moses wrote the record of the wanderings of the Israelites in the wilderness (Num. 33:2), ending the Book of Numbers in this way: "These are the commandments and the judgments which the LORD commanded the children of Israel by the hand of Moses in the plains of Moab by the Jordan, across from Jericho" (36:13). Moses wrote by his hand what God spoke.

Moses wrote the Law and delivered it to the priests and elders of Israel shortly before his death (Deut. 31:9). He also wrote a song, which he taught to the children of Israel (31:22).

Both Israel and Moses knew that he was the human channel through whom God revealed His word. The Bible states: "Then all the people answered together and said, 'All that the LORD has spoken we will do.' So Moses brought back the words of the people to the LORD. And the LORD said to Moses, 'Behold, I come to you in the thick cloud, that the people may hear when I speak with you, and believe you forever.' So Moses told the words of the people to the LORD" (Exod. 19:8–9).

Although Moses did not refer to the ministry of the Holy Spirit on him when he wrote and spoke, he knew that the Spirit of God was in his life in a special way (Num. 11:16–17). The superintending of the Spirit, doubtless, guided Moses for the forty years he served as the administrative leader of Israel.

Balaam

Balak, the king of Moab, hired Balaam to curse the children of Israel (Num. 22:1-6). But God providentially caused the enigmatic prophet to bless Israel instead (23:11). Moses recorded the historical drama, specifically citing the sovereign control of the Holy Spirit on Balaam: "And Balaam raised his eyes, and saw Israel encamped according to their tribes; and the Spirit of God came upon him. Then he took up his oracle and said . . ." (24:2–3). Moses recorded those Spirit-given utterances of Balaam in Numbers 22–24.

David

David himself confessed, "The Spirit of the LORD spoke by me, and His word was on my tongue. The God of Israel said, the Rock of Israel spoke to me" (2 Sam. 23:2–3). What David said was what God spoke. The word of God was also the word of David. David therefore spoke and wrote inerrant truth as the Spirit of truth guided his mouth and pen. The Psalms thus were a divine-human composition, truth revealed and superintended by the Holy Spirit through the thoughts, feelings, and experiences of David (and others).

Isaiah

God commissioned Isaiah to go to Israel and to tell them His words (Isa. 6:8–9). Throughout his book Isaiah asserted that God had spoken to him and that he had faithfully declared the revealed word of God to the people (8:1, 5; 10:24).

He later claimed that the Holy Spirit enabled him to complete his divine assignment. He wrote: "'As for Me,' says the LORD, 'this is My covenant with them: My Spirit who is upon you, and My words which I have put in your mouth, shall not depart from your mouth, nor from the mouth of your descendants, nor from the mouth of your descendants' descendants,' says the LORD, 'from this time and forevermore' " (59:21). There is a significant synchronization of the presence of the Spirit with the revelation of the divine word in the mouth of Isaiah.

Jeremiah

Jeremiah used the Hebrew *rûaḥ* ("spirit") only once in his book, referring to the spirit of the kings of the Medes (Jer. 51:11). He nowhere referred to the Spirit of God, even though he defined the New Covenant which God will make with Israel (31:31–37).

However, he did claim divine origin for his prophetic words. Of his divine commission he testified: "Then the LORD put forth His hand and touched my mouth, and the LORD said to me: 'Behold, I have put My words in your mouth' " (1:9). Even before Jeremiah was born God had sanctified and prepared him to be a prophet (1:4–5). Jeremiah knew that he could speak exactly what God commanded because God was with him (1:7–8).

Ezekiel

Ezekiel claimed that he saw visions of God, that the word of the Lord came to him, and that the hand of the Lord was on him (Ezek. 1:1–3). The prophet reported that when God spoke to him, "Then the Spirit entered me when He spoke to me, and set me on my feet; and I heard Him who spoke to me" (2:2). There was a presence and control of the Spirit in his life when God spoke and ordained him to be a messenger to Israel. Through the Spirit he had the capacity to receive and understand divinely revealed truth. He also was enabled by the Spirit to execute his prophetic office.

Ezekiel reported that the Holy Spirit transported him through space and time to view and record divine revelation. He sensed the hand of God on him when he was sitting in his house in Babylon along with some Jewish elders. He saw a fiery human apparition and reported, "He stretched out the form of a hand, and took me by a lock of my hair; and the Spirit lifted me up between earth and heaven, and brought me in visions of God to Jerusalem, to the door of the north gate of the inner court, where the seat of the image of jealousy was, which provokes to jealousy" (8:3).

On another occasion the Spirit lifted him up and brought him to the east gate of the temple in Jerusalem, where he viewed the wicked leaders (11:1). When God instructed him to prophesy against them, "then the Spirit of the LORD fell upon" him and charged him to speak (11:5). He then voiced the words of God to them. The Holy Spirit subsequently took him up and brought him in a vision to the Jewish captives in Chaldea. There he reported on all the things God had shown him (11:24–25).

Though these adventures of Ezekiel were unique to him, they were nevertheless real and meaningful. His experiences were extraordinary because the Spirit of God willed them. They showed that his message was from God.

Micah

Micah experienced what other prophets lived. The word of the Lord came to him (Mic. 1:1) and he proclaimed to the people, "Hear now what the LORD says" (6:1).

He was confident of his prophetic office and authority. "But truly I am full of power by the Spirit of the LORD, and of justice and might, to declare to Jacob his transgression and to Israel his sin" (3:8). He knew that his gifts were not derived from human choice and attainment. He was not sufficient in himself to complete his divinely given tasks, but he knew that God was actively working in his life through the Holy Spirit (see 2 Cor. 3:15).

THE TEACHING OF JESUS CHRIST

As followers of Jesus Christ we should believe what He believed and taught about any topic. We should accept without any mental reservation His position on the authority of the Old Testament, the Bible available in His day. Christ, of course, lived before the New Testament documents were framed. Although He made no specific mention of the twenty-seven books, He did correlate His authority with the future ministry of the Holy Spirit in the lives of the apostles. In that anticipation of revealed, communicated truth, He laid the foundation for the writing of the inspired New Testament books.

He Accepted the Old Testament

God the Son took to Himself a perfect human nature through the virginal conception and birth. Part of that humanity was His ethnic and racial ancestry. He was Jewish, a descendant of Abraham, Isaac, Jacob, Judah, and David (Matt. 1:1; Rom. 1:3; 9:4–5). He was born under the authority of the Mosaic Law (Gal. 4:4).

He was circumcised at the age of eight days in compliance with the Abrahamic Covenant (Luke 2:21; Gen. 17:9–14). When He was forty days old, Mary and Joseph presented Him to the Lord in the temple in obedience to the Mosaic Law (Luke 2:22–24; Exod. 13:2, 12). His mother and His legal father observed the Passover Feast in Jerusalem each year (Luke 2:41), and in His adult life He attended the synagogue service on the Sabbath (4:16).

On my tours to Israel I have discovered that many knowledgeable Israelis have accepted the Jewishness of Jesus without believing in His messiahship and deity. The tour guides claim that Jesus was an orthodox rabbi, very kosher in His lifestyle.

Its historicity. Whenever Jesus mentioned people, places, and events found in the Old Testament, He accepted their objective historical reality. Some liberals have claimed that Jesus was a child of His culture and that He believed in the historicity of the Old Testament only because everyone in Israel did. Other biblical critics have asserted that Jesus accommodated Himself to the false beliefs of the day in order to have rapport with His audiences.

However, these two false views conflict with the essence of the divine-human person, Jesus Christ. Such critics normally reject the deity of Christ. Christ declared Himself to be the truth (John 14:6). He testified to His own critics, "I do nothing of Myself; but as my Father taught Me, I speak these things" (8:28). He did not have a mere human opinion on history and spiritual authority. His words were of divine origin. He also taught and preached as He was filled with the Holy Spirit. Could the Spirit-anointed Messiah fail to tell the truth, the whole truth, and nothing but the truth? Absolutely not. Christ criticized others for believing error, for embracing the traditions of men, and for being blind leaders (Mark 7:8–10, 13). He would not accommodate Himself to error in order to teach the truth. The end would not justify the means.

Christ accepted the literal historicity of these Old Testament persons and events: Solomon (Matt. 6:29); Moses (8:4); Abraham, Isaac, and Jacob (8:11); Elijah (11:14); the destruction of Sodom (11:24); David and the eating of the tabernacle showbread (12:3–4); Jonah and his experience in the sea creature (12:39–40); the repentance of Nineveh (12:41); the visit of the queen of Sheba to Solomon (12:42); the creation of Adam and Eve (19:4); the murder of Abel (23:35); the martyrdom of Zechariah the priest (23:35); Daniel (24:15); and Noah and the Flood (24:37–39). All these references are found in the Gospel of Matthew. There are others in the other three Gospels, but these are sufficient to prove the point that the teaching of Christ was saturated with allusions to Old Testament history.

If critics deny the historical reality of these persons and events, then they are suggesting that Christ's message is untrustworthy. Christ Himself said, "If I have told you earthly things and you do not believe, how will you believe if I tell you heavenly things?" (John 3:12). Statements about history, geography, and science can be investigated and verified, but concepts about salvation and eternity are beyond human scrutiny. Nevertheless Christ based the truthfulness of His teaching on spiritual regeneration on the accuracy of His allusions to wind currents (3:8) and the historical event of physical healing when Moses lifted up the serpent of brass in the wilderness (3:14).

Its authority. Christ accepted the full authority of the Old Testament over His life and the lives of others. In the Sermon on the Mount He asserted, "Do not think that I came to destroy the Law or the Prophets. I did not come to destroy but to fulfill" (Matt. 5:17). The Law was the first five books written by Moses, and the Prophets referred to the remaining books of the Old Testament canon. To destroy the authoritative Word was to give a faulty interpretation and an erroneous application; to fulfill the authoritative Word meant to give a true interpretation and application.

The critics of Christ charged Him with false interpretations and applications. Christ, however, never violated the divine intention of the meaning of the biblical text. He defended Himself several times with the striking contrasts: "You have heard that it was said to those of old . . . but I say to you" (Matt. 5:21–2; 5:27–28; 5:31–32; 5:33–34; 5:38–39; 5:43–44). Christ compared His interpretation and application with those religious leaders who orally gave wrong interpretations and applications. Christ did not set Himself at odds with Moses or the biblical text. He did not say, "It is written . . . but I say to you."

Christ also accepted the eternal permanence of the authority of the Old Testament. He stated, "For assuredly, I say to you, till heaven and earth pass away, one jot or one tittle will by no means pass from the law till all is fulfilled" (5:18). The Greek letter *iōta* ("jot") corresponds to the Hebrew letter *yod.* Both are the smallest letters in their respective alphabets. The Greek word *keraia* ("tittle") refers to that stroke of the pen which distinguishes one letter from another (for example, note the difference in English between E and F). In other words, Christ believed that divine authority extended down to the very letters that make up the words in the text of Scripture. Only the Spirit of God could guide the biblical authors to write with such accuracy.

Christ proved a theological or moral truth with absolute dogmatism when He boldly stated, "It is written" (4:4, 7, 10; 21:13). He then quoted an Old Testament text. Sometimes He would point to the Old Testament as the final word in the logic of His argument when He challenged His listeners, "Have you not read . . .?" (12:3; 19:4). He also stated, "the Scripture must be fulfilled" (Mark 14:49; John 13:18; 17:12). And He claimed that the Scriptures cannot be broken (10:35).

After His resurrection Christ said to the apostles, "These are the words which I spoke to you while I was still with you, that all things must be fulfilled which were written in the Law of Moses and the Prophets and the Psalms concerning Me" (Luke 24:44). He then opened their mental and spiritual understanding so that they could comprehend His interpretation of the Scriptures (24:45). Here Christ divided the Old Testament into three sections: the Law, the Prophets, and the Psalms (or the Writings, with the Psalms being the first and largest section). He thus accepted the full divine authority of the entire Old Testament canon.

Its inspiration. In His final week of public ministry Christ engaged in intense confrontation with His critics. They asked Him several difficult questions, hoping that He might incriminate Himself. He superbly answered their questions about the payment of taxes to Rome, the nature of the resurrection, and the commandments of the Law (Matt. 22:15–40; Mark 12:13–34; Luke 20:20–38).

Christ then asked them about the identity of the Messiah. They replied that the Christ ("the anointed one") would be the Son of David (Matt. 22:41–42). Christ agreed with their answer, but then asked them, "How is it that the scribes say that the Christ is the Son of David? For David himself said by the Holy Spirit: 'The LORD said to my Lord, "sit at my right hand, till I make Your enemies Your footstool." ' Therefore David himself calls Him 'Lord'; how is He then his Son?" (Mark 12:35–37). The Hebrew text (Ps. 110:1) actually reads, "Yahweh said to Adonai." Yahweh ("the LORD") referred to God the Father, whereas Adonai ("my Lord") referred to God the Son, the son of David. Christ wanted them to see that the promised Messiah had to be both divine and human.

What David said is what David wrote in the Book of Psalms (Luke 20:42). David spoke that messianic, theological truth *en toi pneumati toi hagioi* ("by the Holy Spirit"). The Greek preposition *en* can be translated either "by" (Mark 12:36) or "in" (Matt. 22:43). Literally, David was in the realm of the Holy Spirit, controlled by Him, as he spoke and wrote. Thus Psalm 110 was divinely inspired.

In this critical passage, Jesus Christ affirmed both His deity and humanity. He also asserted His belief that the Holy Spirit superintended David as he composed Psalm 110.

He Anticipated the New Testament

Jesus Christ never wrote a book. He never told the apostles that they would write inspired books. In the great missionary commission He did charge them to teach future believers to observe all things that He had commanded them (Matt. 28:20). Where would there be an authoritative record of the teachings of Christ after the apostles died? Logic presupposes that their oral remembrance and communication would have to be written down for future generations to read and to study.

In the Olivet Discourse (Matthew 24–25), given during our Lord's last week on earth, He declared, "Heaven and earth will pass away, but My words will by no means pass away" (24:35). How would we know what His words were if they had not been written down?

Luke stated that there were eyewitnesses of Christ's ministry who wrote noninspired accounts of events in Christ's life (Luke 1:1–2). Luke consulted those writings in preparing to write his gospel (1:3).

Christ promised that the Holy Spirit would have a ministry of instruction and revelation in the lives of the apostles after His death, resurrection, and ascension. In the Upper Room on the night before His crucifixion, Jesus said, "But the Helper, the Holy Spirit, whom the Father will send in My name, He will teach you all things, and bring to your remembrance all things that I said to you" (John 14:26).

The Gospels. According to the science of cybernetics, all our experiences register on our brains, whether we are conscious or sleeping. Our problem, because we are finite humans, is to retrieve that knowledge at will. Unfortunately we often forget at the most inopportune moments. Have you ever forgotten the name of a person you should know? Have you ever forgotten information that you studied for an exam or for a business presentation?

The apostles, being ordinary men, would have forgotten much of what Jesus said during their lifetimes. If they had been dependent only on themselves, they would have failed in teaching others all that Jesus had commanded. Christ, however, promised that the Holy Spirit would be like a programmer who would enable them to recall the information stored in the computers of their minds.

In fact, when the Gospels were written, the authors selected and arranged only some of the events in the life of Christ. They did not plan to compose exhaustive biographies. The Spirit enabled them to be selective as they wrote to select audiences. John himself wrote, "And there are also many other things that Jesus did, which if they were written one by one, I suppose that even the world itself could not contain the books that would be written" (John 21:25). He earlier stated that he recorded only some of the miracles Jesus performed to prove the deity and messiahship of Christ (20:30–31).

The Epistles. The preauthentication of the Epistles can be seen in the predicted ministry of the Holy Spirit: "[He] will teach you all things" (John 14:26). When Christ was on earth, He could teach the apostles only when they were physically with Him. The Holy Spirit, however, could teach each apostle simultaneously and miles apart because He indwelt each one.

On His way to Gethsemane, Christ informed the apostles, "I have still many things to say to you, but you cannot bear them now. However, when He, the Spirit of truth, has come, He will guide you into all truth; for He will not speak on His own authority, but whatever He hears He will speak; and He will tell you things to come" (16:12–13). The disciples were not in the right mental and emotional frame of mind to receive all that Christ wanted to teach them. Time was short, and they were confused and distressed over the necessity of His coming death. During the forty days of His postresurrection appearances, Christ taught them again "through the Holy Spirit" (Acts 1:2).

Christ's promise, however, was not fulfilled until after His ascension and His sending of the Spirit (John 16:7, 13). When the apostles preached, taught, and wrote, the Spirit guided them into all truth that God planned to reveal. The Spirit spoke all that He heard from the Father and the Son.

Christ added, "He [the Holy Spirit] will glorify Me, for He will take of what is Mine and declare it to you. All things that the Father has are Mine. Therefore I said that He will take of Mine and declare it to you" (16:14–15).

The Spirit did not come to earth to glorify Himself. He came to exalt Jesus Christ through accurate revelation of the things of Christ and of the Father (see 1 Cor. 2:6–13).

Prophecy. Christ said of the coming Spirit, "He will tell you things to come" (John 16:13). The "things to come" formed the content of New Testament prophecy within the Epistles and the Book of Revelation. The apostle John was "in the Spirit" when he saw what he wrote in Revelation (Rev. 1:10; 4:2) and Paul admitted that he received the truth of the Rapture from "the word of the Lord" (1 Thess. 4:15).

Conclusion. The Holy Spirit completed His assigned tasks when He superintended the apostles and their authorized associates as they spoke and wrote. Sinclair Ferguson correctly observed, "The significance of these words is also commonly short-circuited as though they had immediate application to contemporary Christians. But in fact they constituted a specific promise to the apostles which found its fulfillment in their writing of the New Testament Scriptures."[4]

Christ's promises and predictions (John 14:26; 16:12–15) had their primary interpretation and application in Matthew, Mark, Luke, John, Paul, James, Peter, and Jude. Those promises do have a secondary application to us. By the illuminating ministry of the indwelling Holy Spirit, we believers can understand the truth revealed by Him in the Gospels and the Epistles. He can guide us into all truth, which is already contained in the New Testament canon. We should not expect Him to give us new truths that go beyond the Scriptures. He can guide us to understand the plan for the future found in the prophetic sections of the Scriptures, but He will not give us new prophecies. The Bible is the normative standard for our faith and practice.

THE TEACHING OF THE APOSTLES

When the apostles began their ministry, the only written authority they possessed was the Old Testament. As they used it in their public messages and private deliberations, they often referred to the relationship of the Holy Spirit to the biblical text.

The Holy Spirit Directed the Old Testament Writers

Peter. During the ten-day period between the ascension of Christ and the descent of the Holy Spirit, Peter said to the 120 believers, "Men and brethren, this Scripture had to be fulfilled, which the Holy Spirit spoke before by the mouth of David concerning Judas, who became a guide to those who arrested Jesus; for he was numbered with us and obtained a part in this ministry" (Acts 1:16–17). In preparation for the selection of Matthias to replace Judas as the twelfth apostle, Peter referred to a verse in a Davidic psalm: "Even my own familiar friend in whom I trusted, who ate my bread, has lifted up his heel against me" (Ps. 41:9). Jesus Christ had quoted this same verse when He predicted the treachery of Judas (John 13:18). The Holy Spirit enabled Peter to remember those words by Christ and to give an authoritative interpretation of the Davidic verse. Peter also asserted that the Holy Spirit "spoke" by the mouth of David. He equated the speaking of the Spirit with the speaking of David. The speaking of David, subsequently, must be identified with the writing of David. Thus Psalm 41 is the recorded voice of the Holy Spirit.

The messages of Peter are saturated with the content of the Old Testament. He referred to the biblical authors by name. He quoted prophetic passages and stated that they were fulfilled in the redemptive ministry of Jesus Christ: Joel (Acts 2:16–21), David (2:25–28, 34–35; 4:25–26); and Moses (3:22–23).

In his two epistles Peter often referred to the Old Testament (1 Pet. 1:16, 24–25; 2:6–8; 3:10–12; 5:5; 2 Pet. 2:22).

Peter also claimed divine origin for the Old Testament Scriptures: "Knowing this first, that no prophecy of Scripture is of any private interpretation, for prophecy never came by the will of man, but holy men of God spoke as they were moved by the Holy Spirit" (1:20–21). For example, Isaiah did not decide on his own initiative to sit down and write his sixty-six chapters. Rather, God set him apart for the task; in that sense, each writer was "holy." The Holy Spirit then "moved" them by constraining them to write divine revelation through their distinctive burdens and personalities. Just as trade winds moved ancient sailing ships, so the Spirit moved them to write with inerrant authority. The net result was the spoken word of God in written human form, a divine-human book without error.

Apostles. After the Jewish leaders threatened Peter and John and commanded them not to preach in the name of Jesus Christ, the apostles returned to their own group. Together they praised God, saying, "Lord, You are God, who made heaven and earth and the sea, and all that is in them, who by the mouth of Your servant David have said . . ." (Acts 4:24–25). They then quoted a Davidic psalm (Ps. 2:1–2). According to them, God spoke by the mouth of David. Thus, again, what God said and what David said were the same. How do we know what David said? We look at what David wrote. Thus what God said and what David wrote are identical.

Paul. When Paul came to Rome to appeal his imprisonment to Caesar, he met with the Jewish leaders of the city. He expounded "the Law of Moses and the Prophets" and spoke of their relationship to Jesus Christ and the kingdom of God (Acts 28:23). Paul finalized his exposition by saying, "The Holy Spirit spoke rightly through Isaiah the prophet to our fathers" (28:25). What the Holy Spirit spoke is what Isaiah said. How do we know what Isaiah said? We look at what he wrote (Isa. 6:9–10). Thus what the Spirit spoke and what Isaiah wrote are the same. Isaiah had seen and heard the King, the Lord of hosts (6:1, 5, 8–10), and the apostle John said that Isaiah saw the glory of the preincarnate Christ, namely, God the Son (John 12:41). In fact, Isaiah saw the glory of the manifested triune God. He heard the divine commission: "Whom shall I send, and who will go for Us?" (Isa. 6:8). The combination of singular ("I") and plural ("Us") pronouns points to the inner complexity of the divine Godhead. And yet Paul attributed the voice of the Lord to the speaking of the Holy Spirit. Perhaps the triune God spoke as a singular Being, but the Holy Spirit directly superintended Isaiah as he wrote the inscripturated voice of God.

Paul's messages and epistles are permeated with references to the Old Testament. He accepted its full divine authority over his life and the lives of other believers.

Paul testified that Timothy had known "the Holy Scriptures," that is, the Old Testament, from his childhood (2 Tim. 3:15). The apostle then gave this classic statement on divine inspiration: "All Scripture is given by inspiration of God, and is profitable for doctrine, for reproof, for correction, for instruction in righteousness, that the man of God may be complete, thoroughly equipped for every good work" (3:16–17). As noted earlier, the six English words "is given by inspiration of God" are the translation of one Greek word *theopneustos*, which literally means "God-breathed." What is written is what God breathed out. His spoken word is thus equated with the written word. Inspiration therefore refers to the written text of all Scripture.

As the breathed-out Word of God, the Bible thus is the normative basis of faith and practice. It is sufficient to lead the believer into moral and spiritual completeness.

The Book of Hebrews. The unknown writer of the Book of Hebrews gave a stern warning to his readers: "Therefore, as the Holy Spirit says: 'Today, if you will hear His voice, do not harden your hearts as in the rebellion, in the day of trial in the wilderness'" (Heb. 3:7–8). He equated the saying of the Spirit with the written psalm (Ps. 95:7–11). The actual divine speaker in the psalm was the Lord, also referred to as the great God, the great King, the Maker of all. The writer of Hebrews did not state "as God says." Instead, he wrote "as the Holy Spirit says," thereby pointing to the Spirit's ministry in the writing of the psalm, an activity of divine inspiration.

The writer of Hebrews often contrasted the priestly ministry of Christ in redemption with the ministry of the Levitical priests in the tabernacle. On the Day of Atonement, the high priest could go into the inner sanctuary, the Holy of Holies. Other times he could only serve in the outer sanctuary. The author concluded, "The Holy Spirit indicating this, that the way into the Holiest of All was not yet made manifest while the first tabernacle was still standing" (Heb. 9:8). The Holy Spirit guided Moses as he recorded the liturgical obligations of the priests. The specific job descriptions had both divine origin and significance.

In another place the biblical author wrote, "But the Holy Spirit also witnesses to us; for after He had said before, 'This is the covenant that I will make with them after those days, says the LORD: I will put My laws into their hearts, and in their minds I will write them,' then He adds, 'Their sins and their lawless deeds I will remember no more'" (10:15–17). Jeremiah had recorded the content of the New Covenant that God made with Israel (Jer. 31:31–37), and the writer of Hebrews here attributed the content of the covenant to the Holy Spirit. Thus the Spirit was involved in the actual giving of the covenant as well as the writing of it by the prophet Jeremiah.

The Holy Spirit Directed the Apostles

The apostles knew that Jesus Christ had authenticated them, that they were filled with the Holy Spirit, and that they authoritatively spoke and wrote inerrant truth, the basis of faith and practice for the church.

Paul. Paul knew that his message and communication skills did not originate with his wisdom or expertise (1 Cor. 2:14). His ministry was by the "demonstration of the Spirit and of power" (2:4), and he manifested God's wisdom (2:6–7). Several facts may be noted about Paul's relationship to inspiration and the Holy Spirit.

First, he claimed that God revealed this wisdom to him through the Holy Spirit. "But as it is written: 'Eye has not seen, nor ear heard, nor have entered into the heart of man the things which God has prepared for those who love Him.' But God has revealed them to us through His Spirit. For the Spirit searches all things, yes, the deep things of God" (2:9–10). No unaided person could have imagined, reasoned, or sensed the content of the Scriptures. The written Word of God contains divine revelation, the communication of the mind of God to the mind of humans. The Holy Spirit knows the things of God because He is divine.

Paul recognized that he knew divine wisdom because the Spirit had revealed that wisdom to him and his fellow apostles. The first person plural pronouns ("we" and "us" in 2:10–15) referred to a select group, the apostles and the prophets who laid the foundation for the church and who wrote the New Testament books. Charles Hodge commented: "Here, the whole connection shows that the apostle is speaking of revelation and inspiration; and therefore we must mean we apostles."[5] Paul later confessed, "For I think that God has displayed us, the apostles, last, as men condemned to death" (4:9). Thus it is contextually plausible to identify the "we-us" group as the select apostles. In other words believers today should not expect the Holy Spirit to reveal new divine truth to them, either individually or corporately. Such revelation ceased with the writing of the last revealed, inspired canonical book, the Book of Revelation.

Second, Paul claimed that the Holy Spirit illuminated him so that he could understand the divinely revealed truth. "Now we have received not the spirit of the world, but the Spirit who is from God, that we might know the things that have been freely given to us by God" (2:12). The Spirit teaches from within a believer, not from without. Paul knew that the Spirit was within him, instructing and guiding him.

Third, Paul claimed that he spoke and wrote in words the Holy Spirit taught him. "These things we also speak, not in words which man's wisdom teaches but which the Holy Spirit teaches, comparing spiritual things with spiritual" (2:13). Words convey thoughts. The Spirit revealed truth-thoughts and used human words that would correctly express those truths. Spirit-taught words were used to declare Spirit-given truth. The concept of verbal inspiration is seen in this declaration by Paul.

Fourth, Paul distinguished between Spirit-given divine commandments and Spirit-guided human counsel. On one aspect of a husband-wife relationship, he admitted: "But I say this as a concession, not as a commandment" (7:6). Concerning the subject of the marriage of virgins, he confessed, "I have no commandment from the Lord; yet I give judgment as one whom the Lord in His mercy has made trustworthy" (7:25). He gave his personal judgment on the status of Christian widows, and then added "and I think I also have the Spirit of God" (7:40). His disclaimers to divine revelation in these areas actually prove that He had divine revelation in all other areas. The Spirit of God is the Source of truth; thus Paul was truthful about the source of his written comments.

On the issue of spiritual gifts and the contrasts between prophecy and tongues-speaking, he argued, "the things which I write to you are the commandments of the Lord" (14:37).

Fifth, Paul claimed that he had apostolic authority (2 Cor. 10:8), that he had been divinely authenticated by signs and wonders (12:12), and that his apostolic office and message came directly from the resurrected Christ (Gal. 1:1, 11–12).

Sixth, Paul claimed he spoke the Word of God. He joyously reported,

"For this reason we also thank God without ceasing, because when you received the word of God which you heard from us, you welcomed it not as the word of men, but as it is in truth, the word of God, which also effectively works in you who believe" (1 Thess. 2:13). The Holy Spirit worked in the lives of Paul's converts, through what he said. Spiritual transformation into Christlikeness can come only through the word of God animated by the Spirit. Paul commanded his epistles to be read (Col. 4:16), and the churches were instructed to discipline those believers who disobeyed Paul's commands (2 Thess. 3:6, 14–15).

Seventh, Paul accepted and equated the authority of both the Old and New Testaments. To prove that church elders should be financially supported, he wrote, "For the Scripture says, 'You shall not muzzle an ox while it treads out the grain,' and 'The laborer is worthy of his wages'" (1 Tim. 5:18). The first quotation is from Moses (Deut. 25:4) and the second is from Jesus and is recorded in Luke 10:7. Paul grouped both verses under the singular title "Scripture." Thus what Luke wrote was just as binding as what Moses wrote. Since the writings of Moses were Spirit-inspired, then the Gospel of Luke must have been Spirit-inspired also.

Peter. Peter referred to Paul by name in his second epistle: "And consider that the longsuffering of our Lord is salvation—as also our beloved brother Paul, according to the wisdom given to him, has written to you" (2 Pet. 3:15). Peter regarded Paul as his beloved brother. Both were in the family of God and in Christ. Peter asserted that God had given wisdom to Paul. That statement echoes the claim of Paul that God gave him wisdom through the Holy Spirit (1 Cor. 2:6–13). Peter stated that Paul had written about the long-suffering of God. That subject matter bears much resemblance to Paul's own testimony of conversion: "However, for this reason I obtained mercy, that in me first Jesus Christ might show all longsuffering, as a pattern to those who are going to believe on Him for everlasting life" (1 Tim. 1:16). Peter must have read the epistles of Paul to have this working knowledge of them.

Peter then acknowledged that the epistles of Paul are Scripture: "As also in all his epistles, speaking in them of these things, in which are some things hard to understand, which untaught and unstable people twist to their own destruction, as they do also the rest of the Scriptures" (2 Pet. 3:16). When

Peter linked Paul's "epistles" with "the rest of the Scriptures," he testified that the epistles of Paul were also "Scriptures."

Peter earlier indicated that no prophecy of Scripture had human origin, but rather, the Holy Spirit moved the biblical authors to speak and to write (1:20–21). His primary reference, then, was to the Old Testament text. His naming of Paul's epistles as Scriptures, equal to the Old Testament, proves that Peter believed that the Holy Spirit moved Paul to write also.

Peter also claimed that his own epistle was authoritative: "Beloved, I now write to you this second epistle (in both of which I stir up your pure minds by way of reminder), that you may be mindful of the words which were spoken before by the holy prophets, and of the commandment of us, the apostles of the Lord and Savior" (3:1–2). Peter spoke of his personal involvement in the writing process ("I write" and "I stir"). He acknowledged himself to be a part of the apostolic group. He claimed an equality of authoritative position, not a superior one. And he equated the authority of the words of the holy prophets (Old Testament) with the commandment of the apostles (New Testament). The singular usage of the noun ("commandment") shows the corporate oneness of the apostolic word. Thus the writings of Paul, Peter, and the others were equal in authority.

Jude. Jude was a full brother to James, the author of the Book of James (Mark 6:3; Jude 1). He was also a half-brother to Jesus, born to Mary and Joseph after the birth of Jesus.

In his epistle Jude referred to the words of the apostles: "But you, beloved, remember the words which were spoken before by the apostles of our Lord Jesus Christ: how they told you that there would be mockers in the last time who would walk according to their own ungodly lusts" (Jude 17–18). Jude's appeal seems to have a primary reference to Peter's second epistle, where the verses are very similar (2 Pet. 3:2–3). Jude had originally intended to write a treatise on the common salvation of believers, but he found it necessary to change his focus and purpose in writing (Jude 3–4). He probably read the second epistle of Peter, analyzed his contemporary ecclesiastical environment, and sensed a new divine constraint to write a defense of the faith.

IMPLICATIONS FOR US

First, we must realize that the Bible is no mere human book. It is the written Word of God, given by divine inspiration. Many colleges offer a course entitled "The Bible as Literature." The professor and the students then analyze the sixty-six books as they would scrutinize the writings of Shakespeare or Hemingway. In a sense they sit in judgment on the text of Scripture. We believers, however, must allow the Bible to sit in judgment on us.

Second, we must accept the Bible as inerrant truth, the basis of our faith and practice. We must derive our belief system from it. We must not impose our own opinions and prejudices upon it. Thus we must come in humble obedience to the will of God revealed in the sacred text.

Third, we must be yielded to the teaching ministry of the Holy Spirit in order to understand the mind of God revealed in the text. It is good to consult commentaries, encyclopedias, concordances, and lexicons. These helps are valuable. We must recognize that God can teach us by what He has taught others. At the same time we must be aware that the Holy Spirit is the only One who can teach us the intended meaning of a passage. He directed the biblical authors to write and He is the ultimate Interpreter of the text.

Fourth, we must regard all portions of the Bible as equally inspired. We must be seekers of Christ in all the books. What can we learn about Christ in Leviticus or Ezra? What can we learn about godly living from Abraham or David?

Fifth, we must renew our respect for the written Word of God. When Ezra the scribe opened the Scriptures, all the people stood up (Nehemiah 8:5). In the morning service of the church which I pastor, we all stand during the public reading of the Scriptures. We must not be guilty of the sin of bibliolatry, the act of worshiping the Bible, but we must respect the Word and worship the God of the Bible.

CHAPTER SIX

The Ministry of the Holy Spirit in the Gospel Era

The era of the Gospels forms a transition between the Old Testament and the New Testament periods. Israel was prominent in the former age, while the church is central in the new economy. The pre-Christ era (Genesis–Malachi) looked forward to the advent of the Messiah-Redeemer. The Gospel era saw the presence of the Messiah-Redeemer on earth, from His birth through His death and resurrection to His ascension into heaven (Matthew–John.) The post-Christ era looks forward to the second coming of Jesus Christ, the Messiah-Redeemer (Acts–Revelation).

The Gospel era covered less than thirty-five years. In that period, only six people, excluding Christ and the apostles, were said to be filled with the Holy Spirit.

JOHN THE BAPTIST

Jesus said John was the greatest of the prophets (Matt. 11:9–13). The Savior also claimed that the Old Testament predicted the life and ministry of John (11:10, 14). John was God's messenger, the forerunner of Jesus Christ.

His Life

His birth. John's ancestry was priestly. His father was Zacharias, a priest, and his mother was Elizabeth, who could trace her lineage to the first high priest, Aaron (Luke 1:5). The couple had no children before the birth of John. They were elderly, with no normal expectations of having any children.

An angel announced to Zacharias that he and his wife would have a son, who would be named John (1:13). The angel continued, "For he will be great in the sight of the Lord, and shall drink neither wine nor strong drink. He will also be filled with the Holy Spirit, even from his mother's womb" (1:15). John was to be a Nazarite, wholly consecrated to God (Num. 6:2–8). It was predicted that John would be filled with the Holy Spirit while he was still in his mother's womb. He thus was controlled by the Spirit before he was born, before he was circumcised and named, and before he consciously called on God to save him from his sins (Joel 2:32). John was filled with the Spirit before he was saved—an exceptional instance. The Spirit also controlled John throughout his early years and adult ministry.

Since Elizabeth conceived John late in her life, the Holy Spirit probably prevented her from transmitting any genetic birth defects. In addition, the Spirit probably protected her from having a miscarriage. The Spirit sovereignly controlled John from his conception to his birth and throughout his life. God had a special ministry for John to perform, and so He filled John with the Holy Spirit. His experience compares with the sovereign fillings in the Old Testament era.

His coming ministry. The angel then announced what John would do: "He will turn many of the children of Israel to the Lord their God. He will also go before Him in the spirit and power of Elijah, 'to turn the hearts of the fathers to the children,' and the disobedient to the wisdom of the just, to make ready a people prepared for the Lord" (Luke 1:16–17). John was to be a revivalist, preaching repentance basically to Israel. He was to prepare Israel spiritually for the coming of the promised Messiah.

The angel declared that God would give John supernatural enablement. His ministry would parallel that of Elijah, who called Israel to repent of idolatry instituted by Ahab and Jezebel. In fact, John would minister "in the spirit and power of Elijah," which may refer to the Holy Spirit's enabling. Interestingly, John's experiences so approximated those of Elijah that many thought John was actually Elijah (John 1:21).

His early recognition of Jesus. After Mary became pregnant with the Christ child, she visited Elizabeth, who had been pregnant for over six months (Luke 1:24–26, 39–40). When Mary greeted Elizabeth, her baby leaped in her womb (1:41). John, yet unborn, leaped for joy at the presence of Jesus in the womb of Mary. Controlled by the Spirit, John knew and rejoiced because the Messiah-Redeemer was present before him. This mystery of recognition can be attributed only to the filling of the Spirit. John was a living person, even at six months within the womb. In his adult life, he would again sense that joy when Jesus would approach him to be baptized.

His Ministry

His identification of Christ. When John the Baptist began to preach, he announced, "There comes One after me who is mightier than I, whose sandal strap I am not worthy to stoop down and loose" (Mark 1:7). He knew that the Messiah would have supernatural power and would be absolutely holy. Recognizing a qualitative difference between himself and the Messiah, John confessed that he was not even worthy enough to be a servant to the promised One. John was aware of his own finiteness and sinfulness as he compared himself to the Messiah.

When Jesus approached John at the Jordan River, John confessed to Him, "I need to be baptized by You, and are You coming to me?" (Matt. 3:14). John may have had an experience then similar to what he had in the womb of his mother when Mary and Elizabeth exchanged greetings (Luke 1:39–44). Filled with the Spirit, John sensed that he was in the presence of the promised Messiah and needed to be baptized by Him.

This encounter between John and Jesus must be contrasted with that between John and both the religious leaders and the people. He challenged the people to repent and to confess their sins (3:2–3). He called the Pharisees and the Sadducees a "brood of vipers" and warned them to flee from the coming wrath (3:7). He appealed to them to "bear fruits worthy of repentance" (3:8). As an authoritative spokesman for God, he voiced these stern words to his audience.

When John said he needed to be baptized by Jesus, the Lord responded that John was to baptize Him because "it is fitting for us to fulfill all righteousness" (Matt. 3:15). So in obedience to the command of Christ, John then baptized Jesus. John then witnessed the divine confirmation of what he personally sensed. The Holy Spirit, in the form of a dove, descended on Jesus (3:16), and God the Father spoke from heaven: "This is My beloved Son, in whom I am well pleased" (3:17). What John saw and heard witnessed to what he felt and thought.

Later John identified Jesus as "the Lamb of God who takes away the sin of the world" (John 1:29). He then admitted twice that he had not known earlier that Jesus was the promised Messiah (1:31, 33). He then explained why he was now absolutely sure that Jesus Christ is the Messiah, the Son of God: "I saw the Spirit descending from heaven like a dove, and He remained upon Him. I did not know Him, but He who sent me to baptize with water said to me, 'Upon whom you see the Spirit descending, and remaining on Him, this is He who baptizes with the Holy Spirit.' And I have seen and testified that this is the Son of God" (1:32–34). John equated the descent of the Holy Spirit upon Jesus as absolute proof of Christ's true identity.

His message and prediction. John preached a simple, direct theme: "Repent, for the kingdom of heaven is at hand!" (Matt. 3:2). The spiritual-political kingdom was imminent because the coming of the promised Messiah was imminent. John had the responsibility to prepare Israel spiritually for her entrance into the kingdom. His converts, who repented and confessed their sins, were baptized by John in the Jordan River to show their identification with him and other expectant believers. As a result of John's ministry, Israel was divided into two groups—believers who were spiritually prepared and unbelievers who refused to repent.

John thus remarked, "I indeed baptize you with water unto repentance, but He who is coming after me is mightier than I, whose sandals I am not worthy to carry. He will baptize you with the Holy Spirit and fire" (3:11; see also Mark 1:8; Luke 3:16; John 1:33). The baptism of John was in water, visible and outward, but the baptism of Jesus would be in the Holy Spirit, invisible and inward. John's ministry of baptism had divided Israel into two groups; now Christ would do likewise.

Baptism in fire. The baptism in the Holy Spirit and the baptism in fire are not the same. In fact, they are opposites. The baptism in the Holy Spirit is only for believers, whereas the baptism in fire is only for unbelievers. John spoke of "fire" three times (Matt. 3:10–12). First, he equated the people of Israel with trees: "And even now the ax is laid to the root of the trees. Therefore every tree which does not bear good fruit is cut down and thrown into the fire" (3:10). Good fruit was the fruit of repentance (3:8), and so the lack of good fruit demonstrated that the person was unrepentant. The destiny of the unsaved is the fire of judgment, known as the wrath to come and the lake of fire (Rev. 20:14–15; 21:8). Believers, likened to trees that bear good fruit, are not cut down and thrown into the fire.

Second, John compared the spiritual status of the Israelites to wheat and chaff on a threshing floor. "His winnowing fan is in His hand, and He will thoroughly clean out His threshing floor, and gather His wheat into the barn; but He will burn up the chaff with unquenchable fire" (Matt. 3:12). In ancient Israel, the harvesters would bring the wheat or barley to a threshing floor. There they would beat the grain and then they would use their winnowing forks or shovels to throw the grain into the air. As the wind passed through the thrown grain, the heavy kernels would fall directly to the floor but the chaff would be blown away. This repeated action separated the wheat or barley kernels from the chaff. Later, the workers would store the valuable kernels in jars in their barns, but they would burn the useless chaff in fire. The grain kernels represented the people who repented, whereas the chaff symbolized the unsaved. The fire was thus the fire of divine judgment.

Third, the baptism in fire therefore must be a punitive experience for the unsaved. Generally, a symbol or metaphor should be interpreted consistently within its context. Both before and after the baptism of fire is mentioned, the fire referred to the judgment of fire for the unsaved. John predicted that Christ would separate Israel into the saved (the good trees and the grain kernels) and the unsaved (the bad trees and the chaff). Christ would baptize the saved in the Holy Spirit and He would "baptize" the unsaved in fire. For Israel, that experience will ultimately happen when Jesus Christ returns to the earth to establish His kingdom over Israel and the nations of the world.

Some theologians have viewed the baptism in fire as a purifying experience, a postconversion blessing that removes either the sin nature or the desire to sin. In that interpretation the "fire" removes sin from the believer just as a fire removes dross from gold. The hymn "Cleanse Me" contains phrases that speak of this usage of fire: "Cleanse me from every sin / and set me free; Fill me with fire / where once I burned with shame; and, O Holy Ghost / revival comes from Thee / Send a revival / start the work in me." The concepts of spiritual cleansing, freedom, filling, and revival are related to the infusion of holy fire. I approve of the sentiment of this hymn, but the choice of words is not entirely biblical.

Other commentators, especially those of pentecostal persuasion, equate the baptism in fire with what happened to the apostles on the Day of Pentecost. Three unusual phenomena announced the descent of the Holy Spirit: a sound of rushing, mighty wind, the appearance of tongues of fire, and speaking in tongues (Acts 2:1–4). Luke mentioned this occurrence of fire: "Then there appeared to them divided tongues, as of fire, and one sat upon each of them" (2:3).

This event, however, was not a real baptism in fire for the following reasons. First, the fire did not literally fill the room in which the apostles were sitting. If it had, the apostles would have then been "in" the fire, immersed or baptized in it. However, the sound of the wind, representing the Holy Spirit, did fill the room, so they were "in" the wind, that is, the Holy Spirit, but not in the fire. Second, the divided tongues sat on each of the apostles. These tongues were not real fire; they were "as of fire," that is, they looked like fire, but they were not actually fire. Third, Christ informed the apostles that they would be baptized in the Holy Spirit on the Day of Pentecost, but He did not say that they would be baptized in fire (1:5). Fourth, the baptism in fire is never mentioned as a life experience for believers to seek, either in the Book of Acts or in the Epistles.

MARY

Mary was a resident of Nazareth in Galilee. She was a virgin, legally betrothed to Joseph. Both Mary and Joseph were of the house of David. Mary traced her ancestry to the great king through his son Nathan (Luke 3:23–38), whereas Joseph traced his lineage through another son, Solomon (Matt. 1:1–17).

Angelic Announcement to Mary

Choice of Mary. God sovereignly selected Mary to be the woman through whom God the Son would enter the human race (Gal. 4:4). God sent the angel Gabriel to her with this announcement: "And behold, you will conceive in your womb and bring forth a Son, and shall call His name Jesus. He will be great, and will be called the Son of the Highest; and the Lord God will give Him the throne of His father David. And He will reign over the house of Jacob forever, and of His kingdom there will be no end" (Luke 1:31–33). The promises of the Davidic Covenant (2 Sam. 7:16) would be fulfilled through Jesus, the son of Mary.

Virgin conception. Since Mary was a virgin, she asked *how* the conception could happen, not *if* it would occur. The angel then declared, "The Holy Spirit will come upon you, and the power of the Highest will overshadow you; therefore, also, that Holy One who is to be born will be called the Son of God" (Luke 1:35). Though such a birth is humanly impossible, with God nothing is impossible. Mary believed in God's sovereign will and omnipotence, and so she submitted her body and her future to Him (1:34–38).

Technical details about the conception are not recorded. However, as stated in chapter 2, the Holy Spirit came on Mary and controlled her completely at the moment of conception. At the time God the Son entered her body, womb, and ovum, Mary was under the protective guidance of the Spirit. She was able to pass on her humanity to Jesus, but she was prevented from transmitting her sinful nature. God the Son, a divine person with a divine nature, obtained a human nature through Mary. As the result of His incarnation, He is a divine-human person. He did not obtain a second personhood through her. He is one person with two natures, a divine nature and a human nature.

Although the Holy Spirit was upon Mary at the conception, her son did not become the son of the Holy Spirit. The Bible nowhere makes that identification. Jesus Christ is the eternal Son of the Father.

Angelic Explanation to Joseph

His dilemma. Mary did not tell Joseph about the angelic visitation or her pregnancy. How could she? Would he have believed her story? Before Joseph and Mary consummated their legal betrothal with sexual intimacy, Joseph became aware that Mary was pregnant. We are not told how he found out. At his discovery, he did not realize that her pregnancy was caused by the Holy Spirit (Matt. 1:18).

Joseph had to make a difficult decision immediately. He was a just man; therefore he could not go through with the marriage covenant. He did not want to give his family inheritance to a child who was not his. However, because Joseph loved Mary, he didn't want to shame her publicly. So he chose to divorce her privately (1:19).

Explanation. After Joseph made this decision, he fell sleep. An angel appeared to him in a dream and explained, "Joseph, son of David, do not be afraid to take to you Mary your wife, for that which is conceived in her is of the Holy Spirit. And she will bring forth a Son, and you shall call His name JESUS, for He will save His people from their sins" (Matt. 1:20–21).

Several key concepts are found in this explanation. First, Joseph was a physical and legal son of David through the royal line of kings (Matt. 1:1–16). Joseph was prevented from being a Davidic king by God's curse on the descendants of Jehoiachin, the king of Judah, who was captured by the Babylonians (Jer. 22:24–30). Second, Mary had not been unfaithful to Joseph, for her conception was supernatural, caused by the Holy Spirit. Third, the angel instructed Joseph to complete the marriage covenant with Mary. After Joseph realized what God was doing with Mary, he could have been afraid to have sexual relations with her lest he violate her sanctified position as the mother of the Messiah. So the angel told him to take her (into his home) as his wife. Fourth, Joseph had the legal responsibility to name the child. This action established publicly his legal paternity of Jesus. Thereafter Jesus would be known as the son of Joseph. Jesus could then claim the royal, legal birthright to rule as Israel's king from Joseph without receiving the divine curse that rested on Jehoiachin's descendants, including Joseph. Fifth, Joseph now knew that Mary's child would be the Messiah-Redeemer.

Virgin birth. At this point in Matthew's narrative, he wrote, "So all this was done that it might be fulfilled which was spoken by the Lord through the prophet, saying: 'Behold, the virgin shall be with child, and bear a Son, and they shall call His name Immanuel,' which is translated, 'God with us'" (Matt. 1:22–23). Did the angel give these two verses to Joseph? Or, did the Spirit direct Matthew to insert this prophetic explanation? The text does not give a definitive answer, but I prefer the second option.

Isaiah's prophecy declared that the mother of the divine-human Messiah would be a virgin both at the time of her conception and at the time she delivered the child. A virgin loses her status of virginity the moment she has marital relations. In Mary's case, however, she was a virgin from Jesus' conception to birth because she had no sexual intimacy with any man.

Joseph's action. Joseph obeyed the angelic command. He took Mary to be his wife, but he did not consummate the marital union until after Jesus' birth. Matthew wrote that he "did not know her till she had brought forth her firstborn Son" (Matt. 1:25). Later Joseph and Mary had several children together (Mark 6:3), so that Mary did not remain a virgin throughout her life.

In obedience, Joseph named the child of Mary (Matt. 1:25), and thus became the legal father of Jesus. His family and friends must have concluded that Joseph was the actual physical father of Jesus, even though he was not. The biblical record nowhere states that Joseph was ever filled with the Holy Spirit.

ELIZABETH

Elizabeth was the mother of John the Baptist. Although John was filled with the Holy Spirit even when he was in the womb, there is no biblical indication that Elizabeth was filled with the Spirit at her conception. Apparently the Holy Spirit did not superintend her during her pregnancy either.

In one singular event during her life, she became filled with the Spirit. The pregnant Mary visited the pregnant Elizabeth. When Mary greeted Elizabeth, John the Baptist joyously leaped within her womb and she "was filled with the Holy Spirit" (Luke 1:41).

Elizabeth then became a prophetess. She exclaimed to Mary, "Blessed are you among women, and blessed is the fruit of your womb! But why is this granted to me, that the mother of my Lord should come to me?" (1:42–43). This oral pronouncement contained several significant truths.

First, Mary was "blessed." The verbal adjective (*eulogēmenē*) means "one who has been blessed by another." Mary had been blessed by God. God alone is *eulogētos* ("blessed," 1:68; Eph. 1:3). That is, He is blessed in and of Himself. Such blessedness is a divine attribute. Because God is blessed, He can bless others, and Mary was one whom He blessed. Mary was not blessed in and of herself.

Second, Mary was blessed "among" women. The preposition *en* ("among") denotes sphere and can be translated "in" or "within." Thus Mary was blessed within the realm of womankind. She was not blessed over or above other women.

Third, the fruit of Mary's womb was also "blessed." The humanity that Mary transmitted to God the Son was blessed by God the Father in that He chose her ovum. Under ordinary circumstances her human offspring would not be blessed.

Fourth, Elizabeth identified Mary as "the mother of my Lord." She did not call Mary "the mother of my God." Mary did not originate God. The title "my Lord" is messianic (Ps. 110:1; Matt. 22:41–46). Elizabeth knew that Mary was the mother of the promised Messiah.

Fifth, Elizabeth praised Mary for believing the divine announcement through the angel. She stated, "Blessed is she who believed" (Luke 1:45). Mary took God at His word and yielded herself to His divine plan for her and her child.

Sixth, Elizabeth predicted that God would fulfill His prophetic announcement given to Mary. She asserted that "there will be a fulfillment of those things which were told her from the Lord" (1:45). Mary now had a double confirmation of the divine plan—one given by Gabriel and one by Elizabeth. In response to Elizabeth's prophetic, Spirit-filled utterance Mary sang a remarkable hymn of praise (1:46–55).

ZACHARIAS

Zacharias the priest did not believe that he and Elizabeth could become parents so late in their married life (Luke 1:20). Because of his unbelief, God punished Zechariah so that he could not speak from the time of the angelic announcement till John the Baptist was circumcised. When

Zacharias corroborated Elizabeth's desire to name the baby "John," God opened his mouth, and he was able to speak again. This miracle caused the people to fear and to wonder about John's future (1:63–66).

Luke then wrote, "Now his father Zacharias was filled with the Holy Spirit, and prophesied" (1:67). The priest thus became a prophet in the tradition of Old Testament prophets. In the first portion of his Spirit-given prophecy, Zacharias praised God for visiting and redeeming Israel (1:68). He actually focused on the forthcoming birth of the Messiah who would deliver Israel politically from her enemies and the nation spiritually from her sins (1:71, 74–75, 77).

In the second half of his prophecy, Zacharias addressed his son, John the Baptist (1:76). He predicted that John would be the prophet of God, that he would be the forerunner of the Messiah, and that John would give "knowledge of salvation to His people by the remission of their sins" (Luke 1:76–77).

By the Spirit of God, Zacharias thus testified to the persons and ministries of both Jesus Christ and John the Baptist.

SIMEON

Forty days after Jesus was born, Mary and Joseph brought the infant Jesus to the temple to make an offering for the ceremonial purification of Mary and to present Jesus to the Lord (Luke 2:22–24; see also Lev. 12:1–8; Exod. 13:1–16; Num. 3:11–13; 8:16–19). On that occasion they encountered Simeon. Several facts may be noted about Simeon.

First, he was a Spirit-filled believer. "And behold, there was a man in Jerusalem whose name was Simeon, and this man was just and devout, waiting for the Consolation of Israel, and the Holy Spirit was upon him" (Luke 2:25). He was righteous in both his position before God and his practice before people. He obeyed the Mosaic Law both in its moral directives and in the sacrificial system. He anticipated the coming of the Messiah.

Second, the Holy Spirit had revealed to Simeon that he would not die until he had actually seen the Messiah (2:26). How that was revealed to Simeon is not stated.

Third, the Holy Spirit led him into the temple at the very hour Mary, Joseph, and Jesus were there (2:27).

Fourth, when Simeon saw the infant Jesus, he took the child in his arms and blessed God. As a Spirit-guided prophet, he said, "Lord, now You are letting Your servant depart in peace, according to Your word; for my eyes have seen Your salvation which You have prepared before the face of all peoples, a light to bring revelation to the Gentiles, and the glory of Your people Israel" (2:29–32). He equated salvation with the person of the Messiah, not with His redemptive work. He confessed that Christ would have a spiritual ministry to both Gentiles and Jews.

Fifth, Simeon then blessed Mary and Joseph. He declared that Christ would divide Israel into two groups, the saved, that is, who would accept Him, and the unsaved, those who would reject Him (2:34). He informed Mary that her heart would be pierced with sorrow; this was no doubt fulfilled when she witnessed the Crucifixion (2:35).

The Holy Spirit had an unusual ministry in Simeon. He came on him, guided him, and revealed truth to him.

ANNA

Anna was also in the temple when Mary, Joseph, and Jesus entered (Luke 2:36–38). There is no direct statement that the Holy Spirit filled Anna, but Luke identified her as "a prophetess." It is reasonable to assume that the Spirit controlled her as she spoke.

An elderly widow from the tribe of Asher, Anna spent her daylight hours in the temple, serving God "with fastings and prayers night and day" (2:37).

When she saw the infant Jesus, she "gave thanks to the Lord, and spoke of Him to all those who looked for redemption in Jerusalem" (2:38). She became an evangelist for Christ. She believed that God would one day bring spiritual and political redemption to the city of Jerusalem, Israel's capital.

IMPLICATIONS FOR US

First, we should see ourselves as humble servants of God if the Holy Spirit is truly controlling our lives. Neither leaders nor followers should ever be proud or arrogant. John the Baptist saw himself as an anonymous voice crying in the wilderness. He viewed himself as not even worthy to untie and carry the sandals of the Lord Jesus. And Mary saw herself as a maid-servant in full submission to God.

Second, we will exalt Jesus Christ when the Spirit of God controls us. John the Baptist said of Him: "He must increase, but I must decrease" (John 3:30). When the Spirit of God controls us, we will be full of Christ, not full of ourselves.

Third, when we are controlled by the Spirit, we will be biblically firm and accurate in our proclamations. John the Baptist, Mary, Elizabeth, Zacharias, Simeon, and Anna referred to the authority of the written Word of God. They explained the saving plan of God and its proper application to their lives. When the Spirit of God truly controls us, we will point people to God, the Scriptures, and personal redemption.

Fourth, when the Spirit of God controls us, we still maintain our human finiteness. When John the Baptist was in Herod's prison about to be martyred, he had doubts. He needed to trust Christ even when he did not understand what was going on. We must continue to grow in faith and discernment as the Spirit directs us.

CHAPTER SEVEN

The Ministry of the Holy Spirit in the Life of Christ

Our Savior is the Lord Jesus Christ. Those three names each have distinctive significance. "Lord" asserts His deity, "Jesus" points to His humanity, and "Christ" relates to His messianic position. The Greek *Christos* ("Christ") literally means "the anointed One." Isaiah predicted that God would anoint the promised Messiah-Redeemer with His Spirit (Isa. 61:1). Peter, voicing the opinion of the apostles, gave this identification of Jesus: "You are the Christ, the Son of the living God" (Matt. 16:16). In these words Peter recognized that Jesus is divine, human, and the Spirit-anointed One. Jesus once asked the Pharisees: "What do you think about the Christ? Whose Son is He?" (22:42). They identified the Spirit-anointed One as the son of David, but they failed to perceive His deity.

In this chapter, we will focus on two areas: what the Spirit did for Christ in the major events of His life, and what Christ taught about the person and ministry of the Holy Spirit.

WHAT THE HOLY SPIRIT DID FOR CHRIST

John wrote, "For He whom God has sent speaks the words of God, for God does not give the Spirit by measure" (John 3:34). Another translation reads, "for God gives the Spirit without limit" (NIV). Only Jesus Christ experienced the full, infinite, omnipotent ministry of the Holy Spirit in His life. In His public life and ministry Jesus was consciously controlled by the Spirit every moment of every day.

In His Incarnation

Activity of the Holy Spirit. An angel told Mary that the Holy Spirit would come on her and overshadow her at the precise moment of the Incarnation (Luke 1:35). When God the Son, the living Word, became flesh, He entered the body of a woman who was sanctified and superintended by the Spirit. However, the action of the Spirit on Mary did not produce the person of the divine-human Savior, the Son of God. He existed as a divine person within the triune Being before creation and His incarnation (John 1:1, 14).

The Holy Spirit nevertheless enabled Mary to conceive without male fertilization of her egg. He guided the implantation of that egg within her womb. Technical details are omitted in the Scriptures, but the Bible clearly attributes her pregnant condition to the Holy Spirit (Matt. 1:18, 20). The Bible repudiates any suggestion that a male fathered her child.

There is an eternal relationship between the three persons of the triune God (John 1:18; 14:11; 15:26). However, there is no biblical mention that the Holy Spirit filled God the Son when He entered Mary. The emphasis in the biblical narratives is on the relationship between the Spirit and Mary, not the relationship between the Spirit and the Son.

The virginal conception was extraordinary and supernaturally caused, though the nine months of pregnancy and the subsequent birth were basically natural. Although it is plausible to assume that the Spirit remained on Mary throughout her pregnancy, there is no biblical verification of that action. Although she carried within her the incarnate God, Mary nourished and delivered her baby as all mothers do. The miracle occurred at the conception, the exact moment of the divine Incarnation.

Essence of the Incarnation. A number of facts can be noted about the Incarnation. First, the doctrine of the Incarnation and the virgin conception by the Spirit are inseparably linked. We cannot have one without the other. According to the Koran, the sacred book of Islam, Jesus was virgin-born, but He was not God incarnate. In their tenacious acceptance of unitarian monotheism, they must believe that Jesus was only a man, a virgin-born prophet.

Second, the Incarnation does not involve a dual parenthood for Jesus. Liberal theologians believe that Jesus was the natural-born son of Joseph and Mary and that He became the most God-conscious man ever. Some liberals talk about the divinity of the human Jesus, but they deny His eternal deity.

Third, the Incarnation does not involve transubstantiation, an action when one material substance changes into another. Medieval alchemists thus tried unsuccessfully to change lead into gold. According to the Roman Catholic Church, transubstantiation occurs at the sacrament of the Mass when the priest blesses the elements of the wine and the wafer. Their dogma teaches that the wine literally becomes the blood of Christ and the wafer literally becomes His flesh. At the Incarnation, when God became man, He did not cease being God, because deity was not changed into humanity.

Fourth, the Incarnation was not a theophany, an appearance of God in human form. God did appear to man in human form in Old Testament times, but those theophanies did not involve a real Incarnation or a virginal conception.

Fifth, the Incarnation did not cause Mary to become the mother of God. Scripture nowhere gives her that title. A human mother exists before her offspring, but Mary did not exist before God the Son. Mary produced and mothered His humanity, but not His deity.

Sixth, the Incarnation did not cause the Holy Spirit to become the father of Jesus. Jesus is never called the son of the Holy Spirit. Jesus became the human son of Mary, but He always was the Son of God the Father.

Seventh, the Incarnation does not involve the immaculate conception of Mary. In 1854 the Roman Catholic Church pronounced the dogma that Mary herself was conceived apart from sin. This religious tradition believes that Mary had no sin nature, that she lived a life free from sin, that God chose her because of her personal holiness, and that she was unable to pass any sinful disposition to Jesus. Mary, however, confessed that God was her Savior (Luke 1:47).

Eighth, God the Son obtained a true and perfect human nature through the virginal conception (John 1:14; Rom. 8:3; Heb. 2:14; 1 John 4:2–3). He had a normal human birth, experienced normal human development, and had normal emotional and spiritual feelings.

Ninth, at the Incarnation Jesus Christ became a theanthropic person, one person with both a divine nature and a human nature. He did not have a theanthropic nature resulting from a *merger* of the two natures. He was the God-Man, but not the man-God. He was neither a divine man nor a human god.[1]

In His Early Years

Very little is known about the human development of Jesus from His birth to the beginning of His public ministry. He was circumcised at the age of eight days and presented at the temple at the age of forty days (Luke 2:21–24). From this last event to the age of twelve, the Bible gives this summary: "And the Child grew and became strong in spirit, filled with wisdom; and the grace of God was upon Him" (2:40).

When Jesus was twelve years old, Mary and Joseph brought Him to the Passover Feast at Jerusalem. While in the temple, Jesus sat with the teachers, "both listening to them and asking them questions" (2:46). All who heard Him "were astonished at His understanding and answers" (2:47). Jesus manifested unusual biblical and moral insight, not seen in ordinary youth. There are three possible explanations for His wisdom. First, He demonstrated His eternal attribute of omniscience. Second, the Holy Spirit filled Him with this extraordinary wisdom. Third, Jesus displayed the wisdom God intended humans to have before the Fall and the entrance of sin. Without denying the possibility of the first two views, I prefer the third position.

Luke then summarized the next eighteen years of Jesus' human development, from age twelve to thirty: "And Jesus increased in wisdom and stature, and in favor with God and men" (2:52). He underwent mental, physical, spiritual, and social development.

The Scriptures do not state clearly that the Holy Spirit was upon Jesus during those first thirty years. I personally do not think that the Spirit came upon Him until His baptism. However, many theologians believe that the Spirit was upon Jesus from the time He entered Mary's womb. John F. Walvoord, a representative of that view, wrote, "While it is not possible to produce evidence beyond question, it is a matter of reasonable inference that Christ was filled with the Holy Spirit from the very moment of conception."[2] He basically offered three supporting arguments. First, there is an intrapersonal oneness of the three Persons at all times. Thus, God the Holy Spirit has always been in God the Son and God the Son has always been in God the Holy Spirit. Second, since John the Baptist was filled with the Spirit from his mother's womb, then Jesus must have had the same experience. This argument goes from the lesser to the greater, from the lesser person to the greater person. Third, since God gave the Spirit without measure to Jesus, He must have been filled from the beginning of His human experience.

In His Baptism

Various types of water baptism are mentioned in the Scriptures. First, John the Baptist baptized those who had repented and who anticipated the coming of the Messiah and His kingdom. Second, Christians are baptized to show their identification with Jesus Christ in His death, burial, and resurrection (Matt. 28:18–20). Third, there is the baptism of Jesus (3:13–17; Mark 1:9–11; Luke 3:21–22; John 1:31–34).

The event. Jesus began His public ministry when He was about thirty years old (Luke 3:23). Before He did, He was baptized by John and He was tempted by Satan. Christ spent the first thirty years of His human existence in relative obscurity. The Bible gives this comment of that period in His life: "He was in the world, and the world was made through Him, and the world did not know Him" (John 1:10).

The baptism of Jesus marked a transition into public recognition. To use the language of the stage, He went from the dark wings to the center of the stage with the spotlight on Him.

Matthew gave this record of the event: "When He had been baptized, Jesus came up immediately from the water, and behold, the heavens were opened to Him, and He saw the Spirit of God descending like a dove and alighting upon Him. And suddenly a voice came from heaven, saying, 'This is My beloved Son, in whom I am well pleased'" (Matt. 3:16–17). Luke added that the Spirit descended on Jesus as He was praying (Luke 3:21).

The details of the event are clear: Both John and Jesus were in the water, the baptism occurred, the heavens opened, in the visible form of a dove the Holy Spirit descended on Jesus, and God the Father voiced His pleasure over the Son.

Its significance. Since Jesus had no sin, He had no need to be baptized by John. John recognized the moral purity and holiness of Jesus. In fact, at first he refused to baptize the Savior. But finally, in submission to Jesus' request, he baptized Him. Why? Several biblical reasons are given.

First, Jesus was baptized to be made known to John the Baptist (John 1:30–34). John knew that the Messiah was coming, but he did not know Him by name. God revealed to John that he would know Him when he saw the Spirit descending on Him. Witnessing that phenomenon John said, "And I have seen and testified that this is the Son of God" (1:34).

Second, Jesus was baptized to be made known to Israel (1:31). The baptism of Jesus served as His introduction to the covenant people.

Third, Jesus was baptized to identify Himself with John and his converts. By that act He disassociated Himself from the religious leaders who refused to repent and to be baptized. He thus aligned Himself with those who anticipated the establishment of the spiritual-political kingdom.

Fourth, Jesus was baptized to be identified as the Son of God who would baptize believers in the Holy Spirit (1:33–34). The voice of the Father and the descent of the visible dove confirmed that identification.

Fifth, Jesus was baptized to be anointed with the Holy Spirit. The Spirit descended (*katabainō*), alighted or came upon Him (*erchomai*), and remained upon Him (*menō*).

These three actions of the Holy Spirit marked the fulfillment of Old Testament prophecies concerning the Messiah. God said through Isaiah, "Behold! My Servant whom I have chosen, My Beloved in whom My soul is well pleased! I will put My Spirit upon Him, and He will declare justice to the Gentiles" (Matt. 12:18; see Isa. 42:1).

God the Son, the promised Messiah, said through Isaiah, "The Spirit of the Lord GOD is upon Me, because the LORD has anointed Me to preach good tidings to the poor; He has sent Me to heal the brokenhearted, to proclaim liberty to the captives, and the opening of the prison to those who are bound" (61:1–2). When Jesus was in the synagogue at Nazareth, He read those verses and then proclaimed, "Today this Scripture is fulfilled in your hearing" (Luke 4:21). He knew that God the Father anointed Him with the Holy Spirit at His baptism. He knew that the purposes of His messianic mission could be accomplished only through the enabling of the Spirit of God.

Peter informed those who had gathered in the house of Cornelius that "God anointed Jesus of Nazareth with the Holy Spirit and with power, who went about doing good and healing all who were oppressed by the devil, for God was with Him" (Acts 10:38). God officially commissioned Jesus as the Messiah when He anointed Christ with the Holy Spirit. After this event, Jesus actively ministered. Before this event, Jesus did not perform any messianic task, although He was the Messiah.

From His baptism, Christ was full of the Holy Spirit in all He did. Jesus had no future anointings or fillings by the Spirit.

In His Temptation

God cannot be tempted, but people can be (James 1:13–15). Adam and Eve succumbed to the pressure of Satan. Humans sin constantly as they live in a culture dominated by the evil one (1 John 5:19). Satan tempts believers, and they often fall. When God the Son took to Himself a human nature, He exposed Himself to the immoral deceit of Satan, but He gained victory over the devil.

Its description. After His baptism, Jesus "was led up by the Spirit into the wilderness to be tempted by the devil" (Matt. 4:1; see Luke 4:1). Mark stated that the Spirit "drove" (literally, "cast out," *ekballō*) Him into the Judean wilderness (Mark 1:12). Jesus was filled with the Holy Spirit as He went to be tempted (Luke 4:1). Thus it was in the will of God for Jesus to be tempted, but the temptation came from Satan, not from God.

When Jesus experienced temptation for forty days (Mark 1:13), He fasted during that period (Matt. 4:2), and He was surrounded by wild animals (Mark 1:13). After the temptations were over, angels ministered to Him (Matt. 4:11; Mark 1:13).

We believers are tempted in three major areas—"the lust of the flesh, the lust of the eyes, and the pride of life" (1 John 2:16). Satan tempted Eve in these areas, and she yielded, sinning against the revealed will of God. She saw that the tree of the knowledge of good and evil was "good for food" (lust of the flesh), that it was "pleasant to the eyes" (lust of the eyes), and that it was a tree "desirable to make one wise" (pride of life).

Satan used the same lying strategy on Jesus Christ. He tempted Christ to turn stones into bread to satisfy His hunger (lust of the flesh). He tempted Christ to jump from the pinnacle of the temple and to trust God to save His life (pride of life). And he tempted Christ to worship him when he offered and showed Him all the kingdoms of the world (lust of the eyes).

Jesus, however, was not deceived. He fully perceived the essence of the temptation. He yielded Himself to the will of God revealed in the Scriptures (Matt. 4:4, 7, 10). Defeated, Satan left Him.

Its significance. Jesus' temptation is significant for four reasons. First, the temptation demonstrated that the divine-human Son of God could be tempted. He was God manifest in the flesh and He was full of the Holy Spirit, but still He could be tempted. He "was in all points tempted as we are" (Heb. 4:15). Before His conception and birth, God the Son was a divine person with an untemptable divine nature. Through the conception to Mary, He obtained a temptable human nature and thus was able to be tempted by an outside evil force, namely, Satan.

Second, the temptation showed that it is neither sinful nor a sign of weakness to be tempted. Sin only occurs when a person yields to the temptation.

Third, Jesus' temptation demonstrated His holiness and sinlessness. The Bible elsewhere states that Christ "knew no sin" (2 Cor. 5:21), that He was "without sin" (Heb. 4:15), that He "committed no sin" (1 Pet. 2:22), and that "in Him there is no sin" (1 John 3:5). Christ Himself challenged His critics, "Which of you convicts Me of sin?" (John 8:46). Jesus never admitted wrongdoing. He never apologized, never confessed sin, and never offered a sacrifice at the temple. He was holiness personified.

Evangelical theologians all agree that Jesus was tempted and that He was sinless, but they disagree over the essence of His sinlessness. Some say that Jesus could have sinned, but He was able not to sin. They say the reason Jesus did not sin is that He completely submitted Himself to the will of God. These theologians compare the experience of Christ to that of Adam. God created Adam with an ability not to sin, but Adam chose to sin. On the other hand, Christ, they say, chose not to sin. In this view, the humanity of Jesus is emphasized.

Other theologians (including myself) believe that Jesus was not able to sin. He could be tempted because He had a human nature, but He could not sin because He was a divine person with a divine nature. In this view, the deity of Jesus Christ is stressed.

Both positions are acceptable within evangelicalism. Both affirm His deity, humanity, and sinlessness. They simply approach the debatable issue from two different starting points.

Fourth, the temptation demonstrated the full control of the Holy Spirit in the life of Jesus. Christ used the Spirit-inspired Scriptures to rebut the three temptations of Satan. The Spirit enabled Jesus to manifest both His divine and human natures through the trials of those forty days.

In His Ministry

Jesus Christ was always full of the Holy Spirit as He preached, taught, healed, and cast out demons (Matt. 4:23). God had anointed Him with the Spirit to conduct His ministry (12:18–21; Luke 4:18–21; Acts 10:38). To the Gospel authors, it was a foregone conclusion that Jesus did everything by the Spirit's enabling. Thus the four writers rarely related the ministry of the Spirit to the deeds of Christ. They did not debate the issue whether Jesus, in His miracles, used His own divine power or used the power of the Holy Spirit.

After His baptism Jesus "returned in the power of the Spirit to Galilee" to begin His public ministry (Luke 4:14). He ably expounded the Scriptures as He preached the same message John the Baptist proclaimed (Matt. 4:17). He pointed others to His own authority in the interpretation and application of biblical truth (7:29). He performed all types of healings: cleansing lepers, removing paralyses, reducing high fevers. In fact, He healed "every sickness and every disease among the people" (9:35). He also raised the dead, gave hearing to the deaf, restored speech to the mute, and gave sight to the blind. The Bible gives no record of a prophet or apostle ever performing the miracle of restoring sight to the blind. Only the Messiah, the Light of the world, did that.

Jesus Christ demonstrated His authority over the realm of Satan and demons. He restored people to normal human functions when He cast demons out of demonized people. Christ then declared, "But if I cast out demons by the Spirit of God, surely the kingdom of God has come upon you" (Matt. 12:28; see Luke 11:20). Christ performed the exorcism, but He did it by the enablement of the Spirit. Both divine persons were actively involved.

Jesus Christ authorized the twelve apostles to minister. For them to do so, He "gave them power over unclean spirits, to cast them out, and to heal all kinds of sickness and all kinds of disease" (Matt. 10:1). He gave them "power," but the text does not mention that He gave them the Holy Spirit. It is plausible to assume that He did, because usually the Holy Spirit and enabling power cannot be separated. Their ministry, however, was for a specified time and was limited to Israel (10:5–8).

Jesus later authorized seventy others to minister in the cities of Israel (Luke 10:1). They returned with joy, rejoicing over their exorcism of demons (10:17). When Jesus heard that report, He "rejoiced in the Spirit" and thanked God for His revelation of redemptive truth to the converts (10:21–22). In activity and attitude, Jesus was controlled by the Holy Spirit at all times.

In His Crucifixion

The Gospels make no mention of the ministry of the Holy Spirit to Jesus Christ when He suffered and died on the cross. Prior to and during those six hours, Christ "humbled Himself and became obedient to death, even the death of the cross" (Phil. 2:8). Since the Bible nowhere states that the Spirit left Jesus before the Crucifixion, He must have still been filled with the Holy Spirit while He was on the cross.

The Book of Hebrews contrasts the Old Testament sacrifices with the sacrifice of Christ. "For if the blood of bulls and goats and the ashes of a heifer, sprinkling the unclean, sanctifies for the purifying of the flesh, how much more shall the blood of Christ, who through the eternal Spirit offered Himself without spot to God, cleanse your conscience from dead works to serve the living God?" (Heb. 9:13–14). The Holy Spirit, the eternal Spirit, was the intermediate divine Agent by whom Christ offered Himself as a redemptive sacrifice for our sins.

John F. Walvoord ably commented, "The work of the Holy Spirit in relation to the sufferings of Christ on the cross consisted, then, in sustaining the human nature in its love of God, in submission to the will of God and obedience to His commands, and in encouraging and strengthening Christ in the path of duty which led to the cross."[3] God the Son incarnate suffered and died. The Father did not suffer and die. Nor did the Holy Spirit suffer and die, even though He filled Christ when the Savior suffered and died.

In His Resurrection

The Gospels do not mention any ministry of the Holy Spirit to Jesus Christ at the time of His resurrection. The Epistles, however, do connect the Spirit to the resurrection. Walvoord, though, cautioned, "The exact nature of the work of the Holy Spirit in the resurrection of Christ is not revealed."[4]

Paul. Paul centered the gospel in God's Son, "Jesus Christ our Lord, who was born of the seed of David according to the flesh, and declared to be the Son of God with power according to the Spirit of holiness, by the resurrection from the dead" (Rom. 1:3–4). The resurrection authenticated the Spirit-inspired Old Testament Scriptures that the crucified Messiah would be raised from the dead (Acts 2:22–36). The resurrection authenticated the identification of Jesus as the Son of God by the Holy Spirit. Jesus' resurrection and subsequent ascension authenticated Jesus as Israel's Lord and Christ when He poured out the Spirit on the apostles on the Day of Pentecost.

Believers are able to live righteously because the Holy Spirit lives in them. "But if the Spirit of Him who raised Jesus from the dead dwells in you, He who raised Christ from the dead will also give life to your mortal bodies through His Spirit who dwells in you" (Rom. 8:11). God the Father raised Jesus. Elsewhere Christ declared that He could raise Himself from the dead (John 2:19; 10:18). And yet in his encouragement to believers Paul said the

Spirit who indwells us is the "Spirit of Him who raised Jesus from the dead." The Father quickens or gives life to our mortal bodies by the Spirit. Thus the Father must have also used the Holy Spirit to quicken the lifeless body of Jesus. So all three persons of the Godhead were involved in Jesus' resurrection.

Paul recorded an early creedal confession, perhaps even a hymn to be sung in the congregation: "And without controversy great is the mystery of godliness: God was manifested in the flesh, justified in the Spirit, seen by angels, preached among the Gentiles, believed on in the world, received up in glory" (1 Tim. 3:16). The verb "justified" means "to declare righteous." In the experience of Christ, the Holy Spirit declared Him to be righteous through His holy life and supernatural deeds. The Spirit said Christ is who He claimed to be. Christ was "delivered up because of our offenses, and was raised because of our justification" (Rom. 4:25). Thus the Spirit may have declared the validity of Christ's atoning death through the resurrection.

Peter. Peter asserted, "For Christ also suffered once for sins, the just for the unjust, that He might bring us to God, being put to death in the flesh but made alive by the Spirit, by whom also He went and preached to the spirits in prison" (1 Pet. 3:18–19). The words "made alive by (or 'in') the Spirit" show that the Spirit of God was actively involved in the resurrection of Jesus. Some interpreters, though, believe that the noun refers to the spirit of Jesus (in contrast to His flesh), not to the Holy Spirit. It is difficult to know with certainty which view is correct.

If the Spirit of God was involved, then Jesus in the realm of the Spirit (or by means of the Spirit) preached to imprisoned spirits. Theologians have offered several interpretations of this concept. First, Jesus preached by the Holy Spirit through Noah to the unsaved people of his day. Second, Jesus preached to the unsaved in Hades after His death and before His resurrection. Third after His resurrection, Christ by the Spirit proclaimed His victory over sin and Satan to the demonic spirits who were imprisoned in Tartarus, known also as the abyss and the bottomless pit (2 Pet. 2:4; Rev. 9:1; 20:3). The Spirit thus transported the resurrected Christ to this unknown location in the same way He transported Ezekiel, Philip, and John. This is the view I hold.[5]

WHAT CHRIST TAUGHT ABOUT THE HOLY SPIRIT

Christ taught about the ministry of the Holy Spirit during three periods: the three years of His public ministry, the night before His crucifixion, and the forty days of His postresurrection ministry. In the first period He talked about the Spirit to both the multitudes and His disciples. In the second and third periods, He spoke of the Spirit only to the disciples.

During His Ministry

The Holy Spirit could be requested. On one occasion Jesus challenged His disciples, "If you then, being evil, know how to give good gifts to your children, how much more will your heavenly Father give the Holy Spirit to those who ask Him!" (Luke 11:13). At this time, Jesus was filled with the Holy Spirit, but the disciples were not. In fact, the Spirit was not even dwelling within them.

There is no indication that the disciples ever asked for the Spirit. Later they received the indwelling presence of the Spirit only because Jesus prayed for them (John 14:16–17). The Lord never gave this challenge to the crowds.

Today some theologians teach that a believer must ask God in order to receive the Spirit. Proponents of the pentecostal and charismatic movements call this postconversion experience the baptism of the Holy Spirit. The statement of faith of the Assemblies of God denomination reads, "We believe that the baptism of the Holy Spirit, according to Acts 2:4, is given to believers who ask for it."[6] D. V. Hurst, a Pentecostal writer, listed six requirements for receiving the baptism of the Spirit, including "ask in prayer" (Luke 11:13).[7] These same theologians also affirm that speaking in tongues is the sign or evidence of this experience. In effect, they believe that the apostles could have had a pre-Day of Pentecost experience before the Holy Spirit actually descended on the Day of Pentecost.

However, Jesus nowhere equated His challenge to the apostles with the baptism in the Holy Spirit. That view is a presupposition imposed on the biblical text. Also Jesus never mentioned that speaking in tongues would be the evidence of that experience. And He never extended this challenge to believers other than the apostles.

This challenge of faith was given by Christ while He was still on earth—before His crucifixion, resurrection, ascension, and sending of the Spirit. It was a challenge limited to the apostles in the Gospel era. It is not a model to follow in the church age, especially since the Spirit came on the Day of Pentecost in response to the promise of Jesus Christ. Today a believer receives the indwelling presence of the Spirit the very moment he believes in Christ as his Savior (Rom. 8:9).

The apostles in the Gospel era were saved but they did not have the indwelling presence of the Holy Spirit as believers do today in the post-Day of Pentecost period. Since Christ challenged them to ask for the Spirit, they did not have the Spirit in them.

The Holy Spirit gave enablement. When Jesus commissioned the twelve apostles to go only to the lost sheep of Israel, He gave them "power over unclean spirits, to cast them out, and to heal all kinds of sickness and all kinds of disease" (Matt. 10:1; see also Mark 6:7). He charged them to "heal the sick, cleanse the lepers, raise the dead, cast out demons" (Matt. 10:8). What was this power? Did they have an enablement apart from the Spirit? Although the text does not mention that Christ gave them the Spirit at this time, it seems logical that He did so.

This interpretive viewpoint is confirmed in a later encouragement Christ gave to them. Anticipating opposition to their ministries by the religious and civil authorities, He said, "But when they deliver you up, do not worry about how or what you should speak. For it will be given to you in that hour what you should speak; for it is not you who speak, but the Spirit of your Father who speaks in you" (Matt. 10:19–20; see also Mark 13:11; Luke 12:12). Since the Holy Spirit would speak in and through them in their choice of words, Christ must have given them the Spirit when He commissioned them. This unique ministry of the Spirit in the apostles was temporary, only for the duration of their ministry to Israel, and not to Samaritans or Gentiles (Matt. 10:5). Much later, nine apostles tried to cast out a demon, but they were unsuccessful (17:14–21). They no longer had the Spirit or His power. They failed because they did not believe properly (17:19–21).

Jesus Christ claimed that His power to perform miracles came from the Holy Spirit. He defended Himself before His critics who charged that the power of Satan was on His life. He affirmed, "If Satan casts out Satan, he is divided against himself. How then will his kingdom stand? And if I cast out demons by Beelzebub, by whom do your sons cast them out? Therefore they shall be your judges. But if I cast out demons by the Spirit of God, surely the kingdom of God has come upon you" (12:26–28).

The Holy Spirit could be blasphemed. God the Father anointed Jesus Christ with the Holy Spirit and power. As the anointed One, the Messiah or the Christ, He ministered with the total filling of the Spirit on His life. When His critics claimed that He worked miracles by the spirit of Satan, He charged them with the unpardonable sin of blasphemy against the Spirit.

He warned, "Therefore I say to you, every sin and blasphemy will be forgiven men, but the blasphemy against the Spirit will not be forgiven men. Anyone who speaks a word against the Son of Man, it will be forgiven him; but whoever speaks against the Holy Spirit, it will not be forgiven him, either in this age or in the age to come" (Matt. 12:31–32). The religious leaders of Israel blasphemed the Holy Spirit when they asserted that Christ cast out demons by Satan, not by the Spirit of God.

The religious leaders were then confirmed in their sin of unbelief and blasphemy. They could not be forgiven in the age when Jesus was still on earth ("in this age") or in the church age, the age after His death and resurrection ("the age to come"). In the church age as seen in the Book of Acts, they reiterated their rejection of the messiahship of Jesus when they scoffed at His resurrection and repudiated the message of the apostles.

The blasphemy against the Holy Spirit was a unique sin in history. It could be committed only by the unsaved when Jesus was on earth two thousand years ago. It cannot be committed today because Christ is not now personally on the earth performing miracles.

The Holy Spirit affirmed the Old Testament. In chapter 5 we discussed the role of the Holy Spirit in the inspiration of the Scriptures. Christ Himself spoke of the Spirit in relation to the biblical text and its human authors. He asked the leaders, "How then does David in the Spirit call Him Lord saying . . . ?" (Matt. 22:43). He used that rhetorical question to preface His quotation of a verse from one of David's psalms (Ps. 110:1). Jesus knew that David did not speak and write prophetic truth from his own intelligence. He knew that the Spirit guided David in the writing of that psalm. It was inspired, inerrant truth, the authoritative basis of Jesus' comments.

The Holy Spirit regenerated. Jesus told Nicodemus that a person must be born again to see and to enter the kingdom of God (John 3:3, 5). When Nicodemus expressed perplexity over the nature of the second birth, Jesus expanded on His original declaration. In His explanation of a new spiritual birth, He referred to the role of the Holy Spirit three times.

"Most assuredly, I say to you, unless one is born of water and the Spirit, he cannot enter the kingdom of God. That which is born of the flesh is flesh, and that which is born of the Spirit is spirit. Do not marvel that I said to you, You must be born again. The wind blows where it wishes, and you hear the sound of it, but cannot tell where it comes from and where it goes. So is everyone who is born of the Spirit" (3:5–8).

The Holy Spirit is the divine Source of spiritual regeneration. When Jesus spoke of being born of the Spirit, He meant that the second birth comes out of (Greek, *ek*) the Spirit, that is, He is its divine origin.

When Christ claimed to be the Bread of Life (6:48), He affirmed that anyone who would believe in Him would have everlasting life (6:47). When He used the metaphors of eating His flesh and drinking His blood to have spiritual life, many were perplexed at the meaning of His words. He then explained, "It is the Spirit who gives life; the flesh profits nothing. The words that I speak to you are spirit, and they are life" (6:63). The Holy Spirit thus uses the words of the Lord to give spiritual life to the believing sinner. The Spirit and the inspired Word of God are inseparable in the divine work of spiritual regeneration.

At the Feast of Tabernacles Jesus invited people to come to Him: "If anyone thirsts, let him come to Me and drink. He who believes in Me, as the Scripture has said, out of his heart will flow rivers of living water" (7:37–38). The Israelites drank of the water that flowed from the rock Moses had smitten. In fulfillment of that type, Christ claimed to be the Rock, the Source of the water of everlasting life.

John then equated the water with the Holy Spirit. He explained: "But this He spoke concerning the Spirit, whom those believing in Him would receive; for the Holy Spirit was not yet given, because Jesus was not yet glorified" (7:39). In the Gospel era before Christ's death and resurrection, sinners could believe in Christ and be saved. They were regenerated and made members of the family of God. However, those believers were not indwelt by the Holy Spirit because Christ had not yet been glorified. That is, the Savior could not send the Spirit until He had ascended into the presence of the Father.

This passage (John 7:37–39) gives a clear dispensational distinction in the ministry of the Holy Spirit. When believing sinners are regenerated today in the church age, they are immediately indwelt by the Spirit. But in the Gospel era, believing sinners were regenerated by the Spirit, but they could not be indwelt by the Spirit until after Christ's death, resurrection, and ascension.

In the Upper Room Discourse

On the night before His crucifixion, Jesus gathered with the twelve apostles in an upper room of a house in Jerusalem. They ate the Passover meal together, He washed their feet, and He instituted the ordinance of the Lord's Supper. He also taught them. In fact, He extended His teaching as they left the room and walked toward the Garden of Gethsemane.

In His teaching He set forth new relationships and responsibilities that would exist between them and Himself as the result of His death, resurrection, ascension, and the descent of the Holy Spirit (John 13–17). The primary focus of this teaching was thus on believers in the church age. For the first time in His earthly ministry, He gave extensive instruction on the person and ministry of the Holy Spirit. He related the Spirit to the apostles in many new ways.

The Holy Spirit will be sent. He told them God the Father would give them the Spirit in answer to His prayer. "And I will pray the Father, and He will give you another Helper, that He may abide with you forever" (John 14:16). On the Day of Pentecost, the Spirit of God came because Jesus prayed, not because the apostles were praying (Acts 2).

Jesus promised that the Father would send the Holy Spirit in the name of Christ (John 14:26). The "name" of Christ stands for all that He is and does. God thus sent the Spirit in the authority of the Savior and His redemptive work.

Jesus also promised that *He* would send the Spirit: "But when the Helper comes, whom I shall send to you from the Father, the Spirit of truth who proceeds from the Father, He will testify of Me" (15:26). Thus both the Father and the Son sent the Holy Spirit on the Day of Pentecost. Christ could not send the Spirit until He had returned to the Father in heaven. The preposition *para* ("from") denotes that the glorified Christ was literally beside the Father when He sent the Spirit. (The word "parallel" is based on this Greek preposition.)

Jesus promised He would send the Spirit after He departed the earth. "Nevertheless I tell you the truth. It is to your advantage that I go away; for if I do not go away, the Helper will not come to you; but if I depart, I will send Him to you" (16:7). The apostles wanted to keep Jesus in His bodily form in their presence. After the resurrection, they did not want Him to leave them. They were accustomed to walking by sight. Christ knew that the invisible Spirit and He in His human body could not simultaneously be with the apostles. He had to go away before He could send the Spirit.

The Holy Spirit could not come at His own initiative. He had to be sent. That is His role in the divine, redemptive plan.

The Holy Spirit will indwell. Christ promised the disciples, "And I will pray the Father, and He will give you another Helper, that He may abide with you forever—the Spirit of truth, whom the world cannot receive, because it neither sees Him, nor knows Him; but you know Him, for He dwells with you and will be in you" (John 14:16–17). These two verses reveal clear dispensational distinctions between the ministry of the Spirit in the Gospel era and His role in the present church age.

First, the Spirit was dwelling "with" the apostles in the Gospel era. In Greek the words "with you" literally mean "beside you." In that sense, the Holy Spirit had a companion ministry to the apostles. He was beside them, but not inside them.

Second, Christ predicted that the Spirit would be in them. After the death, resurrection, and ascension of Christ, the same Spirit who was beside them would be inside them. Christ also changed verbal tenses to show the difference in the two relationships of the Spirit to the apostles. The verb *menei* ("dwells") is in the present tense, whereas the verb *estai* ("will be") is in the future tense.

Third, the abiding presence of the Holy Spirit in the believer is forever. The Father gave the Spirit "that He may abide with you forever." Here the Greek prepositional phrase translated "with you" is different from the other two phrases ("with you" and "in you"). It signifies association. The verb "may abide" literally means "may be." Thus the Spirit would be associated with the believers forever. In the church age the Holy Spirit indwells a believing sinner the moment he or she is saved, and will never leave the believer. This abiding presence of the Spirit is not based on the faithfulness of the child of God; rather, it is based on the faithfulness of the Father and the Son to their pledged word.

Fourth, unredeemed sinners have no relationship to the Holy Spirit. In this church age there are only two classes of people: the saved, who have the Spirit in them, and the unsaved, who do not have the Spirit in them (Rom. 8:9). As Sinclair Ferguson observes: "As a result, when he comes to Christians to indwell them, he comes as the Spirit of Christ in such a way that to possess him is to possess Christ himself, just as to lack him is to lack Christ."[8]

The Holy Spirit will teach. The Lord Jesus Christ was a Jewish rabbi, a master Teacher. He discipled both men and women. Knowing that the apostles needed further instruction, He said, "But the Helper, the Holy Spirit, whom the Father will send in My name, He will teach you all things, and bring to your remembrance all things that I said to you" (John 14:26). The apostles enjoyed the teaching ministry of Jesus when He was visibly present with them. In His localized human body, He could be present in only one place at one time. After His departure to heaven, the Father would send the Spirit to be the new Teacher. He would teach each apostle from within them. Thus no matter where the apostles were, whether together or apart, each one could enjoy the teaching ministry of the Spirit. What was true of the apostles is also true of us today. Each believer today has the divine Teacher, the Holy Spirit, within him.

Later Jesus promised, "However, when He, the Spirit of truth, has come, He will guide you into all truth; for He will not speak on His own authority, but whatever He hears He will speak; and He will tell you things to come" (16:13). These two verses (14:26; 16:13) point out four areas of His didactic ministry to the apostles.

First, the Holy Spirit would teach truth. Because He is the Spirit of truth, He teaches in accord with who He is. He never teaches error. Truth is both God-originated and God-centered. Truth is consistent with the essence of the triune God. Since God is the source of creation and redemption, then genuine moral and redemptive truth must manifest His revealed plan in the Scriptures. The Bible is truth (17:17); therefore the Holy Spirit teaches truth that manifests the real meaning of the Scriptures.

Second, the Holy Spirit would cause the apostles to remember all that Jesus said to them. In our human finiteness, our memories fail us. I often forget names, places, events, and conversations. As I grow older, I find that I must write down daily reminders for future tasks. Under ordinary circumstances, the apostles would have had collective and individual difficulty in recalling the actual words and deeds of Christ. The indwelling Spirit, however, worked through their minds so that they could remember accurately all Jesus said. This divine enablement assisted them in their preaching and in their writing of the Gospels.

Third, the Holy Spirit would teach them everything God wanted them to know. There is no indication that the apostles would become omniscient. The Spirit spoke only what He heard from the Father and the Son. This concept of limited revelation is what Moses stated to Israel: "The secret things belong to the LORD our God, but those things which are revealed belong to us and to our children forever, that we may do all the words of this law" (Deut. 29:29). Paul knew that he knew "in part" (1 Cor. 13:12). He did not know everything, but what he knew, he knew accurately. Truth, though it be partial and not comprehensive, is nevertheless still truth. The apostles embodied this teaching ministry of the Spirit in the messages they proclaimed and in the inspired epistles they wrote.

Fourth, the Holy Spirit would reveal the future to them. Predictive prophecy is found in both the oral sermons and the inspired writings of the apostles. They wrote about the Rapture, the future of Israel, the Great Tribulation, the Antichrist, Armageddon, the return of Jesus Christ to the earth, the millennial kingdom, the Great White Throne judgment, the eternal holy city, the lake of fire, and the eternal state. They lived to see some of their prophecies fulfilled in their own lifetime, but others remain unfulfilled to this very day. Truth permeated all their predictions because the Spirit of truth guided them in their prophetic teaching.

The predicted teaching ministry of the Holy Spirit had its primary and immediate fulfillment in the lives of the authenticated apostles. In a secondary sense believers today also enjoy the teaching ministry of the Spirit. He teaches us to understand what He taught the apostles and what the apostles taught in their Spirit-inspired books, namely, the New Testament. We should not expect the Spirit to teach us new redemptive truth that goes beyond the scope of the canonical Scriptures. He can guide us in the application of biblical truth to our contemporary problems.[9]

The Holy Spirit will glorify Christ. God the Son became incarnate to glorify God the Father (John 17:1, 4). The Holy Spirit descended in order that He might glorify Christ. Jesus said, "He will glorify Me, for He will take of what is Mine and declare it to you. All things that the Father has are Mine. Therefore I said that He will take of Mine and declare it to you" (16:14–15).

All three divine persons share equally the glory of the divine essence. The Westminster Confession of Faith states that the chief end of man is to glorify God and to enjoy Him forever. Whenever we truly glorify God, we glorify the Trinity, not just one of the divine persons.

However, God the Son subordinated Himself in order to glorify the Father. In the same sense the Holy Spirit subordinated Himself in order to glorify the Son. Thus when a believer is truly controlled by the Holy Spirit, he, too, glorifies Jesus Christ. The Spirit-filled saint will glorify neither himself nor any other believer. The Spirit-filled believer also will not glorify the Holy Spirit. Although we can discuss and desire the ministry of the Holy Spirit, we must not exalt Him beyond His role in redemption.

Christ asked the Father to glorify Him so that He in turn would glorify the Father (John 17:1, 5). And Paul exclaimed, "But God forbid that I should boast except in the cross of our Lord Jesus Christ, by whom the world has been crucified to me, and I to the world" (Gal. 6:14). Paul nowhere stated that he wanted to boast in the Holy Spirit. Paul's passion was Christ (Phil. 1:21), not the Holy Spirit. And yet Paul was as full of the Spirit as any believer has been.

The Holy Spirit will convict the world. The Holy Spirit has always been the Restrainer of sin within the fallen human race (Gen. 6:3). He has reproved the wickedness of sinners through the personal holiness of believers, Israel, and the church. The Spirit-filled Christ, was, of course, Himself a rebuke to His culture. As the Light of the World, He revealed the darkness of the world system.

When Christ was about to depart from the earth, He informed the apostles of the forthcoming ministry of the Holy Spirit to the world. "And when He has come, He will convict the world of sin, and of righteousness, and of judgment" (John 16:8). *Elenchō*, the Greek verb for "convict," is a legal term. It involves a moral and mental awareness of wrongdoing, an indictment of legal guilt beyond a reasonable doubt, and a willing admission of shame and guilt.

Today many criminals are often sorry—sorry that they were caught, but not sorry for what they did. But this is not the same as willfully admitting their guilt.

According to the Scriptures believers can rebuke or convict other believers (for example, Matt. 18:15; 1 Tim. 5:20). The saved convict the unsaved (Luke 3:19; 1 Cor. 14:24; Eph. 5:11, 13). God can convict the saved (Heb. 12:5; Rev. 3:19) and the unsaved (John 3:20–21; 8:9). Christ challenged his religious critics to convict Him of any sin, but they were not able to do so (8:46).

Christ claimed that the Holy Spirit would convict "of sin, because they do not believe in Me; of righteousness, because I go to My Father and you see Me no more; of judgment, because the ruler of this world is judged" (John 16:9–11). The Holy Spirit convicts sinners through the witness of believers in what they say, in how they say it, and in how they live (15:27). The Spirit also convicts the lost through the truths of the inspired Scriptures.

The Holy Spirit reveals the truth that a person can be accepted by God only through the redemptive work of Christ, and that only through belief in Christ can a person have His righteousness imputed to him or her. When the Holy Spirit convicts a lost sinner in this area, that person will be aware of the folly of trusting in Buddha, the gods of Hinduism, Jewish traditions, Islamic fervor, or his own self-righteousness.

The judgment of Satan was secured by the death and resurrection of

Jesus Christ. If the originator of sin will be cast into eternal judgment, then all sinners who fail to believe in Christ will also be cast into eternal judgment. The Spirit convicts sinners of their moral accountability and the eternal consequences of their sins—and thus of their need for Christ. As the Bible states, "It is appointed for men to die once, but after this the judgment" (Heb. 9:27).

Summary. The apostles experienced the promised ministry of the Spirit in their lives, as recorded in the Book of Acts. The Spirit came to them on the Day of Pentecost. The Spirit indwelt and taught them. The Spirit glorified Christ through them. The Spirit convicted both Jews and Gentiles through their preaching of the gospel. Thousands were saved and added to the true church.

Believers today are indwelt and taught by the Spirit. As they witness to others of their need for Christ, they can observe the convicting and regenerating ministries of the Holy Spirit.

After His Resurrection

Christ "presented Himself alive after His suffering by many infallible proofs" (Acts 1:3). During the forty days between His resurrection and ascension into heaven Christ appeared to individuals, small groups, and large crowds (1 Cor. 15:5–8). Believers saw, heard, and touched Him. He appeared in public and private places, in Galilee and Judea, and in the daytime and at night. He manifested Himself to both men and women. Again, however, He directed His ministry to the apostles.

He gave them the Holy Spirit. On the evening of His resurrection, Jesus appeared to ten apostles. (Thomas was absent.) Recommissioning them to the gospel ministry, He said to them, "Peace to you! As the Father has sent Me, I also send you" (John 20:21).

"And when He had said this, He breathed on them, and said to them, 'Receive the Holy Spirit'" (20:22). This impartation of the Spirit was not the fulfillment of Christ's prayer and promise given earlier on the night before His crucifixion (14:16–17, 26; 15:26–27; 16:7–15). That fulfillment occurred on the Day of Pentecost. Why then did Christ impart the Spirit before His ascension and the actual descent of the Spirit? As John Walvoord has suggested, "Apparently a temporary filling of the Spirit was given to provide for their spiritual needs prior to Pentecost."[10] In that sense they received a prechurch age filling of the Spirit in anticipation of the Day of Pentecost so they could fully understand the Savior's instructions.

He commanded them through the Holy Spirit. Luke introduced the Book of Acts in this way: "The former account I made, O Theophilus, of all that Jesus began both to do and teach, until the day in which He was taken up, after He through the Holy Spirit had given commandments to the apostles whom He had chosen" (Acts 1:1–2). Christ taught them for over three years between His baptism and His death, and then for forty days after His resurrection, He continued to teach them through the Holy Spirit who was imparted to them. In this postresurrection ministry Christ further developed what He had earlier taught. With the events of Christ's death and resurrection behind them, the apostles then had a better historical and spiritual capacity to perceive the significance of Christ's words.

He predicted the baptism in the Holy Spirit. On the day of His ascension into heaven, Christ told the apostles "not to depart from Jerusalem, but to wait for the Promise of the Father, 'which,' He said, 'you have heard from Me; for John truly baptized with water, but you shall be baptized with the Holy Spirit not many days from now'" (Acts 1:4–5). Ten days later, they were baptized in the Spirit when sound of the rushing wind filled the room where they were gathered (2:1–2).

Christ compared His predictions about the future baptizing ministry of the Spirit with the prediction given by John the Baptist over three years earlier. This was the only time Jesus mentioned the baptizing work of the Holy Spirit.

He commissioned them through the Holy Spirit. Jesus predicted, "But you shall receive power when the Holy Spirit has come upon you; and you shall be witnesses to Me in Jerusalem, and in all Judea and Samaria, and to the end of the earth" (Acts 1:8). The apostles' task was worldwide evangelism. They were to become His witnesses throughout the world.

However, they could not carry out this assignment in their own strength and ingenuity. They needed supernatural "power" (*dynamis*), available through the Holy Spirit, who came on them as Jesus predicted on the Day of Pentecost.

Elsewhere, Jesus had said to the apostles, "Behold, I send the Promise of My Father upon you; but tarry in the city of Jerusalem until you are endued with power from on high" (Luke 24:49). Some denominational groups believe that to "tarry" means to pray fervently and to ask for a postconversion giving of the Holy Spirit. However, this Greek verb *kathizō*, used forty-eight times in the New Testament, simply means "to sit," and it is translated that way forty-six times in the King James Version (for example, Matt. 5:1; 13:48; Luke 5:3; 16:6). Once it is translated "continued" (Acts 18:11) and once "tarry" (NIV). Modern translations use the verb "stay" rather than "tarry" (NASB). The verb does not suggest fervent religious devotion, a state of desperate spiritual supplication.

Thus Christ instructed the apostles to stay in Jerusalem until He sent the promised Spirit. The Spirit did not come because the apostles prayed for Him to come or because they had a successful "tarrying" experience. The apostles lived in a transitional, historical, dispensational period, the ten-day period between Christ's ascension and the descent of the Spirit on the Day of Pentecost. Their experience is not a model for us to follow today.

IMPLICATIONS FOR US

First, we believers must be controlled by the Holy Spirit if we want to have an effective spiritual ministry to others. In our culture, which emphasizes programs and personalities, we need to be yielded to the person of the Spirit. Christ did not begin His ministry until the Spirit came on Him. He served others always under the fullness of the Spirit. We must do likewise. And when we do, we will manifest the moral qualities of the Savior as we seek to impact others with the Word of God.

Second, even when we are controlled by the Holy Spirit, we still may be tempted by Satan. In fact, it may be the will of God for us to be tempted, as it was for Christ. However, the best way to have victory over temptation is to be yielded to the Spirit and to the Word of God. It is wrong to think we can avoid temptation by becoming more spiritual.

Third, believers need not ask God for the gift of the Holy Spirit because God has already given them the indwelling Spirit at the very moment they believed in Christ. We must not seek a Gospel-era experience (Luke 11:13) that does not pertain to the present church age.

Fourth, we must glorify Christ in all we do. We must not become preoccupied with the Holy Spirit or His work in us. We must understand the activities of the Spirit, but we must thank the Father and the Son through the Spirit. The Holy Spirit came to glorify Christ, therefore we, too, when controlled by the Spirit, must exalt the Savior.

Fifth, we must become people committed to truth. God is truth, the Holy Spirit is the Spirit of truth, and the Word of God is truth. We must be biblically critical as we analyze various moral and doctrinal viewpoints. We must prove all things and hold to what is good and true (1 Thess. 5:21).

Sixth, we must become witnesses for Christ, enabled by the Holy Spirit. We must not depend on our techniques, personalities, intelligence, or past experiences in soul-winning. Salvation is of God, so we must allow the Spirit of God to do His works of convicting and regenerating others. We must be sensitive to the guidance of the Spirit in our witnessing to the unsaved.

CHAPTER EIGHT

The Ministry of the Holy Spirit in the Book of Acts

The Book of Acts give us a historical record of the early life of the church. It relates the advance of the gospel message from Jerusalem to Rome, primarily through the ministries of Peter and Paul. It records the first apostolic sermon (2:14–40), the first apostolic miracle of healing (3:1–11), the first instance of persecution (4:13), the first defense of the gospel (4:5–12), the first divine chastisement (5:1–11), the appointment of the first deacons (6:1–7), the first martyrdom (7:54–60), the first missionary journey (13:1–14:28), and the first church council (15:1–35). The book has a progressive and transitional character in that the redemptive program of God leaves the old dispensation of Law, passes into the early life of the new church dispensation, and advances into a later, more mature stage.

Although the book is known as the Acts of the Apostles, many believe a better title would be The Acts of the Holy Spirit. This is because the Holy Spirit is mentioned about sixty times in the Book of Acts, more than He is mentioned in all four Gospels put together.

The Holy Spirit thus had a prominent role in the activity of the early church.

THE RECEPTIONS OF THE HOLY SPIRIT IN ACTS

Five unique receptions of the Holy Spirit are recorded in the Book of Acts. Four involve groups, and one involves an individual. The phenomenon of speaking in tongues accompanied at least three of them.

The Apostles

Background. The first unsual reception of the Holy Spirit occurred on the Day of Pentecost (Acts 2:1). The Day of Pentecost received this name because it was celebrated on the fiftieth day after the presentation of the first harvested sheaf of the barley harvest. The name "Pentecost" transliterates the Greek word *pentēkostē.* It was the fiftieth day from the first Sunday after Passover (Lev. 23:15). It was also known as the Feast of Weeks (Exod. 34:22; Deut. 16:10), and it was also called "the day of the firstfruits" because it was the day when the firstfruits of the wheat harvest were presented to God (Exod. 23:16; 34:22; Num. 28:26).

This particular Day of Pentecost was special because it occurred fifty days after Christ's crucifixion and resurrection. It also happened ten days after His ascension into heaven.

The city of Jerusalem was the location for this unusual reception of the Spirit. After Christ ascended, the apostles returned to Jerusalem (Luke 24:52; Acts 1:12), where Christ told them to remain until He sent them the Spirit (Luke 24:49). They obeyed His command. When the Spirit of God came, Peter preached his sermon to Jews who had traveled to Jerusalem from many parts of the Roman world (Acts 2:5).

The apostles "were all with one accord in one place" (2:1). That place is further identified as "the whole house where they were sitting" (2:2). What house was this? One possibility is that this was the temple. In the Old Testament the temple was called a house (Isa. 6:4), and Stephen referred to the temple as a house (Acts 7:47). In the ten-day period before the Day of Pentecost the apostles "were continually in the temple praising and blessing God"(Luke 24:53). On this special feast day it would be logical to find the apostles in the temple. Since a crowd of over three thousand heard Peter preach, the people may have been gathered in and around the public courtyard of the temple. It is difficult to imagine such a large crowd gathered in a private house or even in a narrow street and courtyard outside of a house.

Another possibility is that the house was the one with the upper room where Jesus and the apostles gathered on the night before His crucifixion. This could have been the house where earlier about 120 believers congregated for the election of Matthias to be the apostle to replace Judas (Acts 1:15). Many view this as the house owned by the parents of John Mark (12:12).

I have been to Israel on eight tours. Most tour groups are taken to a place called the Upper Room, identified by some as the actual room mentioned in the Gospels. However, since the building is less than one thousand years old, it cannot be the actual biblical site. The building may be in the general geographical area where the biblical Upper Room was located, but again, there is no archeological certainty for this speculation.

It is difficult to say with absolute certainty just where the apostles were. The city is certain, but the actual site is not.

Recipients. Who received the Holy Spirit in an unusual way on the Day of Pentecost? To whom do the personal pronouns "they" and "them" refer (Acts 2:1–4, 6)?

Henry Alford believed the group was "all the believers in Christ, then congregated at the time of the feast in Jerusalem."[1] He said this group consisted of the twelve apostles, the 120 disciples (1:15), and many others.

Most commentators identify the group as the 120 disciples including the twelve apostles (1:15), a group that included both men and women (1:12–14). Proponents of this viewpoint state that the selection of Matthias by the 120 is recorded just before the events of Pentecost are recorded (1:15–26; 2:1). To them, the grammatical antecedent of the pronouns "they" and "them" must be the 120. Thus the 120 were filled with the Spirit and spoke in tongues, and tongues as of fire appeared on each of the 120.

However, several factors suggest that only the twelve apostles received the Holy Spirit in an unusual way on this first day. First, the nearest antecedent of the pronoun "they" in 2:1 is the group of eleven apostles plus Matthias (1:26).

Second, although the 120 are mentioned in the immediate context (1:12–26), it must be remembered that ten days intervened between the selection of Matthias and the Day of Pentecost. Also it need not be assumed that the twelve apostles spent all their time with the 120 during that ten-day interval.

Third, Christ gave the promise of the Spirit only to the apostles. Speaking only to them, He said, "Behold, I send the Promise of My Father upon you; but tarry in the city of Jerusalem until you are endued with power from on high" (Luke 24:49). When Christ announced that the baptism in the Holy Spirit would occur soon, He was speaking only to the apostles (Acts 1:1–7).

Fourth, when the listeners heard the speaking in tongues, they asked with amazement, "Look, are not all these who speak Galileans? And how is it that we hear, each in our own language in which we were born?" (2:7–8). When Jesus ascended into heaven, two angels addressed the apostles as "men of Galilee" (1:11). When Peter denied the Lord three times, an accuser said to him, "Surely you are one of them; for you are a Galilean, and your speech shows it" (Mark 14:70). The apostles were definitely Galileans, but it is doubtful that all 120 disciples were.

Fifth, there is no mention of the 120 in connection with the events that occurred on the Day of Pentecost. When the tongues-speakers were mocked for supposedly being drunk, Peter stood up with the eleven apostles and rebutted their critics (Acts 2:14). When those who heard his sermon were convicted of their sin, they spoke "to Peter and the rest of the apostles" (2:37).

Features. The descent of the Holy Spirit was authenticated by three spectacular phenomena. The first was "a sound from heaven, as of a rushing mighty wind, and it filled the whole house where they were sitting" (Acts 2:2). The apostles were literally "in the wind," that is, they were totally immersed in it. The apostles heard the sound and felt the wind.

The second phenomenon was the "divided tongues, as of fire, and one sat upon each of them" (2:3). Apparently one fiery tongue divided into twelve smaller ones. The apostles witnessed this miracle. It was not actual fire, so no one felt any heat nor was anyone burned. It doubtless signified the division of one native language into multiple languages and dialects that they subsequently spoke.

The third phenomenon was that "they were all filled with the Holy Spirit and began to speak with other tongues, as the Spirit gave them utterance" (2:4). The apostles spoke in foreign languages and dialects they had never spoken before. Each spoke and each heard the others speaking.

A large crowd of devout Jews and Gentile proselytes also heard the speaking in tongues (2:5–11).

Significance. Four facts may be noted about this experience. First, it was a postconversion experience for the apostles. They were definitely saved men before the events of Pentecost occurred (Matt. 16:16–17; John 1:41–49; 6:68–69). Jesus had pronounced them spiritually clean (13:10; 15:3); He said they belonged to Him and to the Father (17:10); He had earlier given them a temporary ministry of the Spirit (20:22) and He had commissioned them to preach (Acts 1:8).

Second, the apostles did not seek this unusual experience. They did not pray that they or others would receive it. In fact, there is no biblical indication that they were praying at the time the Spirit came. They were sitting together, but this does not require that a prayer meeting was going on. They simply waited in Jerusalem for Christ to do what He had promised to do.

Third, the apostles did not expect others to have the same experience they had. They never taught anyone that the three phenomena would accompany the entrance of the Holy Spirit into the lives of the converts. Nor did the apostles teach that believers would receive the Spirit in a postconversion experience. When three thousand people gladly received the truth of Peter's sermon, repented, and believed in Jesus Christ, they immediately received the gift of the Holy Spirit (2:36–41). The pattern for believers to receive the Holy Spirit in the church age is seen in the experience of the three thousand converts, not in that of the apostles.

Fourth, the phenomena that announced the descent of the Holy Spirit gave evidence to the Jewish multitudes that Jesus, whom they crucified, had been raised from the dead, that He had been exalted to the right hand of the Father, and that He had poured out the Spirit (2:22–36). Thus they saw that Jesus is the divine-human Messiah, the only one who could save Israel from her sins. The phenomena authenticated the fulfillment of prophecy.

The Samaritans

Background. After the martyrdom of Stephen there was a great persecution against the church at Jerusalem (Acts 8:1). Believers were scattered into the regions of Judea and Samaria. Stephen, a deacon who was full of faith and the Holy Spirit, had gone to the city of Samaria and preached Christ (6:5; 8:5). He also performed miracles of healing and demon exorcism. The Samaritans were intrigued by his ministry and many rejoiced over the results of the miracles he performed.

Recipients. Many Samaritans responded to the gospel. Luke wrote, "But when they believed Philip as he preached the things concerning the kingdom of God and the name of Jesus Christ, both men and women were baptized" (Acts 8:12). They were converted, but at this point there is no mention of the relationship of the Holy Spirit to their lives.

Who were the Samaritans? They were a mixed race (2 Kings 17:24; Ezra 4:2). When the Assyrians conquered Israel, the northern kingdom (722 B.C.), they removed many Israelites from the land and repopulated the region with pagan Gentiles whom they had conquered elsewhere (2 Kings 17:24). Subsequently these transplanted Gentiles intermarried with Israelites who remained in the land. Their offspring became the Samaritan people, half-Jewish and half-Gentile.

The Samaritans practiced a different religion from that of the Jews in the southern region of Judea (17:27; John 4:20–22). These two facts of racial mixture and rival religion caused a great separation and intense hatred between the Jews and the Samaritans in the first century (Ezra 4; Luke 9:52–53; John 4:9).

Features. When the apostles in Jerusalem heard about Philip's successful ministry, they sent Peter and John to Samaria (Acts 8:14). When the two apostles arrived, they prayed for the Samaritan converts "that they might receive the Holy Spirit. For as yet He had fallen upon none of them" (8:15–16). The Samaritans thus had believed and had been baptized in water, but they did not have the indwelling presence of the Holy Spirit.

The apostles then "laid hands on them, and they received the Holy Spirit" (8:17). The Samaritan believers thus received the Spirit in this postconversion experience.

No outward, visible phenomena occurred when the Samaritans received the Spirit. There is no mention of a sound like a rushing wind and no occurrence of cloven tongues like fire (2:2–3). Although speaking in tongues is not explicitly mentioned, many commentators believe that the phenomenon occurred then.[2] That viewpoint is based on the reaction of

Simon to the ministry of the apostles: "And when Simon saw that through the laying on of the apostles' hands the Holy Spirit was given, he offered them money, saying, 'Give me this power also, that anyone on whom I lay hands may receive the Holy Spirit' " (8:18–19). What did Simon see? Pentecostalists believe Simon saw the converts speaking in tongues. Carl Brumback, an Assembly of God theologian, admitted that this position rests on circumstantial evidence, but he added, "The burden of proof would most certainly seem to lie upon those who assert that speaking with tongues was not present on this occasion."[3]

But the Bible suggests that speaking in tongues did not occur when the Samaritan believers received the Holy Spirit. First, the phenomenon is not mentioned. This fact takes on importance because Luke did record that speaking in tongues occurred when Cornelius believed and when the disciples of John the Baptist came into a new understanding of God's program (10:44–48; 19:1–7). If Luke wanted to present a pattern of receiving the Holy Spirit accompanied by speaking in tongues, he would not have omitted its occurrence here if it had actually occurred.

Second, the use of the verb "saw" is not conclusive. The phenomenon of speaking in tongues would appeal more to the sense of hearing than to the sense of seeing. The phenomena on the Day of Pentecost were both seen and heard by the observers (2:33).

Third, what Simon saw was the apostles placing their hands on the converts, and he coveted that ability. Actually the burden of proof rests on those who say tongues-speaking occurred in Acts 8 when it is not specifically mentioned.

Significance. The unusual reception of the Holy Spirit by the Samaritans does not provide a model for all future believers to follow. In fact, it would be impossible to duplicate their situation. There are no apostles in Jerusalem who could come to our towns and lay hands on us.

Nor did the converts seek a postconversion experience. They did not pray for themselves. Philip, who evangelized them, did not pray for them. Rather, Peter and John, with delegated apostolic authority, were the ones who prayed for them to receive the Holy Spirit.

The delay in the Samaritan converts' reception of the Holy Spirit was a sign to them that they needed to be under the spiritual authority of the apostles. The rivalry and separation between Jews and Samaritans had to be eliminated. The apostles had earlier laid hands on Philip, and he recognized their authority over him (Acts 6:1–6). Now the Samaritans, although saved through the ministry of Philip, had to submit to the apostles, who were Jewish.

Paul

Background. Saul, later known as Paul, assented to the killing of Stephen (Acts 7:58; 8:1). Afterward, "he made havoc of the church, entering every house, and dragging off men and women, committing them to prison" (8:3). After his conversion, Paul admitted he had persecuted the church of God beyond measure and had tried to destroy it (Gal. 1:13). In his rage he was "breathing threats and murder against the disciples of the Lord" (Acts 9:1).

He went to the high priest "and asked letters from him to the synagogues of Damascus, so that if he found any who were of the Way, whether men or women, he might bring them bound to Jerusalem" (9:2). On the road a heavenly light shone around him and blinded him (9:3, 8–9), and Christ said to him, "Saul, Saul, why are you persecuting Me?" (9:4). The Lord told Saul to enter Damascus and to wait for further instructions.

Later the Lord directed Ananias, a disciple at Damascus, to lay hands on Saul so that his sight would return (9:10–12). Ananias did so and said, "Brother Saul, the Lord Jesus, who appeared to you on the road as you came, has sent me that you may receive your sight and be filled with the Holy Spirit" (9:17). Subsequently Saul regained his vision and was baptized.

Features. Three facts may be noted about Saul's experience. First, this event is permeated with extraordinary divine activity. There is the blinding, heavenly light, the appearance and voice of the resurrected Christ, Saul's vision, Ananias's vision, and the miraculous return of Saul's sight.

Second, there is no record that Saul spoke in tongues when he was filled with the Holy Spirit. The only accompanying phenomenon seems to be his return of sight.

Third, the exact time of Saul's conversion is not given. Was he saved when Christ appeared to him on the road to Damascus? Or was he saved through the witness of Ananias? Or was he saved when he called on the name of the Lord at the time of his baptism (22:16)?

Paul then experienced the filling of the Spirit either at the time of his conversion or in a postconversion event. Since Scripture is silent here, we cannot know for sure.

Significance. Paul's conversion and infilling by the Spirit do not give us a model to follow. His spiritual experience was unique to him. No person, whether sinner or saint, should expect the resurrected, ascended Christ to appear and to speak to him. Even Paul knew that his conversion was extraordinary. When he offered proof about the historical veracity of the physical resurrection of Christ, he pointed to the many appearances of the Savior (1 Cor. 15:3–7) and wrote, "Then last of all He was seen by me also, as by one born out of due time" (15:8). Paul knew that Christ sovereignly revealed Himself to him out of His gracious mercy.

The Gentiles

Background. Christ had commissioned the apostles to preach the gospel to all peoples. In the early history of apostolic activity, however, they limited their ministry to Jews and to the region around Jerusalem (Acts 1–9).

Cornelius, a Gentile and a Roman centurion, was stationed at Caesarea, a town on the Mediterranean coast on the great road between Tyre and Egypt (10:1, 24; 11:11–12). In a vision, an angel told him to summon Peter from Joppa. Meanwhile, Peter himself received a vision in which God told him not to regard anyone as morally unclean or inferior. The Holy Spirit commanded Peter to go to Caesarea with the representatives sent by Cornelius (10:9–20).

Cornelius had gathered his relatives and close friends into his house. Peter informed them of his reluctance as a Jew to associate himself with Gentiles, but he also expressed his willingness to obey God's directive. Cornelius then responded, "Now therefore, we are all present before God, to hear all the things commanded you by God" (10:33). Peter then preached about Christ's earthly life, crucifixion, and resurrection (10:24–43).

Recipients. Cornelius was a religious Gentile. He was "a devout man and one who feared God with all his household, who gave alms generously to the people, and prayed to God always" (10:2). Apparently he had repudiated his pagan, polytheistic past and embraced the single God of Judaism.

However, he was still unsaved. Later, when Peter recounted the events at Caeserea to the church at Jerusalem, he quoted the words of the angel who spoke to Cornelius: "Send men to Joppa, and call for Simon whose surname is Peter, who will tell you words by which you and all your household will be saved" (11:13–14). Thus Cornelius was not saved at the time the angel appeared to him.

Features. Five features of this experience may be noted. First, Cornelius and the other Gentiles were converted when they believed in Christ. Peter had told them that faith in Christ alone brings "remission of sins" (10:43). Luke then wrote, "While Peter was still speaking these words, the Holy Spirit fell upon all those who heard the word" (10:44). They heard, believed, were saved, and were immediately indwelt by the Spirit.

Second, the Gentile converts received the Holy Spirit at the very moment they believed. This was their original salvation experience, not a postconversion experience which they sought.

Third, the Gentile converts spoke in tongues when they received the Spirit. As Luke observed, "And those of the circumcision who believed were astonished, as many as came with Peter, because the gift of the Holy Spirit had been poured out on the Gentiles also. For they heard them speak with tongues and magnify God" (10:45–46). In his message Peter did not speak about the phenomenon of speaking in tongues. It just happened, sovereignly and spontaneously, to the surprise of all.

Fourth, Peter did not pray for them to receive the Spirit as he had done in Samaria. Nor did he lay hands on them. He simply was speaking and the people were listening. Then God graciously saved the Gentiles and imparted the Holy Spirit to them. Peter's message was abruptly interrupted by this intervention by God.

Fifth, the gentile converts were subsequently baptized in water and discipled by Peter (10:47–48).

Significance. First, the experience of Cornelius and the other gentile converts was different from that of the apostles (Acts 2), the Samaritans (chap. 8), and Paul (chap. 9). There was no rushing mighty wind nor fiery tongues. There was no laying on of hands or intercessory prayer.

Second, the Gentiles received the Holy Spirit as soon as they believed in Christ. There was no delay. In that sense their experience became a model for today. People today who believe in Christ are sealed with the Holy Spirit at the moment of salvation (Eph. 1:13).

Third, speaking in tongues was an outward evidence that the Gentiles were truly saved and filled by the Spirit. It was a sign given basically to Peter and his Jewish Christian friends that God could save Gentiles. When the believers in Jerusalem heard all the details, they glorified God and exclaimed, "Then God has also granted to the Gentiles repentance to life" (Acts 11:18).

Fourth, the experience of Cornelius marked the first time the gospel penetrated the Gentile world. It was an epochal event. God used it to transform the thinking of Peter and the Jewish church. Jewish believers finally realized that Gentile Christians could be equal to them. In subsequent records in Acts of the conversion of Gentiles there is no mention of any unusual receptions of the Holy Spirit. The extraordinary phenomena of speaking in tongues did not need to be repeated.

The Disciples of John the Baptist

Background. On his third missionary journey (Acts 18:23–21:17) the apostle Paul came to Ephesus (19:1), the main city of the Roman province of Asia, an area now known as western Turkey. His three-year ministry there (20:31) occurred about twenty-five years after Christ's death (that is, in about A.D. 52–55).

Recipients. In Ephesus Paul found "some disciples," actually twelve in number (19:1, 7). They turned out to be disciples of John the Baptist. No information about their conversion is given, but on a pilgrimage to the Holy Land they may have heard John the Baptist preach, and then repented and been baptized. More likely, however, they heard the gospel from Apollos, "an eloquent man and mighty in the Scriptures" (18:24). Apollos "had been instructed in the way of the Lord; and being fervent in spirit, he spoke and taught accurately the things of the Lord, though he knew only the baptism of John" (18:25).

Aquila and Priscilla, a Christian couple who were saved through the ministry of Paul, heard Apollos speak in the Ephesus synagogue. They "took him aside and explained to him the way of God more accurately" (18:26). Apollos then believed that Jesus was the promised Christ, the one John the Baptist predicted would come.

In a similar way twelve disciples of John the Baptist needed more information about the actual identity of the Messiah. When Paul asked them, "Did you receive the Holy Spirit when you believed?" they responded, "We have not so much as heard whether there is a Holy Spirit" (19:2). These twelve simply did not know that the promised Messiah had already come. In a sense they were Old Testament saints living in the New Testament church age. They were looking for the Messiah, but He in fact had come over twenty-five years earlier.

Years after World War II was over, some Japanese soldiers were found in the deep forests of the Philippine Islands. They thought the war was still going on, so they remained in their military outposts.

These twelve disciples were much like these Japanese soldiers. They were looking ahead, but they should have been looking back.

Features. Paul then explained that Christ Jesus is the promised Messiah. In a sense he put a name and a face on the anonymous Savior whom John preached (Acts 19:4). Then they believed in Jesus Christ and were baptized in His name (19:5). The new baptism was necessary because Christian baptism depicts identification with Christ in His death and resurrection.

Luke then reported, "And when Paul had laid hands on them, the Holy Spirit came upon them, and they spoke with tongues and prophesied" (19:6). There is no mention that Paul prayed for them to receive the Holy Spirit or that they themselves prayed.

Significance. First, this reception of the Holy Spirit was unique to these twelve men. In the three years that Paul taught in Ephesus, this situation was not repeated in the lives of any others.

Second, God gave the Holy Spirit to these twelve in an unusual way so that they would know that Paul's explanation of the identity of the Messiah was correct. The speaking in tongues validated the presence of the Holy Spirit in the world and in their lives.

Third, the apostolic authority of Paul was authenticated to these twelve in Ephesus through the laying on of hands and speaking in tongues. In this way they submitted themselves to the discipling ministry of Paul.

Fourth, the historical situation at Ephesus cannot be duplicated today. There are no saints alive on earth today who have passed from the old dispensation of Law into the new church age. The experience of the twelve disciples of John the Baptist in Ephesus should not be viewed as a model for us to follow.

Basic Principles

Acts is a transitional book. It bridges the gap between the Gospels and the Epistles, between the ministry of Christ and the activities of the apostles. It is therefore an introductory book, full of historical background. Great care must be exercised lest one build an entire theological position of doctrine and practice on what is found in its chapters. Doctrine must be primarily based on the Epistles, in which apostolic teaching is spelled out in detail.

Acts is more descriptive than prescriptive. We can read about what happened two thousand years ago; that is descriptive. Does God command us to have the same experiences? If so, that would be prescriptive.

Many events recorded in Acts were never intended to become a pattern for every generation of Christians to follow. For instance, no one should expect to be personally taught by the resurrected Christ as were the apostles (Acts 1:1–3). The phenomena of wind, fiery tongues, and speaking in tongues should not be anticipated by believers today. Christians do not have to sell their possessions (2:45; 4:34). Deliberate liars are not immediately struck dead today (5:1–11). Imprisoned Christians should not expect to be released by angels (5:19; 12:7).

Should martyrs today expect to see the resurrected Savior, as Stephen did (7:55)? Should preachers expect to be transported from one geographic location to another by the Spirit as was Philip (8:39)? Should people expect to see the resurrected Christ before their conversion, as Paul did (9:1–6)? Should unsaved men expect an angel to inform them what evangelist to secure, as Cornelius did (10:1–8)? Obviously the answers to these questions are negative.

Acts introduced the Holy Spirit. The Holy Spirit entered the lives of four groups in an unusual fashion. He came on Jews, namely, the apostles (Acts 2). He came on the Samaritans (chap. 8). He came on the Gentiles (chap. 10). And He came on Old Testament saints, namely, the twelve disciples of John the Baptist (chap. 19).

In all the other chapters in Acts where conversions are recorded, no mention is made of a spectacular introduction of the Spirit. The reason is that He was already introduced to that particular group. If there is a pattern for the reception of the Spirit, it is to be found in the lives of those people.

THE WORKS OF THE HOLY SPIRIT IN ACTS

We have just seen how the Spirit of God entered some lives. Now we want to look at what He did in their lives.

Filling

Throughout the Book of Acts, we read how the Spirit filled both groups and individuals.

Groups. On the Day of Pentecost the apostles were all filled with the Holy Spirit (Acts 2:4). The infilling happened individually, corporately, and simultaneously. They did not ask God for this experience. They did not lay hands on each other. They spoke in foreign languages and dialects "as the Spirit gave them utterance." Others could understand the tongues-speaking without the need of translation.

Later the religious authorities ordered Peter and John not to preach the gospel. The two apostles went to their own group and reported the incident (4:23). The group then asked God to give them boldness to speak the Word of God and power to perform miracles (4:29–30). "And when they had prayed, the place where they were assembled together was shaken; and they were all filled with the Holy Spirit, and they spoke the Word of God with boldness. . . . And with great power the apostles gave witness to the resurrection of the Lord Jesus" (4:31, 33). And they performed signs and wonders (5:12). Thus this spectacular filling did come in response to apostolic prayer.

The apostles needed administrative assistance in their daily tasks. They asked the church body to select "seven men of good reputation, full of the Holy Spirit and wisdom" (6:3). This group probably became the first church deacons.[4] After the selection, the apostles showed their authoritative approval by laying their hands on the seven men, two of whom were Stephen and Philip.

In Paul and Barnabas's missionary journey, both Jews and Gentiles were saved in Antioch in Pisidia (13:14–52). Because of persecution, the two apostles had to leave the region.. The new disciples who lived there, in spite of the expulsion, "were filled with joy and with the Holy Spirit" (13:52).

Individuals. The same religious council that tried Jesus summoned Peter and John and questioned them about their power (Acts 4:5–7). Peter, "filled with the Holy Spirit," responded with a bold evangelistic witness (4:8). It cannot be determined whether this was a second infilling or just the maintenance of a Spirit-controlled life since the Day of Pentecost.

Stephen was an exceptional deacon. He was "a man full of faith and the Holy Spirit" (6:5). "Full of faith and power, [he] did great wonders and signs among the people" (6:8). As a deacon, authenticated by the apostles and associated with them, he had delegated authority to perform the same miracles they did. When Stephen debated with his synagogue critics, he spoke by the Holy Spirit (6:10). Later, when he was stoned to death, he was "full of the Holy Spirit" when he saw the resurrected Christ standing at the right hand of the Father (7:55).

Paul was filled with the Holy Spirit when Ananias laid his hands on the apostle (9:17). And Paul was "filled with the Holy Spirit" when he imposed blindness on Elymas for resisting the gospel (13:9).

Barnabas, an apostle and an associate of Paul, is described as "a good man, full of the Holy Spirit and of faith" (11:24). He manifested the control of the Spirit in his life when he encouraged new believers to be faithful to Christ (11:23).

Guiding

The leading of the Holy Spirit is an evidence of spiritual sonship (Rom. 8:14–15). Such guidance is within the will of God for all areas of life.

Philip. The Holy Spirit directed Philip, the deacon-evangelist, to witness to the Ethiopian eunuch. In fact, He spoke directly to Philip (Acts 8:29). After the conversion of the eunuch, the "Spirit of the Lord caught Philip away" and transported him to Azotus (8:39–40).

Peter. Peter was confused over the meaning of the divine vision of the unclean creatures (Acts 10:9–17). At that time the Spirit spoke to Peter and commanded him to go with the representatives of Cornelius to Caesarea (10:19–20). In fact, the Spirit said that He had actually sent the emissaries. Later in Jerusalem Peter recounted how the Spirit had guided him in his decision to go to the Gentiles (11:12).

Agabus. Agabus was a prophet in the church at Jerusalem. He "showed by the Spirit that there was going to be a great famine throughout all the world" (Acts 11:28). The famine occurred during the reign of Claudius Caesar. That prophetic announcement caused the church at Antioch to send relief to the believers in Judea (11:29–30).

Much later, Agabus met Paul in Caesarea after the apostle finished his third missionary journey. He took Paul's belt and bound his own hands and feet, and said, "Thus says the Holy Spirit, 'So shall the Jews at Jerusalem bind the man who owns this belt, and deliver him into the hands of the Gentiles' " (21:11). Though Agabus and others tried to prevent Paul from going to Jerusalem, the apostle was determined to go.

Paul. On his second missionary trip Paul and his companions "were forbidden by the Holy Spirit to preach the word in Asia" (Acts 16:6). They wanted to enter the province of Bithynia, "but the Spirit did not permit them" (16:7). How did the Spirit do that? Did He speak orally? Did the team sense a mental and emotional restraint, an intuitional burden of heart? No biblical specifics are given.

When Silas and Timothy rejoined Paul in Corinth, he "was compelled by the Spirit" to intensify his witness to the Jews (18:5). Their opposition caused him to refocus his evangelistic outreach to the pagan Gentiles (18:6).

After three years of ministry in Ephesus, Paul "purposed in the Spirit" to go to Jerusalem after passing through the regions of Macedonia and Achaia, the northern and southern sections of modern Greece (19:21). From Jerusalem he wanted to go to Rome.

When Paul addressed the Ephesian elders at Miletus, he said he was "bound in the Spirit" to go to Jerusalem (20:22). He admitted that he did not know what would happen to him there "except that the Holy Spirit testifies in every city saying that chains and tribulations await me" (20:23). In addition to his personal burden brought about by the Spirit, he had the outward confirmation of Spirit-given warnings (21:4).

Commissioning

Missionaries. Prophets and teachers labored in the church of Antioch in Syria (Acts 13:1). Two of them were Barnabas and Saul, later known as Paul. As they all ministered to the Lord and fasted, the Holy Spirit said, "Now separate to Me Barnabas and Saul for the work to which I have called them" (13:2). The Spirit sovereignly selected them for the first major missionary thrust into the Gentile world. The Spirit revealed His will when He spoke. Again, we do not know whether He spoke orally or through the spiritual intuition of the group.

In obedience, the leaders fasted, prayed, laid hands on Barnabas and Saul, and sent them (13:3). Actually, they were "sent out by the Holy Spirit" (13:4). The leaders recognized and did the will of the Spirit.

Paul was an apostle, chosen and sent directly by the resurrected Christ (9:15–16; see also Gal. 1:1, 11–12). And yet both the Father and the Spirit sent Him.

Elders. At Miletus, Paul summoned the Ephesian elders to meet with him. In his challenge to them, he warned, "Therefore take heed to yourselves and to all the flock, among which the Holy Spirit has made you overseers, to shepherd the church of God which He purchased with His own blood" (Acts 20:28). Three names describe the position of administrative leaders in the local church: elders, bishops or overseers, and pastors (20:17, 28; 1 Tim. 3:1–2; Titus 1:5, 7; 1 Pet. 5:1–2). Both the leader and the laymen must realize that the Holy Spirit has gifted the elder, prepared him, and placed him in the role of leadership.

The elder-bishop-pastor is not a chief executive officer. Some churches have had this mistaken notion: "We hired him, therefore we fired him." But this attitude is neither biblical nor Spirit-driven. A chosen, Spirit-given leader should be treated with love and respect (1 Thess. 5:12–13). Whenever the pulpit and the pew recognize that the primary and ultimate responsibility of the leader is to obey God through the Holy Spirit, that church will be blessed by God.

Resolving

A council at Jerusalem convened to debate the issue of justification (Acts 15:1–29). The doctrinal question was clear: Is a person, whether Jew or Gentile, justified by grace alone through faith alone in Christ alone, or is he justified by faith plus circumcision? The council, composed of apostles and church elders, determined that the rite of circumcision was not necessary. The council, however, did have some concerns over some personal life choices that would be offensive to Jews who lived in the Gentile world.

In a signed statement the council wrote, "For it seemed good to the Holy Spirit, and to us, to lay upon you no greater burden than these necessary things" (15:28). The council witnessed interpretive disagreement, vigorous exchange of opinions, and conciliatory resolution. They came to a firm, united conclusion, knowing that the Spirit guided them as they interacted. What the Holy Spirit wanted, they wanted, for they were sensitive to the will of the Holy Spirit.

Inspiring

Peter. Peter accepted the Spirit-inspired authority of the Old Testament. He said, "Men and brethren, this Scripture had to be fulfilled, which the Holy Spirit spoke before by the mouth of David concerning Judas" (Acts 1:16). What the Spirit spoke could be known through what David said and wrote. The voice of the Holy Spirit is binding on the child of God, whether that voice is heard or is seen in the written text.

Paul. Paul also accepted the Spirit-inspired authority of the Old Testament. He said, "The Holy Spirit spoke rightly through Isaiah the prophet to our fathers" (Acts 28:25). The word of the Spirit is found in the written prophecy of Isaiah. They are one and the same.

Indwelling

It is a gift. Peter preached that repentance would bring the remission of sins and "the gift of the Holy Spirit" (Acts 2:38). He then notified his Jewish listeners, "For the promise is to you and to your children, and to all who are afar off, as many as the Lord our God will call" (2:39). The gift and the promise are the same, namely, the Spirit Himself.

Paul explained that Christ redeemed us from eternal judgment when He became a curse on the cross (Gal. 3:13). One purpose of His redemptive death was "that the blessing of Abraham might come upon the Gentiles in Christ Jesus, that we might receive the promise of the Spirit through faith" (3:14). Repentant faith alone in Christ causes the believing sinner to receive the gift and the promise of the Spirit. A person does not have to be circumcised or baptized to receive the Spirit.

Several times in Acts the initial indwelling of the Holy Spirit is defined as a gift (Acts 8:15–19; 10:44–47; 11:15–17; 15:8). God is the Giver, the Spirit is the Gift, and the believing sinner is the recipient. He does not work to get the Holy Spirit; instead he must simply believe in Christ.

Peter did say that God has given the Holy Spirit "to those who obey Him" (5:32). Some commentators have concluded that this obedience takes place after the initial salvation experience; thus the Spirit does not begin to indwell a believer at the moment of justification. But what must a person obey to receive the Spirit? In the context Peter announced that Jesus was the exalted Savior who could "give repentance to Israel and forgiveness of sins" (5:31). People must obey God's command to repent for the forgiveness of sins. It is this obedience to the gospel message that brings the gift of the indwelling Spirit.

It brings comfort and joy. Believers in the churches in Judea, Galilee, and Samaria walked "in the fear of the Lord and in the comfort of the Holy Spirit" (9:31). The believers at Antioch in Pisidia were filled "with joy and with the Holy Spirit" (13:52). The Holy Spirit is the *paraklētos*, the divine Comforter or Encourager. His presence manifests His essence. Wherever He is, He provides love, joy, comfort, peace, and encouragement. Those spiritual qualities are an evidence of His gracious indwelling.

IMPLICATIONS FOR US

First, we must be aware of the transitional nature of the Book of Acts. We must not try to pattern our lives after all of the details of the experiences of those first-century believers. We must distinguish between the normal and the miraculous, and discern between what the apostles did and what they taught. We must examine the events of Acts against the clear teaching of the Epistles.

Second, we must depend on the Holy Spirit in our thinking, serving, and decision-making. We must be sensitive to His silent voice as He moves on our thoughts and feelings. Where should we serve? What should we do? With whom should we do it? We should submit these questions to private and corporate prayer, the study of the Scriptures, and the counsel of godly believers. In all areas we must be yielded to the will of the Holy Spirit.

Third, we must be involved in evangelistic outreach, the discipleship of believers, and the numerical growth of the church. However, to have effective, lasting results, we need the power of the Spirit. We need organization and programs, but we must never let them replace the enabling of the divine Spirit.

Fourth, we must look for church leaders who are full of the Holy Spirit and wisdom. We must demand Spirit-caused, Christlike character for our pastors and lay leaders. We must not substitute superficial, extrovert personality traits for the Spirit-produced fruit of moral excellence.

CHAPTER NINE

The Baptism in the Holy Spirit

The baptism in the Holy Spirit is a divine work accomplished only in the church age. It is not mentioned in the Old Testament.

ITS DESCRIPTION

There are eleven references in the New Testament to the baptism in the Holy Spirit, but only four persons referred to it by name: Jesus Christ, John the Baptist, Peter, and Paul.

Predicted by John the Baptist

All four Gospel writers attributed the first mention of the baptism in the Holy Spirit to John the Baptist. The forerunner predicted that the coming Messiah would baptize repentant Jews "with the Holy Spirit" (Matt. 3:11; see also Mark 1:8; Luke 3:16). The preposition *en* ("with") is normally translated "in," although it can be translated "with" or "by." According to John, Jesus Christ would be the Baptizer and the Holy Spirit would be the element or sphere of the baptism. In his ministry John the Baptist was the baptizer and water was the element or sphere of the baptism. John also said the baptism in the Holy Spirit was a future event.

John the Baptist knew that Jesus Christ was the Son of God who would baptize believers in the Holy Spirit. God the Father informed John that the descent of the Spirit on Jesus at His baptism in the Jordan River identified Jesus as the Spirit-baptizer (John 1:33).

Guaranteed by Jesus Christ

Jesus Christ did not baptize anyone in the Holy Spirit during His earthly ministry. In fact, He did not mention the baptism in the Holy Spirit in His teaching before the Crucifixion.

On the day of His physical ascension into heaven He announced to the eleven apostles, "For John truly baptized with water, but you shall be baptized with the Holy Spirit not many days from now" (Acts 1:5). The period of days turned out to be ten. On the Day of Pentecost the Holy Spirit filled the room where the apostles were sitting (2:2). They were "in" the Spirit, immersed or baptized in Him.

Thus the predictions of John the Baptist and Jesus Christ were first fulfilled on the Day of Pentecost, the beginning of the church age.

Declared by Peter

Peter recounted the conversion of the Gentile Cornelius and his household to the church in Jerusalem (Acts 11:1–15). He said their experience was the same as that of the apostles on the Day of Pentecost. "And as I began to speak, the Holy Spirit fell upon them, as upon us *at the beginning*. Then I remembered the word of the Lord, how He said, 'John indeed baptized with water, but you shall be baptized with the Holy Spirit' " (11:15–16, italics added).

With Cornelius and his household the indwelling presence of the Spirit and the baptism in the Holy Spirit occurred at the very moment they believed and repented (10:43–44; 11:18). Their experience, rather than that of the apostles, is the normative standard for believers in this age.

The apostles had to wait for the events of Christ's death, resurrection, and ascension to occur before they could experience the baptism in the Holy Spirit. For them, it was a postconversion experience, but their experience was transitional, connected to Jesus' ministry while He was on the earth.

Defined by Paul

Paul clearly referred to the baptism in the Holy Spirit once (1 Cor. 12:13). He mentioned it four other times (Rom. 6:3–5; Gal. 3:27; Eph. 4:5; Col. 2:12), but these passages are disputed. Many people believe these passages refer to water baptism only. Some advocates of this view believe in baptismal regeneration, and others stress the importance of believer's baptism almost to the neglect of Spirit baptism.

Of course, Paul did refer to water baptism (1 Cor. 1:13–17). However, the five passages mentioned above are in contexts that discuss spiritual realities common to all believers. If these verses are restricted to participants in water baptism only, then a great host of believers who have not received water baptism would be eliminated from the enjoyment of the spiritual blessings mentioned in the verses.

What, therefore, does the baptism in the Holy Spirit accomplish in each believer?

It identifies every believer with Jesus Christ in His death, burial, and resurrection. Every believer is in Christ, and Christ is in every believer. We are in Him, one in Him, united in Him forever.

On the night before His crucifixion, Christ said to the apostles, "At that day you will know that I am in My Father, and you in Me, and I in you" (John 14:20). The essence of Christianity is seen in those six words: "You in Me" and "I in you." Because we are in Christ, we have an acceptable position before God. He sees us in Christ and through Christ, and we are just as righteous as Christ is. On this basis, God can justify us.

Because Christ is in us, we have power to become Christlike in our daily living. We can have victory over the sinful disposition that still affects our human experience.

Our positional oneness in Christ and His presence in us have been made possible by the baptism in the Holy Spirit. "Or do you not know that as many of us as were baptized into Christ Jesus were baptized into His death? Therefore we were buried with Him through baptism into death, that just as Christ was raised from the dead by the glory of the Father, even so we also should walk in newness of life" (Rom. 6:3–4). When we were baptized in the Holy Spirit at the moment of our conversion, we were placed into Christ. We became identified permanently with Him—in who He is and in what He did. God positionally views us in Christ. Thus when Christ died and rose again, believers positionally died and rose again in Him and with Him. Just as sin and death do not have dominion over Him, neither do they have dominion over believers.

The unsaved are "in Adam," positionally condemned. But when a person is saved, he or she is in Christ, positionally justified (5:12–21). Should believers continue to practice sin now that they are saved? As Paul responded, "Certainly not! How shall we who died to sin live any longer in it?" (6:2). Our death to sin occurred through our positional presence in Christ, accomplished by the baptism in the Holy Spirit.

Paul's testimony in Galatians 2:20 is that of all church-age believers: "I have been crucified with Christ; it is no longer I who live, but Christ lives in me; and the life which I now live in the flesh I live by faith in the Son of God, who loved me and gave himself for me." Like me, put yourself into that verse. I, Bob Gromacki (or your name), have been crucified with Christ. He now lives in me, Bob Gromacki (or your name).

This positional identification is true of all believers. Unfortunately many Christians are not aware of this blessed truth. Many do not appropriate by faith the victory over sin that Christ won. Having won that victory, we must believe it and act appropriately.

In a related passage, Paul wrote, "Buried with Him in baptism, in which you also were raised with Him through faith in the working of God, who raised Him from the dead" (Col. 2:12). Once dead in sins, we were "made alive together with Him" (2:13; see also Eph. 2:4–7).

It places every believer into the spiritual body of Christ, the true church. After Christ died and rose from the dead, He ascended to heaven where He began His headship over "the church which is His body" (Eph. 1:22–23). During His ministry, Christ had said, "I will build My church" (Matt. 16:18). There are several key features in this prediction. First, Christ is the Builder ("I"). Second, the building would take place in the future ("will build"). In fact, in this chapter (16:21), Christ spoke for the first time about His intention to die and to rise again. Third, the church would be His ("My"). Fourth, the church is singular. Local churches should manifest the essence of the one true, universal church. The Greek *ekklēsia* ("church") means literally "called-out" ones. In this church age, the dispensation between the Day of Pentecost and the Rapture, Christ is calling out a redeemed group, formed from believing Jews and believing Gentiles.

We who are called of God to salvation are placed into the body of Christ, namely, the true church, by the baptism in the Holy Spirit. "By one Spirit we were all baptized into one body—whether Jews or Greeks, whether slaves or free—and have all been made to drink into one Spirit" (1 Cor. 12:13). The Greek preposition *en*, here translated as "by," is better translated as "in," that is, "one Spirit."

There are some key doctrinal points found in this verse. First, all believers have been baptized in the Holy Spirit ("we all"). Nowhere does the Bible suggest that only some believers have been baptized in the Spirit. Second, this baptism places every believer into one body, the true church. The goal of Spirit baptism is positional oneness within the called-out group in this church age. All church-age believers are in the church; there are no believers outside the spiritual body of Christ. Third, normal racial, social, and sexual distinctions remain in ordinary life experiences, but they are irrelevant within the body. Jews and Greeks are positionally one in the church. So are the slaves and free citizens. And so are males and females.

Fourth, the baptism in the Holy Spirit is a work that Christ does for us. It is not an experience we should seek after conversion. It is an automatic part of spiritual regeneration. Fifth, the baptism in the Spirit establishes our sphere of ministry within the true church. Paul explained, "But now God has set the members, each one of them, in the body just as He pleased" (12:18). Although we believers are one in our spiritual position in the body, we have different functions to perform.

Sixth, the baptism in the Holy Spirit is not evidenced by speaking in tongues. Later Paul asked, "Do all speak with tongues?" (12:30). The expected answer was no. All were baptized in the Holy Spirit, but not all spoke in tongues. Thus speaking in tongues is not the initial evidence of the baptism in the Holy Spirit.

It enables believers to be clothed with Christ. "For as many of you as were baptized into Christ have put on Christ" (Gal. 3:27). The baptism in the Holy Spirit places us into Christ, into total union and identification with Him. Positionally, He is around each one of us. As in 1 Corinthians 12:13, Paul wrote in Galatians 3:28, "There is neither Jew nor Greek, there is neither slave nor free, there is neither male nor female; for you are all one in Christ Jesus." The baptism in the Spirit eliminates human distinctions; it does not exacerbate them. It does not create two peoples of God—one that has the baptism and one that doesn't.

It is a spiritual reality that marks every believer in this church age. Paul challenged believers to walk worthy of their divine calling and "to keep the unity of the Spirit in the bond of peace" (Eph. 4:1–3). The spiritual oneness created by the ministry of the Holy Spirit in the life of each believer is true whether believers live in accord with that truth or not. Yet, the daily practice of believers should display their spiritual position.

What is the unity of the Spirit? Paul explained, "There is one body and one Spirit, just as you were called in one hope of your calling; one Lord, one faith, one baptism; one God and Father of all, who is above all, and through all, and in you all" (4:4–6). Here Paul used the word *one* seven times to point out seven realities that mark the spiritual position of every believer.

First, we believers are all in the one body, the true church. Second, we are all indwelt by one Spirit, the Holy Spirit. Third, we all have one hope, the hope of being like Christ when He returns to rapture the church. Fourth, we all have one Lord, Jesus Christ, the crucified, resurrected, ascended Head of the church. Fifth, we all have one faith, that belief in the deity and the redemptive work of Christ. Sixth, we are all marked by one baptism, the baptism in the Holy Spirit, which placed us into Christ and His body. Seventh, we all have one God and Father, the sovereign Ruler of our lives.

The words "one baptism" must refer to the baptism in the Holy Spirit. It cannot refer to water baptism because not all Christians have been baptized in water. Those who have, have not all been baptized in the same method. Some have been immersed backward once, whereas others have been immersed forward once or three times. Many have been sprinkled or poured on. Some were baptized when they were infants, whereas others have been baptized as adults. Water baptism is not a singular reality true of all believers.

Since all believers are marked by the six other spiritual realities, the "one baptism" must also be true of all believers. It is part of the unity of the Spirit, which is to be maintained.

ITS CONTRASTS

Baptism and Indwelling

Both the baptism in the Holy Spirit and the indwelling presence of the Spirit occur at the moment of salvation. Both are divine works done in our lives apart from our human efforts or requests. And both are permanent.

Old Testament believers could be indwelt by the Spirit, but they were never baptized in the Holy Spirit. They never became members of the spiritual body of Christ, the true church that Christ is building in this dispensation.

We were in the Spirit when we were baptized in the Holy Spirit. In indwelling, the Spirit is in us. We were immersed in the Spirit (baptism), but we "have all been made to drink into one Spirit" (indwelling, 1 Cor. 12:13).

This baptism is a nonrepeatable event that occurs at the point of salvation, and the indwelling of the Spirit also occurs at the point of salvation and of course, continues on.

Baptism and Filling

The baptism in the Holy Spirit and the filling of the Holy Spirit are two separate divine works. Although several groups try to equate them, the biblical evidence contrasts them.

First, the baptism in the Holy Spirit is a once-for-all operation, whereas filling is a continuous process. The command to be filled (Eph. 5:18) is in the present tense, indicating an experience that can be repeated. The disciples were repeatedly filled (Acts 2:4; 4:8, 31). The baptism, however, is a single event (Eph. 4:5), described as completed (Rom. 6:3–4; 1 Cor. 12:13; Gal. 3:27; Col. 2:12).

Second, the baptism in the Holy Spirit is nonexperiential, whereas filling is a reality to be experienced. The baptism in the Spirit is something God does for us without our knowing about it at the time. Filling is an experience to be desired and to be achieved.

Third, there is no command for any believer to be baptized in the Holy Spirit, but there is a command to be filled with the Spirit (Eph. 5:18).

Fourth, the baptism in the Holy Spirit is universal among all Christians (1 Cor. 12:13; Eph. 4:5). The command to be filled with the Spirit implies that some believers were not filled.

Fifth, the baptism in the Holy Spirit is different from filling in its results. Baptism unites us to Christ and makes us members of the body of Christ (Rom. 6:3–4; 1 Cor. 12:13). Filling produces joy, thanksgiving, submission, service, and Christian character (Gal. 5:22; Eph. 5:19–21).

Sixth, the baptism in the Holy Spirit is different from filling in the conditions by which it is received. When a person believes in Christ for salvation, at that very moment he or she is baptized in the Holy Spirit. When a believer is separated from known personal sin and is totally yielded to the indwelling Spirit, he will be filled with the Spirit.

ITS CONTROVERSY

The doctrine of the baptism in the Holy Spirit is marked by hermeneutical and denominational controversy. Local churches have been split over its meaning and application. Within the evangelical family there are several divergent opinions. I have already presented my personal understanding, a viewpoint that marks the typical dispensational position of interpretation. Now, let's look at differing views.

The Baptism Is the Filling

R. A. Torrey and D. L. Moody embraced this equation of terms. Torrey wrote, "The Baptism with the Holy Spirit is the Spirit of God coming upon the believer, taking possession of his faculties, imparting to him gifts not naturally his own, but which qualify him for the service to which God has called him."[1] To them, this event usually occurred after salvation. The experience gave special enablement for Christian service. All these biblical terms referred to the same experience: "filled" (Acts 2:4), "receive" (1:8), "come upon" (19:6), "promise" (1:4), "endued with power" (Luke 24:49), and "gift" (Acts 2:38). In this view the baptism/filling experience basically provided power for effective evangelism. Tongues-speaking was not seen as an evidence of this experience.

The Baptism Is Sanctification

Vinson Synan, a theologian-historian, has written an excellent book on the history of the Holiness-Pentecostal Movement.[2] He himself embraces this doctrinal position. He traced this movement back to John Wesley, who stressed two separate experiences for the believer, namely, salvation and sanctification. Sanctification, Wesley said, is a postconversion experience which produces a perfection of moral motives and desires. In the Wesleyan holiness tradition, some viewed this experience of sanctification as the baptism in the Holy Spirit.

This holiness position is generally noncharismatic and nonpentecostal. Its advocates deny that tongues-speaking is a sign of the experience. The emphasis, rather, is on a postconversion experience, which leads to a life free from sin.

The Wesleyan church and the Church of God (Anderson, Indiana) are representatives of this theological position.

The Baptism Is Charismatic

Pentecostalism is basically a twentieth-century movement. Charles F. Parham (1873–1929), sometimes identified as the father of the modern Pentecostal movement, established the Bethel Bible College in Topeka, Kansas, in 1900. He asked the student body to research the question, "What is the Bible evidence of the baptism of the Holy Ghost?" The students responded that speaking in tongues was the evidence. The students then sought the experience. Agnes Ozman subsequently spoke in tongues on January 1, 1901. Klaude Kendrick, a Pentecostalist, observed, "Although Agnes Ozman was not the first person in modern times to speak in tongues, she was the first person to have received such an experience as a result of specifically seeking a baptism in the Holy Spirit with the expectation of speaking in tongues."[3]

Pentecostalists believe that the baptism in the Holy Spirit is a postconversion experience. However, some see the baptism as a "third blessing," and others view it as a "second blessing."

The baptism is a third blessing. The Reformers, such as Luther and Calvin, emphasized the blessing of justification by grace alone through faith alone in Christ alone. John Wesley and the Holiness tradition affirmed that there is a second blessing, a postconversion experience known as sanctification. Some Holiness proponents equated this second blessing with the baptism in the Holy Spirit. Benjamin Irwin of the Fire-Baptized Holiness Church later distinguished the second blessing of sanctification from the third blessing of the baptism in the Holy Spirit. The third blessing was evidenced by speaking in tongues.

Nearly one-half of worldwide Pentecostalism holds to the three-blessings concept. The Church of God (Cleveland, Tennessee) adheres to this Holiness-Pentecostal position. These people are Holiness in that they accept sanctification as a second work of grace. They are also Pentecostal because they believe Christians should seek the baptism in the Holy Spirit with the expectation of speaking in tongues.

The baptism is a second blessing. In 1914 the Assemblies of God, a major Pentecostal denomination, rejected the concept that sanctification is a second blessing. They teach that positional sanctification occurs at conversion and that progressive sanctification takes place throughout the lives of believers. The Assemblies thus moved the third blessing, the baptism in the Holy Spirit, into the second position. A true Pentecostalist, therefore, is not Holiness in doctrine.

David duPlessis was known as "Mr. Pentecostalist" in his generation. He was a key figure who promoted the Pentecostal distinctives among traditional Protestant churches and Roman Catholics. He defined a Pentecostal as "someone who can testify to having enjoyed the very same experience as that which the Apostles of our Lord had on the day of Pentecost according to Acts 2."[4]

He defined the Pentecostal movement in this way: "On the whole this term includes all those societies and movements or missions which teach and preach that all Christians should receive the baptism in the Holy Spirit as they did on the day of Pentecost according to Acts 2:4, with the evidence of speaking with other tongues as the Spirit gives utterance. This seemed to be the 'proof' of the baptism in the Spirit that the Apostles recognized."[5]

The typical second-blessing Pentecostal thus believes that the baptism in the Holy Spirit is a postconversion experience that should be sought through prayer. This experience, it is believed, will introduce the believer to the charismatic life. The sign of receiving the experience is the ability to speak in tongues.

There are two baptisms. Howard Ervin, a neoPentecostal Baptist, claimed that there are two separate baptisms in the Holy Spirit. "It should be noted that the baptism in the Spirit in 1 Cor. 12:13 is not the same as the baptism in the Spirit at Pentecost. The former places one in the body of Christ, the Church. The latter is for power manifested in charismatic witnessing."[6]

Ervin's mentor, David du Plessis, held the same position. He wrote, "All too often we hear people talk about the baptism *of* the Spirit when they mean *in* or *with.* The baptism *of* the Spirit comes at conversion or regeneration. . . . The Holy Spirit is the baptizer, the Church is the element into which He baptizes, and the unregenerated sinner is the object that is baptized."[7] He also identified this event as the baptism by the Spirit.

This distinction of two baptisms in the Holy Spirit is a minority view within the Pentecostal movement, although both duPlessis and Ervin are very influential. However, this distinction cannot be maintained exegetically because the same Greek construction is used in all the passages. To be consistent, the preposition *en* should be translated "in." It cannot arbitrarily be translated "of" or "by" just to conform to a predetermined view.

There are three movements. Church historians have identified three major movements within Pentecostalism, all occurring within the twentieth century. First, from 1900 to 1960, the Pentecostal experience basically remained within Pentecostal denominations. These groups were viewed as outside of evangelicalism and the liberal ecumenical movement.

Second, the charismatic movement began around 1960 when the Pentecostal experience began to penetrate the historic denominations, including Baptists, Methodist, Lutheran, Presbyterian, Roman Catholic, and others. For the most part the people who claimed that they had spoken in tongues after they received the baptism in the Holy Spirit remained in their home denominations. These charismatics also viewed tongues-speaking as *a* sign of the baptism, not necessarily *the* sign, as traditional Pentecostalists did. For example, Laurence Christenson, a Lutheran charismatic, admitted, "Many people have received the baptism with the Holy Spirit as a definite experience and reality. In their life and ministry there has been the unmistakable evidence of increased power and effectiveness. Yet they have not spoken in tongues."[8]

Third, the Third Wave manifested itself in 1980–1990 with the Vineyard movement, led by John Wimber. Offshoots have been seen in the Toronto and Pensacola revivals. The Vineyard movement stressed power evangelism, the manifestation of signs and wonders to attest the gospel message. The role of tongues-speaking was minimized in this group. This Third Wave has also seen the rise of prophecy and unusual physical manifestation. People who claim to be controlled by the Spirit may laugh incessantly, bark like dogs, and roar like lions. Some fall to the floor, asserting that they have been slain in the Spirit. Such acts are neither commanded nor seen in the New Testament.

IMPLICATIONS FOR US

First, we need to recognize the distinctiveness of the present church age. The true church, the body of Christ, which He is building, consists of saved Jews and saved Gentiles. The difference between local churches and the true church needs to be recognized. Some truths relate to church believers today that were not true of the Old Testament saints. Also some truths relate only to ethnic Israel and not to the church.

Second, we must exalt our spiritual oneness in Christ and in the body of Christ—two results produced by the baptism in the Holy Spirit. Our oneness in Christ transcends our denominational and doctrinal differences. We can fellowship with those who are genuinely saved even if they do not interpret the Scriptures in the same way we do.

Third, we must evaluate our experiences by the clear teachings of the

Word of God. We must not view our experiences as more authoritative than the Bible. We must exercise spiritual discernment when people claim experiences that are not supported by Scripture.

Fourth, we need to examine carefully the various meanings and applications that are attached to the doctrine of the baptism in the Holy Spirit, including our own. Is it true that those who have not spoken in tongues in a postconversion experience are deficient in spiritual gifts and evangelistic success? What about Billy Graham? Charles Swindoll? Charles Stanley? These men, and many nonPentecostal and noncharismatic believers like them, have not spoken in tongues nor do they believe in a postconversion baptism in the Holy Spirit. Even Pentecostalists and charismatics admire such men.

Fifth, let's rejoice in all the spiritual blessings God has bestowed on us in Christ (Eph. 1:3). We need not seek a second or a third postconversion blessing, something beyond what the Bible teaches. Our position in Christ is complete.

CHAPTER TEN

The Indwelling and Filling of the Holy Spirit

These two ministries of the Holy Spirit are related, but they are not identical. A person must be indwelt by the Spirit before he can be filled with the Spirit. A person, however, can be indwelt by the Spirit without being filled by the Spirit.

The conditions for indwelling and filling are entirely different. In order for a person to be indwelt by the Spirit, he must receive Jesus Christ as his Savior from sin. For a believer to be filled by the Spirit, he must be yielded to His sovereign control.

THE INDWELLING OF THE HOLY SPIRIT

Its Reality

It is true of all believers. The apostle Paul wrote, "But you are not in the flesh but in the Spirit, if indeed the Spirit of God dwells in you. Now if anyone does not have the Spirit of Christ, he is not His" (Rom. 8:9). Genuine believers are in the Spirit, and the Spirit is in them. There is no true believer who does not have the indwelling presence of the Holy Spirit. At the very moment of personal salvation the Holy Spirit begins to dwell within the child of God. There is no interval of time between salvation and the reception of the Spirit. The new Christian can immediately live a righteous life through the enabling of the indwelling Spirit (8:10–11).

God's right of ownership of believers follows the act of redemption. As Paul wrote, "Or do you not know that your body is the temple of the Holy Spirit who is in you, whom you have from God, and you are not your own? For you were bought at a price; therefore glorify God in your body and in your spirit, which are God's" (1 Cor. 6:19–20). When Christ redeems a person from the penalty of sin, He demonstrates His ownership over that individual by causing the Holy Spirit to dwell within him or her. Believers become living temples of God at the very moment of salvation, because the Spirit then begins to live in them.

The indwelling of the Spirit begins at the very moment of redemptive faith in Christ (Gal. 3:1–5). When one is born into the family of God, God sends forth "the Spirit of His Son into [our] hearts, crying out, 'Abba, Father' " (4:6).

It is a gift from God. Jesus Christ declared that after He was glorified every believer would receive the Holy Spirit (John 7:37–39). The Holy Spirit is identified as "the gift" (Acts 2:38; 11:17).

Paul wrote, "Now hope does not disappoint, because the love of God has been poured out in our hearts by the Holy Spirit who was given to us" (Rom. 5:5). We can know that God loves us through that assurance created by the indwelling Spirit. And we can love God only because the Spirit of God enables us to do so. We can immediately produce the fruit of the Spirit, permeated by love (Gal. 5:22–23).

God has "given us the Spirit in our hearts as a guarantee" (2 Cor. 1:22; see also 5:5). The indwelling Spirit is the divine pledge that God loves us, that we belong to Him, and that we will enjoy all the blessings of salvation throughout time and eternity.

It is permanent. There is no indication in the New Testament that any believer in this church age could lose the indwelling presence of the Holy Spirit. When the apostles appealed to their readers to live godly lives, they never said that they might lose the Spirit if they failed to do so.

The permanent presence of the Holy Spirit in the lives of all believers is guaranteed by the Father's response to Christ's prayer: "And I will pray the Father, and He will give you another Helper, that He may abide with you forever" (John 14:16). There are no conditions or exceptions to this promise.

The Corinthian believers were carnal, not spiritual. They had the Spirit of God, but they chose to yield to their sinful disposition. Some of them were divisive, immoral, selfish, compromising, insubordinate, loveless, and doctrinally incorrect. And yet Paul identified them as saints, who were the temple of God, indwelt by the Holy Spirit (1 Cor. 1:2; 3:16–17, 6:19–20). Some groups allege that the Spirit of God will leave a Christian when he sins. If that were true, then the Holy Spirit should have left the believers at Corinth. But He didn't. That is the reason Paul exhorted them. The carnal Christians needed to remember that they were "in Christ"and that the Holy Spirit was living in them.

All believers are sealed with the indwelling Spirit "until the redemption of the purchased possession" (Eph. 1:14). That event will be the Rapture at the end of the church age (1 Thess. 4:13–18). All believers in the church, Christ's body, are positionally perfect, but they are all practically flawed. Though Christians sin, they remain sealed, indwelt by the Spirit.

It includes anointing. God anointed Jesus Christ with the Holy Spirit (Luke 4:18; Acts 4:27; 10:38; Heb. 1:9). When that happened at His water baptism, Christ began to preach and to perform miracles. Some groups have concluded that Christians, too, should be anointed with the Spirit in order to do wondrous works for God. However, there is no scriptural basis for this theological presupposition of a postconversion experience.

The verb *chriō* ("anoint") is used only once of believers: "Now He who establishes us with you in Christ and has anointed us is God, who also has sealed us and given us the Spirit in our hearts as a guarantee" (2 Cor. 1:21–22). All believers, with Paul, are divinely established, placed in Christ, anointed, sealed, and indwelt by the Spirit. The anointing of the Spirit, as John Walvoord notes, is the "initial act of indwelling."[1]

The noun *chrisma* ("anointing" or "unction") occurs only three times in the New Testament. The apostle John used this word to describe the indwelling presence of the Holy Spirit (1 John 2:20, 27 [twice]). "But you have an anointing from the Holy One" (2:20). In this context the Spirit of God affirms the deity and the incarnation of Jesus Christ by His teaching witness. No genuine believer would ever deny the deity of Christ. The Spirit of God would not allow him to do so.

It is not experienced by the unsaved. "Now if anyone does not have the

Spirit of Christ, he is not His" (Rom. 8:9). Jude added that the unsaved are people "not having the Spirit" (Jude 19). From God's perspective, there are only two groups of people in the world today—the saved, who have the Holy Spirit in them, and the unsaved, who do not have the Holy Spirit in them.

Its Blessings

Purity. After Paul commanded believers to flee sexual immorality, he reminded them that their bodies were the temples of the indwelling Spirit (1 Cor. 6:18–20). Our bodies are sacred, sanctified, the very sanctuary of the Spirit, who is holy. No believer should involve the Spirit in the immoral acts of adultery, fornication, or homosexuality (6:9–11).

Believers should treat the bodies of themselves and others "in sanctification and honor" (1 Thess. 4:4). In our culture people justify immoral acts with these rationalizations: "We love each other," "We are consenting adults," "No one is getting hurt." The child of God must reject this kind of nonbiblical logic for one basic reason: The Holy Spirit is hurt when a Christian violates the proper sexual usage of his body (4:8). All sin is ultimately against God, and sexual sin by a believer violates the sanctity of the indwelling Spirit.

Worship. Genuine worship of God is "in spirit and truth" (John 4:24). All believers should be "praying in the Holy Spirit" (Jude 20). The Spirit unifies the communion or fellowship of believers (2 Cor. 13:14). The true church is the "dwelling place of God in the Spirit" (Eph. 2:22). Saved Jews and saved Gentiles, made one in Christ, now "both have access by one Spirit to the Father" (2:18). True biblical worship is Spirit-guided, personal, and relational. It is biblically accurate, in accord with the Spirit-inspired Word of God.

Assurance. How can anyone know he is really a child of God? One answer is that "the Spirit Himself bears witness with our spirit that we are children of God" (Rom. 8:16). The silent communication between the Holy Spirit and the human spirit occurs when we understand the written Scriptures. When we receive salvation by grace alone through faith alone in Christ alone (John 3:16; Rom. 10:9–10), the Spirit gives assurance to our hearts that we are His. As John wrote, "By this we know that we abide in Him, and He in us, because He has given us of His Spirit" (1 John 4:13).

Service. In this church age Christians should serve God "in the newness of the Spirit and not in the oldness of the letter" (Rom. 7:6). That is, serving God must be generated from within us, Spirit-driven, and marked by love. It is not to be legalistic, in forced conformity to ecclesiastical tradition.

The true church is built on the foundation of Jesus Christ (1 Cor. 3:11). All Christians must build on that foundation, knowing they will give an account of their accomplishments at the judgment seat of Christ (3:12–15). Toward that end, Paul warned, "Do you not know that you are the temple of God and that the Spirit of God dwells in you? If anyone defiles the temple of God, God will destroy him. For the temple of God is holy, which temple you are" (3:16–17). Believers must be aware that the Spirit of God dwells within each of us. We must edify one another. We dare not offend the indwelling oneness of the Spirit in the corporate body of believers.

Growth. All Christians need to grow from spiritual infancy to adulthood (2 Pet. 3:18). As we understand and apply the Scriptures to our lives, we grow spiritually. We can know God's truth only as the Holy Spirit teaches us. We all have the indwelling Spirit "that we might know the things that have been freely given to us by God" (1 Cor. 2:12).

To grow we must rely on the Spirit. We cannot grow into Christlikeness through conformity to man-made lists of do's and don'ts. "Are you so foolish? Having begun in the Spirit, are you now being made perfect by the flesh?" (Gal. 3:3). We must not substitute human effort for the divine power of the Spirit. We must be yielded to Him, sensitive to His teaching and guidance.

THE FILLING OF THE HOLY SPIRIT

In a prayer to be sung as a benediction, Andrew Reed wrote, "Spirit Divine, hear our prayer, / And make our hearts Your home; / Descend with all Your gracious pow'r, / Come, Holy Spirit, come. Amen."[2] There are other prayers, hymns, and praise songs that express identical appeals. I appreciate the sentiment and the cry of the heart found in these words, but I respectfully disagree with their content for three reasons. First, no prayer in the Bible is ever addressed directly to the Holy Spirit. It may not be wrong, but there is no scriptural command or precedent to do so. Second, such cries of the heart suggest that the Holy Spirit is living outside the believer. But, in his entire divine personhood, the Spirit of God dwells within each believer. Third, the Spirit's filling of the believer originates from within, not from outside.

Yet we must not allow this difference of opinion to set aside the importance of believers needing to be filled with the Holy Spirit. As Walvoord wrote, the filling of the Spirit is "the source of all vital spiritual experience in the life of the Christian."[3]

Its Meaning

The terms. The verbs *pimplemi* and *plēthō,* lengthened forms of *plēō,* are used of both mundane and spiritual fillings. A wedding was filled with guests (Matt. 22:10), a sponge was filled with vinegar (27:48), a time period was filled or accomplished (Luke 1:23, 57; 2:6, 21–22), and boats were filled with fish (5:7).

In addition, people were filled with fear (5:26), rage (6:11), awe (Acts 3:10), indignation (5:17), envy (13:45), confusion (19:29).

The above verbs also describe those who were filled with the Holy Spirit (Luke 1:15, 41, 67; Acts 2:4; 4:8, 31; 9:17; 13:9).

Another key verb, *plēroō,* is translated "to fill" or "to fulfill." It is used of the fulfillment of Old Testament prophecy (Matt. 1:22; 2:15), righteousness (3:15), the times of the Gentiles (Luke 21:24), the sayings of Jesus (John 18:32), periods of time (Acts 7:23, 30; 9:23), the work of the ministry (12:25), the Law (Gal. 5:14), and the Word of God (Col. 1:25).

The verb *plēroō* also is used of being filled with wisdom (Luke 2:40), joy (John 15:11), sorrow (16:6), unrighteousness (Rom. 1:29), peace (15:13), knowledge (15:14), comfort (2 Cor 7:4), and the fruits of righteousness (Phil. 1:11).

Filling can happen in several ways. What is empty can be filled from outside, or a filling can originate from within a person, such as being filled with anger or fear.

Does the Holy Spirit fill a believer from outside or within him? Since the Spirit began to dwell within a believer at conversion, He must consequently fill from within.

The command. The command to be filled with the Spirit is stated in Ephesians 5:18: "And do not be drunk with wine, in which is dissipation; but be filled with the Spirit." Literally the second part of the verse reads, "Be you [plural] filled in spirit." There is some debate whether "spirit" refers to the Holy Spirit or to the human spirit. While the grammar permits either interpretation, most theologians believe that the Holy Spirit is referred to here.

Some key observations must be noted. First, believers can either obey or disobey this command. It is up to them. Paul has issued a directive, not a suggestion.

Second, we are not commanded to ask or pray for the filling of the Holy Spirit. Rather, we are commanded to be obedient. As Andreas Kostenberger observes, "We may conclude that there is not a single reference in the NT that enjoins believers to ask to be filled with the Spirit."[4] Lewis Sperry Chafer concurred.[5] As believers, we do not need to pray earnestly, to fast, to tarry, or to follow a set of human directives. Rather, we must obey the conditions for filling prescribed in the Scriptures.

Third, believers do not fill themselves, nor do they actively command the Spirit to fill them. The verb *plērousthe* in Ephesians 5:18 is in the passive voice, meaning that we are acted on by Him. But we are active when we obey Him and yield to Him.

Fourth, we must be filled with the Spirit over and over. The verb is in the present tense, and it can be translated, "Be you continuously filled." Although a believer may consciously yield himself to the Holy Spirit for the first time in a crisis experience, that act of submission must be repeated daily. It is possible to be filled with the Spirit on Sunday and not be filled on Monday. Each Christian must ask himself or herself, "Am I at this moment spiritually clean and submissive to the leadership of the Spirit?"

Fifth, we are filled with the Spirit when we are obedient to the Word of God. Paul wrote that we are to "let the word of Christ dwell in [us] richly in all wisdom" (Col. 3:16). The Holy Spirit fills us when we understand and apply the Scriptures to our lives. The Spirit works according to the Scriptures, not apart from them.

Sixth, we are filled with the Spirit when we are controlled by Him. When I was a young person, I saw many people who were intoxicated. My dad was a part-time bartender, and I often saw drunks do things they did not do when they were sober. They were under the control or influence of the alcohol in their bodies. We are all acquainted with traffic violators who are DUI—"driving under the influence of alcohol."

Paul used this graphic, cultural experience to illustrate the filling of the Spirit. The Spirit wants to influence us in all areas of our lives—mental, emotional, vocational, sexual, and relational. He wants to control us as we apply the Scriptures to those areas. When we are filled with the Spirit, we will do things that we would not ordinarily do.

William Longstaff, in the fourth stanza of his hymn "Take Time to Be Holy," correctly stated the truth: "Take time to be holy, be calm in thy soul; / Each thought and each motive, beneath His control; / Thus led by His Spirit to fountains of love, / Thou soon shall be fitted for service above."[6]

The results. After Paul commanded believers to be filled with the Spirit, he listed four results or evidences of His control. He used four participles to define the characteristics of filling: speaking, singing, giving, and submitting.

The first result is ministry to others. Spirit-filled believers will be "speaking to one another in psalms and hymns and spiritual songs" (Eph. 5:19). They will be spiritually concerned for others. They will purposely relate to others. They will share the Word of God with others.

The second result is joy. If you are a Spirit-controlled saint, you will be "singing and making melody in your heart to the Lord" (5:19). Paul elsewhere charged, "Rejoice in the Lord always. Again I will say, rejoice!" (Phil. 4:4). Even in the experiences of grief and sadness, we can rejoice because God loves us and He is in control. The Spirit-filled believer will see life from the divine perspective.

The third result is thanksgiving. Spirit-influenced saints will be "giving thanks always for all things to God the Father in the name of our Lord Jesus Christ" (Eph. 5:20). Elsewhere Paul wrote, "In everything give thanks; for this is the will of God in Christ Jesus for you" (1 Thess. 5:18). We believers can thank God for all things and in everything. With all of the tragedies and disappointments in life, this spiritual quality may seem to be an impossible dream. But the Spirit-filled child of God knows that God is present and that He is working out His sovereign will.

The fourth result is mutual submission. Spirit-controlled believers will be "submitting to one another in the fear of God" (Eph. 5:21). Equally accepted in Christ before God, believers must be submissive to each other in personal humility. Paul subsequently discussed the marks of role submission when he spoke of the submission of wives to husbands, children to parents, and slaves to masters (5:22–6:9). Spirit-control is necessary in these family and cultural activities, but there is a mutual submission of believers to each other as persons. My wife, Gloria, is in submission to me as her husband. But I must be in submission to her as a coequal person and believer. Only the Spirit of God can cause us to understand and apply this principle of mutual submission and service.

Spirit-filled believers will be marked by Spirit-produced character and conduct. When the Spirit permeates all areas of our lives, the fruit of the Spirit will be displayed, which "is love, joy, peace, longsuffering, kindness, goodness, faithfulness, gentleness, self-control" (Gal. 5:22–23). These nine virtues manifest Christlikeness. As we are yielded to the Holy Spirit, others will see Christ in and through us.

Its Conditions

How can we be filled with the Spirit? Stanley Toussaint correctly observed, "The New Testament gives no specific instructions on this subject."[7] At first glance, that comment seems unbelievable. If the filling of the Spirit is so crucial, why are there no explicit instructions? Of course, there are many commands and examples for us to follow. As we obey these directives, we manifest the surrender of ourselves to the Spirit (Rom. 12:1–2). Toussaint thus concluded, "Evidently, any heart that is open toward God and is in submission to the Scriptures will be filled with the Spirit."[8]

There are, however, three direct commands that involve the person and ministry of the Holy Spirit. If these are obeyed, we are filled or controlled by the Spirit.

Walk in the Spirit. "Walk in the Spirit, and you shall not fulfill the lust of the flesh" (Gal. 5:16). The imperative "walk" is in the present tense, denoting a continuous walk. It could be translated, "Keep on walking." The noun *pneumati* ("Spirit") can be translated "in the Spirit" or "by the Spirit."

The essence of a Spirit-filled walk is dependence and enablement. No believer has the capacity in himself to become what God wants him to be. No one is sufficient in himself to do what God wants him to do.

To live physically, we need air. We must be in the air and the air must be in us.

Fish must be in the water in order to live. If you take a fish out of the water and place it on a table, it will flop around helplessly. Its natural habitat is water, not air.

So it is with us. The supernatural habitat for successful Christian living is the Holy Spirit. We must depend on Him for our spiritual lives and strength.

Don't grieve the Spirit. "And do not grieve the Holy Spirit of God, by whom you were sealed for the day of redemption" (Eph. 4:30). We grieve Him when we deliberately sin. We delight Him when we live in holiness. If we do grieve Him, we must seek immediate restoration to fellowship through repentance and confession of sin (1 John 1:9).

God wants us to be holy as He is holy (1 Pet. 1:16). We should desire not to sin (1 John 2:1). How can we achieve these lofty goals? First, we must study and apply the Word of God to our lives. As the psalmist testified, "Your word I have hidden in my heart, that I might not sin against You" (Ps. 119:11). Second, we must daily resist the temptations of sin by the help of the Spirit. Third, we must prayerfully attempt to glorify God in all that we do.

Don't quench the Spirit. Paul simply cautioned, "Do not quench the Spirit" (1 Thess. 5:19). We quench the Spirit when we resist His attempts to produce Christlikeness in us. The essence of quenching is active selfishness, the failure to yield our wills to God.

The Spirit is like a fire who wants to warm and enlighten our lives. We quench Him when we purposefully disregard His directives.

We must desire to do the will of the Spirit, even before we know what it is. We must will to do it because of our love for the Lord.

Our submission must manifest our gratitude for His gracious mercy.

We will not quench Him if we obey Paul's appeal in Romans 12:1–2: "I beseech you therefore, brethren, by the mercies of God, that you present your bodies a living sacrifice, holy, acceptable to God, which is your reasonable service. And do not be conformed to this world, but be transformed by the renewing of your mind, that you may prove what is that good and acceptable and perfect will of God."

Summary. Dependence, cleanliness, and yieldedness are necessary to achieve the Spirit-filled life. Such conditions must be met daily. They may be realized for the first time in a postconversion act of total commitment to the will of God, but they must be reaffirmed daily.

Its Contrasts

Spirituality and carnality. A believer is spiritual when he is yielded to the Holy Spirit; he is carnal when he is not yielded to Him. A believer chooses whether to yield himself to the Spirit or to his sinful disposition.

A Christian, one day old in the faith, can be spiritual even though he knows little about the faith. On the other hand, a Christian who has been saved a long time is carnal if he is submissive to his fleshly desires. The carnal believer thus acts like an unsaved person (1 Cor. 3:3).

Think about radio frequencies. The Holy Spirit communicates through HBS (the Heaven Broadcasting System). The sinful world communicates through WBS (the World Broadcasting System). The believer is like an AM-FM radio. In our analogy, he can turn on the HBS or the WBS dial. He has both the Holy Spirit and the flesh within him. When he chooses to dial HBS, he is in tune with the Spirit; thus he is spiritual. If he chooses to dial WBS, then he is in tune with the world system; thus he is carnal at that moment.

We therefore vacillate between spirituality and carnality moment by moment. We are either controlled by the Spirit (spirituality) or we are not (carnality).

Maturity and immaturity. All Christians are immature when they are first saved. They are like babies, and they need to grow into maturity. Such growth involves effort, time, and experience. Peter encouraged new Christians: "As newborn babes, desire the pure milk of the word, that you may grow thereby" (1 Pet. 2:2). To grow properly, infants and children need nourishment, rest, exercise, and health.

Unfortunately, in real life some people may be thirty years old with only the mental and emotional capacities of a five-year-old. In the Christian world there are similarities. Some people have been saved for over twenty years, but their biblical understanding and spiritual activity seem childlike. The Bible indicates that those who should have been teachers were still spiritually immature by choice and neglect (Heb. 5:11–14). This type of immaturity was caused by a lack of true spirituality.

Spirituality and maturity. The ideal situation is for a Christian to be spiritual (yielded to the Spirit) as he grows from normal immaturity into maturity. His goal should be Spirit-filled adulthood, full conformity to Christ.

The worst scenario is for believers to be carnal and immature. Such Christians are difficult to distinguish from the unsaved. Mature Christian leaders fail when they are not yielded to the Spirit at a key moment. They sin because they are carnal, even though they have matured in spiritual things.

On the other hand, immature (undeveloped) spiritual believers fail because of inexperience. Their sins are caused by immaturity, not from failure to be yielded to the Spirit.

IMPLICATIONS FOR US

First, we should stand in awe that the infinite God dwells within us. God is so great that He can fill the created universe with His presence, and yet He dwells within each believer. What a wonderful truth! What an amazing mystery! May we never get over the joy of knowing that God is with us and in us.

Second, we need to be careful not to profane the temple of God, that is, our physical bodies. We need to be pure, always striving for holiness of body and spirit. And we should avoid abusing our bodies with harmful substances.

Third, we should be filled with the Spirit, praying that He will produce His fruit in us.

Fourth, we must avoid sinning against the Spirit by acts of divisiveness, selfishness, and greed.

Fifth, we should seek to appoint spiritually qualified local church leaders, men and women who are Spirit-filled and maturing.

Sixth, we must teach our people the biblical blessings of indwelling and filling, carefully avoiding wrong interpretations and applications of these two key doctrines.

CHAPTER ELEVEN

The Holy Spirit and His Ministry in Believers

God has already blessed believers with every conceivable spiritual blessing (Eph. 1:3).[1] Among those blessings is the ministry of the Holy Spirit toward us, in us, and through us. Some of His numerous activities occurred when we were saved, whereas others are now happening after our salvation.

AT OUR SALVATION

In Relationship to God

He regenerated us. When we were born into the family of God through faith in Jesus Christ, we were "born of the Spirit" (John 3:5–6, 8). He brought us out of our spiritual death and gave us new life. He convicted us of sin, righteousness, and judgment (16:8); He caused us to understand the redemptive truth of the Word of God (1 Pet. 1:22); He graciously invited us to come to Christ (Rev. 22:17). Paul summarized this magnificent event in these words: "Not by works of righteousness which we have done, but according to His mercy He saved us, through the washing of regeneration and renewing of the Holy Spirit" (Titus 3:5).

Even before we were saved, the Holy Spirit set us apart to prepare us for the moment of our salvation. Paul wrote that "God from the beginning chose you for salvation through sanctification by the Spirit and belief in the truth" (2 Thess. 2:13). In our unsaved days He created needs and attitudes in us whereby we would respond favorably when the gospel was presented to us.

He was a divine gift. At the very moment we called on Christ to save us, God gave us the gift of the Holy Spirit (Acts 2:38). We received Him by the "hearing of faith," not by "the works of the law" (Gal. 3:2). We did not do anything to merit this divine gift.

At the moment of our conversion we were able to love God as our spiritual Father. We could do so only by the Holy Spirit, which He gave us. "Now hope does not disappoint, because the love of God has been poured out in our hearts by the Holy Spirit who was given to us" (Rom. 5:5).

He secured our acceptance. When we were saved, we changed from an unrighteous position to a righteous one before God. After describing the sinful lifestyles of the unsaved, Paul wrote, "And such were some of you. But you were washed, but you were sanctified, but you were justified in the name of the Lord Jesus and by the Spirit of our God" (1 Cor. 6:11). The triune God has saved us once and for all time. The Holy Spirit has secured our position of permanent cleansing from sin, of sanctification, and of justification. As sanctified people, we are now "saints," set apart in Christ by the Spirit forever (1:2).

The Spirit has guaranteed our acceptance before God by His indwelling presence. Paul attested, "Now He who establishes us with you in Christ and has anointed us is God, who also has sealed us and given us the Spirit in our hearts as a guarantee" (2 Cor. 1:21–22). God's pledge of eternal security is corroborated by the witness of the Spirit to the truthfulness of His word (5:5). We have been sealed with the Holy Spirit until we are changed into total Christlikeness at the return of Jesus Christ (Eph. 1:13–14).

He confirmed our sonship. How can a person know he is really saved? Should he trust the circumstances of his professing Christ, such as raising his hand, walking an aisle, or praying a prayer? Should he trust his feelings or the comments of a friend? No, assurance of salvation is based on the Word of God, which affirms that the Holy Spirit testified to our hearts that we are children of God by faith.

Paul wrote, "For you did not receive the spirit of bondage again to fear, but you received the Spirit of adoption by whom we cry out, 'Abba, Father.' The Spirit Himself bears witness with our spirit that we are children of God" (Rom. 8:15–16). In a similar passage, the apostle said, "And because you are sons, God has sent forth the Spirit of His Son into your hearts, crying out, 'Abba, Father!'" (Gal. 4:6). In Romans Paul said believers cry out, and in Galatians he said the Spirit cries out. As the Spirit of the Son of God, He causes us to affirm that God is our Father, even as Jesus acknowledges the Father.

Sinclair Ferguson has beautifully expressed this truth of the Father-child relationship: "What Paul is saying, however, is that even in the darkest hour there is a co-operative and affirmative testimony given by the Spirit. It is found in the very fact that, although he may be broken and bruised, tossed about with fears and doubts, the child of God nevertheless in his need cries out, 'Father!' as instinctively as a child who has fallen and been hurt calls out in similar language, 'Daddy, help me!' Assurance of sonship is not reserved for the highly sanctified Christian; it is the birthright of even the weakest and most oppressed believer. This is its glory."[2]

The Spirit of God has borne witness to the testimony of God in the Scriptures (1 John 5:9–10). When we read the gospel message (John 1:12; 3:16; Rom. 10:9–10, 13), the Spirit testified that it was true. We did what we were supposed to do (we believed) and God did what He promised to do (He saved us).

He indwelt us. The Holy Spirit entered us when we were saved. His indwelling presence is the evidence that we belong to Jesus Christ (Rom. 8:9). Our bodies are now living temples. His habitation within us is forever.

The true church, composed of saved Jews and saved Gentiles, is "being built together for a dwelling place of God in the Spirit." All true believers in this church age are built on the foundation laid by the apostles and prophets, with Christ being the cornerstone. Church-age believers, as a corporate body, are like a temple building. In Christ "the whole building, being fitted together, grows into a holy temple in the Lord." We believers are living stones or blocks, individually and corporately indwelt by the Spirit who fills the entire church with His presence (Eph. 2:20–22).

In Relationship to Believers

He united us. As discussed in chapter 9, the action of the baptism in the Holy Spirit is unique to the church age. It makes all believers one in Christ and one in the church, the body of Christ. "For as the body is one and has many members, but all the members of that one body, being many, are one body, so also is Christ. For by one Spirit we were all baptized into one body—whether Jews or Greeks, whether slaves or free—and have all been made to drink into one Spirit" (1 Cor. 12:12–13). At the moment of salvation, we became united with all living believers, regardless of their race, gender, age, ecclesiastical affiliation, and geographic location. We also became united with all believers who died between the Day of Pentecost and our present day. Thus, each believer today is united with Paul, Peter, Martin Luther, John Calvin, William Carey, Adoniram Judson, and the missionaries martyred by the Auca Indians. Every Christian is part of the spiritual bride of Christ, the body of Christ. Their spiritual position, privileges, and eternal destiny are inseparably united with all the saints during the past two thousand years.

Concerning Jews and Gentiles, Paul wrote, "For He Himself is our peace, who has made both one" (Eph. 2:14). Christ has created "one new man from the two, thus making peace" (2:15). In past ages God saved both Jews and Gentiles, but their racial distinctions remained. In the Old Testament age of the Law, no saved Gentile could serve, for example, as a priest in the temple at Jerusalem. Nor could saved Gentiles enter temple areas restricted to Jews. Through our oneness in Christ, however, we all "have access by one Spirit to the Father" (2:18).

He bestowed gifts. When believers are baptized in the Holy Spirit into the body of Christ, the Spirit gives them abilities to function in the ministries assigned to them. These gifts (discussed in the next chapter) are denoted as *pneumatika* ("spiritual gifts") or *charismata* ("grace gifts"). God has bestowed them on us out of His grace and through His Spirit. Every believer has received at least one gift (1 Cor. 12:7). A believer may have more than one gift, but he cannot have all the gifts (12:27–30). The Spirit sovereignly distributed gifts "to each one individually as He wills" (12:11).

These gifts are equated with the functions of body members (12:12). An eye can do what the ear cannot, and a hand can do what the foot cannot. In like manner, we believers are all in the same spiritual body. The life of Christ energized by the Spirit permeates every Christian. But we have different tasks to perform for the edification of others and for the glory of God.

These gifts may function through natural abilities and learned skills. Since God chose us in Christ for salvation and made us with distinctive genetic codes, He prepared us for that moment when He would place us into the body of Christ (12:18).

AFTER OUR SALVATION

In Relationship to God

He assists us in prayer. When we are controlled by the Spirit, we will be people of prayer. Jude spoke of "praying in the Holy Spirit" (Jude 20), that is, praying in His strength and in accord with the revealed will of God.

At difficult times, however, we often do not know how to express our burdens in words. We may see alternative solutions to our problems, but we may not be able to determine which solution is God's will. In such puzzling moments the Holy Spirit assists us. "Likewise the Spirit also helps in our weaknesses. For we do not know what we should pray for as we ought, but the Spirit Himself makes intercession for us with groanings which cannot be uttered" (Rom. 8:26). The Spirit thus prays in us, through us, and for us. He knows us better than we know ourselves. He knows our needs, our concerns, and the best solutions to our needs.

He strengthens us. Paul prayed that believers might be "strengthened with might through His Spirit in the inner man" (Eph. 3:16). Inner courage, fortitude, and spiritual stamina are necessary to persevere through hardships to perfect spiritual maturity, and to achieve the abundant life. In a similar prayer Paul asked that believers might be "strengthened with all might, according to His glorious power, for all patience and longsuffering with joy" (Col. 1:11). The Spirit of God gives us ability to endure joyfully situations such as accidents, disease, death, layoffs, demotions, gossip, and false accusations.

The Spirit strengthens us when we are persecuted for our faith. As Peter wrote, "If you are reproached for the name of Christ, blessed are you, for the Spirit of glory and of God rests upon you" (1 Pet. 4:14). Spirit-filled people have always been persecuted, but they overcome.

He leads us. Believers who are "led by the Spirit of God" thereby give evidence that they "are sons of God" (Rom. 8:14). The Spirit leads us into truth, holiness, and discernment of the will of God. People have many decisions to make in life. Which college should I attend? Which career should I pursue? Whom should I marry? Specific answers to such questions, however, aren't found in the Scriptures. There are biblical directives, however, which the Spirit of God uses to guide us. We need to be willing to do God's will. I like this guideline: Take a piece of blank paper, write your name at the bottom, and ask God to give the directions. Too often, we want to see the will of God before we make our decision to do it, but that attitude will not work.

The Spirit leads those who are yielded to Him and to the will of God taught in the Scriptures. Have we presented our bodies—our minds, our feelings, our decisions—to Him? Do we want to discern "that good and acceptable and perfect will of God" (12:1–2)?

He gives hope. "For we through the Spirit eagerly wait for the hope of righteousness by faith" (Gal. 5:5). Several truths may be noted in this verse about this Spirit-given hope. First, the Spirit fosters within us spiritual optimism. We eagerly wait[3] for the coming of Christ (Rom. 8:19). A genuine believer looks back at the cross and forward to the return of Christ (Titus 2:11–14).

Second, the Spirit assures us of "the hope of righteousness." That hope is to be fully righteous, that is, Christlike, when we see Him.

Third, the Spirit enables us to walk "by faith." Elsewhere Paul testified, "For we walk by faith, not by sight" (2 Cor. 5:7). We trust God to do what He has promised to do. And as we do, we please Him (Heb. 11:6). Faith grows as the Spirit causes us to understand and apply the Scriptures.

In Relationship to Sin

He delivers us from sin. Within every believer are two natures—a disposition to sin and a disposition to holiness.[4] As unsaved humans, we inherited from our parents a sinful disposition, which permeates and controls our human activities—our thoughts, feelings, choices, and value systems.

When we were saved, we still retained that sinful disposition; however, God gave us a new disposition. As Renald Showers noted, "The new nature is the confirmed new disposition, consisting of the law of God in the heart, which God places inside a human being through the regenerating work of the Holy Spirit."[5]

Believers face a struggle, a conflict, a decision: Will we sin or will we become holy? Paul explained, "For the flesh lusts against the Spirit, and the Spirit against the flesh; and these are contrary to one another, so that you do not do the things that you wish" (Gal. 5:17).

Just as we cannot trust our will power to be saved, neither can we trust our will power to become holy. We must exercise our wills, but we must submit our wills to the indwelling Holy Spirit. "Walk in the Spirit, and you shall not fulfill the lust of the flesh" (5:16).

Paul expressed the frustration of all of us when he testified, "For what I am doing, I do not understand. For what I will to do, that I do not practice; but what I hate, that I do" (Rom. 7:15). Many Christians try to live the Christian life, but they fail because they are trusting in their own will power and ingenuity. Rather, we must allow the Holy Spirit to work through our submissive wills. "For the law of the Spirit of life in Christ Jesus has made me free from the law of sin and death" (8:2).

He delivers us from Satan. We are engaged in holy warfare. We need to be "strong in the Lord and in the power of His might" (Eph. 6:10). As spiritual soldiers, we need to be clothed with the whole armor of God in order "to stand against the wiles of the devil" (6:11). Our equipment includes the belt of truth, the breastplate of righteousness, the shoes of peace, the shield of faith, the helmet of salvation, and "the sword of the Spirit, which is the word of God" (6:17). We must read, memorize, understand, and apply the Spirit-inspired Scriptures. Just as Christ quoted the Scriptures in His temptation to defeat Satan, so must we. Only God is more powerful than Satan, and only His word is more powerful than satanic assaults.

There is one other divine resource we must employ. Paul added, "praying always with all prayer and supplication in the Spirit, being watchful to this end with all perseverance and supplication for all the saints" (Eph. 6:18). We must watch and pray. We must be dependent on God under the control of the Holy Spirit. We are not alone in our conflict, for we have the Holy Spirit in us.

In Relationship to the Scriptures

He gives understanding. The Holy Spirit is directly involved in the revelation, inspiration, illumination, and communication of the Scriptures (1 Cor. 2:9–13). Both revelation and inspiration have already occurred. The biblical canon (Genesis–Revelation) is complete. It alone is the normative basis of our evangelical faith and practice.

Illumination and communication, however, are happening every day. Through the teaching ministry of the Holy Spirit, we can understand the true meaning of the Scriptures and we can teach that truth to others.[6] "Now we have received, not the spirit of the world, but the Spirit who is from God, that we might know the things that have been freely given to us by God" (2:12). The Spirit teaches us from within us as we read and hear the Word of God, and He can teach us through what He has taught others.

There is only one divinely intended meaning in each biblical passage, although the Spirit can apply that truth to various life situations. Unfortunately well-intentioned readers of Scripture differ over that one intended meaning. Roy Zuck has listed four criteria by which we should judge an interpretation: the spirituality of the interpreter, logical consistency, the harmonization of Scripture with Scripture, and the viewpoint of historic evangelical Christianity.[7] He concludes: "All four tests are necessary. Each is a test of harmony: the interpreter's life must be in harmony with the Spirit, the interpreter's thinking must be in harmony with the laws of logical thinking; the interpreter's Scriptural views must harmonize with the rest of Scripture; and his views must harmonize with the stream of Christian theology. If any of these tests is disregarded, inaccurate views may be admitted, and the Bible content of Christian education may be susceptible to misinterpretation and insufficient application."[8]

Thus we can know the meaning of God's Word as we read and study it in prayerful dependence on the Spirit, as we consult study helps (such as

Bible maps and dictionaries), and as we double-check our interpretations with the opinions of other Spirit-directed believers (through personal conversations, sermons, and commentaries).

He enables us to proclaim the message. We are not sufficient in ourselves to communicate the true meaning of the Word of God to others. God, however, does not command us to witness without first giving us the enablement to do so. That ability is found in the indwelling Holy Spirit.

Christ informed the apostles that they would be witnesses to the entire world once the Holy Spirit came upon them (Acts 1:8). Charles Swindoll presents four key changes that the Spirit worked in the apostles' lives.[9] First, their human frailties were transformed into supernatural gifts and abilities. Second, their fearful reluctance was transformed into bold confidence. Third, their fears and intimidation were transformed into a sense of invincibility. Fourth, their lonely, grim feelings of abandonment were transformed into joyful perseverance.

Paul himself said his speech and preaching (that is, his content and style of proclamation) were "not with persuasive words of human wisdom, but in demonstration of the Spirit and of power" (1 Cor. 2:4). He also admitted that his proclamation of the gospel came not "in word only, but also in power, and in the Holy Spirit" (1 Thess. 1:5).

Peter claimed that his believing readers heard the message of salvation from those who preached the gospel to them "by the Holy Spirit sent from heaven" (1 Pet. 1:12).

Both in evangelism and teaching, we must allow the Holy Spirit to permeate our motivation, to select our content, and to craft our rhetoric. Paul testified, "These things we also speak, not in words which man's wisdom teaches but which the Holy Spirit teaches, comparing spiritual things with spiritual" (1 Cor. 2:13). The Spirit within us can teach the true meaning of the Spirit-inspired Scriptures to others who are also indwelt by the Spirit.

In Relationship to Holiness

He produces righteous character. The citizens of the spiritual kingdom of God should be identified by "righteousness and peace and joy in the Holy Spirit" (Rom. 14:17). Outward, legalistic conformity to religious traditions only constructs a facade for self-righteous pride. As someone has well said, reputation is what people think we are; character is what God knows we are.

True Christian character can be produced only by total yieldedness to the indwelling Spirit. Paul described godly character in this way: "But the fruit of the Spirit is love, joy, peace, longsuffering, kindness, goodness, faithfulness, gentleness, self-control" (Gal. 5:22–23). These are nine characteristics of the believer who is spiritual, controlled by the Spirit. Just as edible fruit is not produced in one moment, neither is the fruit of the Spirit. It is His fruit, produced by Him as His life flows through us.

In another analogy, we must sow to the Spirit and not to the flesh (6:7–8). Whenever we do, we will reap the essence of everlasting life, namely, the abundant life that exalts Christ (John 10:10).

He enables us to serve God. In this church age believers should serve God "in the newness of the Spirit and not in the oldness of the letter" (Rom. 7:6). Spirit-controlled living stresses grace and not law. It is marked by freedom, freshness, and faith.

Paul saw himself as a "minister of Jesus Christ to the Gentiles, ministering the gospel of God, that the offering of the Gentiles might be acceptable, sanctified by the Holy Spirit" (15:16). Successful service must be controlled and set apart by the Spirit. Genuine spiritual transformation within true converts can be achieved only by Him. Unfortunately in our flesh we can fabricate faulty professions and assume a false spirituality. Converts are easy to obtain, but disciples of Christ are more difficult to develop.

We should seek to "commend ourselves as ministers of God . . . by purity, by knowledge, by longsuffering, by kindness, by the Holy Spirit, by sincere love" (2 Cor. 6:4, 6). Why did Paul mention the Spirit in this list of moral virtues? It is because apart from Him, these qualities are not possible. Apart from Him, no believer can be a commendable servant of God.

He guides us. Daily guidance in the development of personal holiness comes through the Holy Spirit. His leading is in holiness, not apart from it. Just as the Son of God, Jesus Christ, was led daily by the Spirit, so must we be led by Him (Rom. 8:14). His leading is always in moral truth according to the Scriptures. His guidance is always in the good, acceptable, and pleasing will of God (12:2).

He gives courage. One day I was walking through a shopping mall when I noticed a young man wearing a T-shirt with these words printed in bold letters: "No Retreat! No Return! No Regret!" Underneath those three exclamations was this verse: "For God has not given us a spirit of fear, but of power and of love and of a sound mind" (2 Tim. 1:7). Exactly! God the Holy Spirit is the source of power, love, and right thinking. He is not the source of fear.

A Spirit-filled believer is not timid, afraid of other people or even of himself. He respects his satanically controlled enemies, but he does not fear them. Fear is the opposite of faith. When we walk by faith, controlled by the Spirit, we will not be afraid. The shepherd-psalmist rejoiced, "Yea, though I walk through the valley of the shadow of death, I will fear no evil; for you are with me; your rod and your staff, they comfort me" (Ps. 23:4). We can have the same confidence because the Holy Spirit permanently indwells us.

He changes us into Christlikeness. "Now the Lord is the Spirit; and where the Spirit of the Lord is, there is liberty. But we all, with unveiled face, beholding as in a mirror the glory of the Lord, are being transformed into the same image from glory to glory, just as by the Spirit of the Lord" (2 Cor. 3:17–18). As we read the Scriptures and see Christ revealed in its pages, the Holy Spirit changes us into the moral character of Christ. He changes us from the inside out. As we submit to Christ, the Spirit can cause us to be like Him. We can glorify Christ as we manifest His character in us. We experience a spiritual metamorphosis. The Greek verb *metamorphomai* ("to transform") is the same verb used of Christ's "metamorphosis" on the Mount of Transfiguration (Matt. 17:2). The glory of His deity manifested itself through the human flesh and garments of Christ. Similarly, as the Spirit of God changes us into Christlikeness, others will be able to see the glory of the indwelling Christ.

IMPLICATIONS FOR US

First, we must realize that the Holy Spirit is indispensable to the process of salvation. He set us apart before we were saved, regenerated us, and continues to work in us. We need to know the full scope of His ministry in order that we might better relate to Him.

Second, we must understand the essence of true spirituality. It consists in what we are and what we are becoming. We must not equate it with abilities or mere knowledge of biblical facts. Instead, we must manifest true spiritual character in true spiritual conduct.

Third, we must not substitute programs for the person of the Spirit. We cannot become spiritual through mere participation in spiritual seminars and retreats. We must not equate the euphoria of high-powered, well-planned conferences with the achievement of genuine spirituality. Nor does spirituality come automatically through the reading of books on the Holy Spirit and spirituality.

Fourth, we must seek a one-on-one relationship with the Spirit. We must pray, walk, and serve in the Spirit. We must be taught, led, and controlled by Him.

CHAPTER TWELVE

The Gifts of the Holy Spirit

What is your spiritual gift? Some Christians are confused when they first hear that question. They are not aware that spiritual gifts exist. They do not know what they are, nor do they know whether they have one. Other Christians do not seem to appreciate the importance of spiritual gifts; they either abuse or neglect them. Still other believers, fortunately, do understand the biblical nature and usage of spiritual gifts.

THEIR NATURE

Lists of Gifts

The New Testament records five lists of the spiritual gifts, four by Paul and one by Peter. No two lists are identical. James Boyer remarked that "these gifts were not a fixed and unchanging catalog or just so many specific functions in the church."[1] Twenty gifts are mentioned by name, with the possibility that two may refer to the same gift. There may be other spiritual gifts not mentioned by name in the Scriptures.

Romans 12:3–8. In our position of salvation and in our practice of spiritual gifts, we should be humble and thankful. Each gifted believer is like a body part or member. Each believer therefore has a different function to perform. All gifted believers are one in Christ and should manifest interdependence on one another.

Paul then gave this listing: "Having then gifts differing according to the grace that is given to us, let us use them: if prophecy, let us prophesy in proportion to our faith; or ministry, let us use it in our ministering; he who teaches, in teaching; he who exhorts, in exhortation; he who gives, with liberality; he who leads, with diligence; he who shows mercy, with cheerfulness" (12:6–8). Paul here listed seven gifts: prophecy, ministry, teaching, exhortation, giving, leadership, and showing mercy.

1 Corinthians 12:4–11. There are diverse gifts, ministries, and activities. The Holy Spirit, the Lord Jesus Christ, and God the Father provide and energize the gifts. Every believer has received a gift, a manifestation of the Spirit, and should use it for the profit of all other believers.

Paul then gave this listing: "For to one is given the word of wisdom through the Spirit, to another the word of knowledge through the same Spirit, to another faith by the same Spirit, to another gifts of healings by the same Spirit, to another the working of miracles, to another prophecy, to another discerning of spirits, to another different kinds of tongues, to another the interpretation of tongues" (12:8–10). Paul here listed nine gifts: wisdom, knowledge, faith, healings, miracles, prophecy, discernment of spirits, speaking in tongues, and interpretation of tongues.

The Spirit energizes the gifts, and distributes them to each believer as He sovereignly chooses.

1 Corinthians 12:28–30. The body of Christ and the church are synonymous. Each member of the body of Christ is thus in the true church.

Paul then gave this listing: "And God has appointed these in the church: first apostles, second prophets, third teachers, after that miracles, then gifts of healings, helps, administrations, varieties of tongues. Are all apostles? Are all prophets? Are all teachers? Are all workers of miracles? Do all have gifts of healings? Do all speak with tongues? Do all interpret?" (12:28–30). Paul here listed nine gifts: apostles, prophets, teachers, miracles, healings, helps, administration, tongue-speaking, and interpretation of tongues.

Paul ranked some of these gifts in importance, from the gift of apostleship to the gift of interpretation of tongues (12:28). In a series of questions he pointed out that not all believers have the same gift (12:29–30).

Ephesians 4:7–16. After His death and resurrection, Christ ascended to heaven to become the head of the church (4:7–10; see also 1:20–23). He gave gifts to believers and gifted leaders to the church (4:8, 11).

Paul then gave this listing: "And He Himself gave some to be apostles, some prophets, some evangelists, and some pastors and teachers" (4:11). Paul here listed four gifts: apostles, prophets, evangelists, and pastor-teachers. There may be a difference between pastors and teachers, although most commentators see one group with a double function.

These gifted leaders are supposed to equip the saints so that the trained saints will minister and cause the body of Christ to mature (4:12–16).

1 Peter 4:10–11. Every believer has received a gift. Each should therefore minister to one another. As each gifted believer serves one another, he reveals that he is a good steward of what God has entrusted to him.

Peter then gave this listing: "If anyone speaks, let him speak as the oracles of God. If anyone ministers, let him do it as with the ability which God supplies, that in all things God may be glorified through Jesus Christ, to whom belong the glory and the dominion forever and ever. Amen" (4:11). Here Peter listed two gifts: speaking and ministering.

Dedicated believers can speak divine content with divine authority, ministering with the ability God has provided. By exercising their gifts, they can glorify God.

Meaning of Gifts

Contrasts with general commands. God has issued general commands to all believers. We all should exhort one another (Heb. 10:25), but only some have the actual gift of exhortation. We all should give (2 Cor. 9:7), but only some have the actual gift of giving. We all should walk by faith (5:7), but only some have the actual gift of faith. We all should witness for Christ (Acts 1:8), but only some have the actual gift of evangelist. We should all test truth claims and their advocates (1 Thess. 5:21), but only some have the actual gift of discerning spirits.

Contrasts with natural talents. Charles Ryrie claimed that natural talents are given by God through one's parents to benefit others, that skills are learned throughout life to benefit others, and that spiritual gifts are given by the Holy Spirit at conversion to benefit the church.[2] Of course, all abilities and opportunities ultimately come from God, to whom we should be most thankful (1 Cor. 4:7). Ryrie honestly admitted: "I am frank to acknowledge that I do not always know what differences would be seen, for instance, between a naturally talented teacher, a teacher who has been well trained, and one who has been given the spiritual gift of teaching."[3] Both Ferguson [4] and Erickson[5] agree with Ryrie, and I concur with all of them.

Since God has an eternal plan in which believers have been chosen in Christ before the foundation of the world, it is very plausible to believe that God programmed our genetic code and disposition before we were born and before we were saved. At conversion, the Holy Spirit entered us and caused us to use those talents and skills for the glory of Christ. He also gifted us to have spiritual impact on other believers through our areas of ministry.[6]

Contrast with office. A believer can have the gift of teaching without having the formal office of a teacher in a college or seminary. Both men and women may have the gift of pastoring without holding the office of senior pastor in a local church.

The Bible Department at Cedarville College, which I chaired at the time, invited Dr. Lucy Mabery-Foster, associate professor of pastoral ministries at Dallas Seminary, to lecture on the place of women in the ministry. In her excellent presentation she said she believes God has given her the gift of pastoring, but she also stated that the church office of pastor should be held only by males. Ryrie also affirms this position. So do I.

The demarcation between gift and office can be seen throughout Scripture. David had the gift of prophecy, but he did not have the office of prophet. Philip had four virgin daughters who had the gift of prophecy, but they did not have the office (Acts 21:8–9), whereas Agabus had both the gift and office of prophet (21:10).

Spiritual in essence. The Greek construction *tōn pneumatikōn* ("spiritual gifts," 1 Cor. 12:1) can be translated as either "spiritual things" or "spiritual persons."[7] That's because the Greek can be understood as either neuter or masculine. It is difficult to distinguish between the gift and the person who has the gift. In both situations the Holy Spirit lives inside the child of God and enables him to have a spiritual relationship and ministry to others. The gift is "the manifestation of the Spirit" (12:7). Paul explained: "But one and the same Spirit works all these things, distributing to each one individually as He wills" (12:11). A spiritual gift then is an ability given to a Christian by the Holy Spirit and controlled by the Spirit for spiritual service and growth.

Functions of divine grace. Paul also called the gifts *charismata* (Rom. 12:6; 1 Cor. 12:4), a word based on *charis* ("grace").

Thus spiritual gifts are gifts of grace. We did not deserve salvation, but God redeemed us by His grace (Eph. 2:8–9). Also, we do not deserve to serve Him, but God has given us abilities out of His grace to serve Him.

Thus a spiritual gift is an ability given to the Christian out of the grace of God through the Holy Spirit and controlled by the Spirit in spiritual service and growth.

Divinely given. Each person of the Godhead is involved in bestowing spiritual gifts. Paul wrote, "There are diversities of gifts, but the same Spirit. There are differences of ministries, but the same Lord. And there are diversities of activities, but it is the same God who works all in all" (1 Cor. 12:4–6). These are sovereign impartations of spiritual ability, given as God desires (12:11, 18). They cannot be gained through human initiative or produced by praying for them.

Designed to edify. The gifts were never intended to be used in isolation for a person to edify himself. Instead, believers are to use their spiritual gifts for the profit of the church (1 Cor. 12:7).

"From whom [Christ] the whole body, joined and knit together by what every joint supplies, according to the effective working by which every part does its share, causes growth of the body for the edifying of itself in love" (Eph. 4:16). Within the body of Christ, every believer must function as the Spirit energizes him. Every believer must be engaged in "the work of ministry" (4:12). God never intended that Christian work be done only by professional Christian workers. We are all "created in Christ Jesus for good works" (2:10). Thus every believer should actively participate in a local church, the manifestation of the true church in a given location.

THEIR DESCRIPTION

Apostle

The Greek *apostolos* ("apostle") comes from the verb *apostellō,* "to send away with a commission to do something." The original twelve apostles were selected from among many disciples to be with Christ and to be sent by Him to preach, heal, and cast out demons. Their ministry at that time was restricted to the Jewish world (Matt. 10:5–8; Mark 3:13–15). After His resurrection Christ reappointed the group of eleven to preach the gospel to all peoples (Matt. 28:16–20).

Apostles thus were believers who had seen the resurrected Christ and who had been commissioned directly by Him to preach and to lay the foundation for the church age (1 Cor. 9:1; Eph. 2:20). Their ministries were authenticated by the performance of miracles and healings (Acts 5:12; 2 Cor. 12:12). They possessed both administrative and prophetic authority over the churches.

Only a few males had the gift and office of apostleship: the Twelve, Paul (Rom. 1:1), Barnabas (Acts 14:14), and James (Gal. 1:19). Others, such as Titus and Timothy, had delegated apostolic authority, but they did not have the office.

Some say missionaries are apostles. Although there are some general similarities, contemporary missionaries have not seen the resurrected Christ and have not been authenticated by signs and wonders.

Prophet

Although the gift and the office of apostleship were given only at the beginning of the church age, the gift and the office of prophet can be seen in both the Old Testament era and the outset of the church age.

Moses became the pattern of all future prophets within Israel (Deut. 18:15–22). The fulfillment of short-range predictions authenticated the genuine prophet. Prophets spoke the very words God put on their lips (Jer. 1:9). They were both foretellers and forthtellers. Their proclamations, therefore, were authoritative and infallible.

Some advocates of the charismatic movement today claim that modern prophets have divinely given insight but not necessarily infallibility. They believe that such prophets can be wrong in their counsel and predictions. They also assert that the prophetic declarations do not supplant the Scriptures as the normative basis of faith and practice. To me, this seems like an attempt to keep the title of prophet without having the biblical essence of a prophet.

Both the New Testament apostles and prophets laid the foundation of the church (Eph. 2:20). Only a few people were specifically named as prophets: Agabus (Acts 11:27–28), some anonymous leaders at Antioch (13:1), and some believers at Corinth (1 Cor. 14:29).

Some prophets only spoke, whereas others both spoke and wrote. In either case, what they said and wrote became the standard of doctrine and behavior. A prophetic message produced edification, exhortation, and consolation (14:3). Apparently the apostles and the writers of the New Testament had the gift of prophecy, although some of them did not have the office of prophet.

Evangelist

Christ gave the gift and office of evangelist to some (Eph. 4:11). However, only Philip is actually denoted as an evangelist (Acts 21:8). Paul encouraged Timothy to do the work of an evangelist, so he may also have had the gift and office (2 Tim. 4:5).

The Greek word *euangelistēs* ("evangelist") denotes one who is committed to the proclamation of the gospel of Jesus Christ. Literally, he is a "good-news person." Little is known about the specific work of New Testament evangelists. Modern-day preachers, such as Billy Graham, are known as evangelists. It is uncertain, however, whether such men have the same gifted office Philip and Timothy had.

Pastor

The Greek *poimēn* ("pastor") is usually translated "shepherd." Christ, of course, is the great and good Shepherd of the sheep (John 10:14; Heb. 13:20).

Like a shepherd with sheep, a pastor feeds, provides for, and protects those under his care. *Poimēn* is used only once to describe the leader of a local church (Eph. 4:11).

The terms *elder* and *bishop* are also used of the pastor (Acts 20:17, 28; 1 Tim. 3:1–7; Titus 1:5–9; 1 Pet. 5:1–4). The term *presbyteros* ("elder") depicts a mature believer who presides over others. The noun *episkopos* ("bishop"), literally "one who has oversight," describes one who has spiritual supervision of others. Both within Israel and the church, the office of spiritual administrator was restricted to men.

A pastor also had the gift of teaching, although a person could teach without having the gift of pastoring (Eph. 4:11).

Teacher

A believer who has the gift of teaching has the "ability to explain and apply the truths which had been already received by the church."[8] Both men and women can understand the truth of the Spirit-inspired Scriptures through the teaching ministry of the Holy Spirit. The Spirit can also guide them as they seek to communicate that truth to others. As they merge content with pedagogical technique, they have Spirit-given insight to relate the Word of God to contemporary experiences and needs.

I have personally admired men like John MacArthur, Charles Ryrie, Charles Swindoll, and Warren Wiersbe. They have the Spirit-given ability to put complex, profound truth into simple, clearly illustrated statements. They stimulate interest and guide our learning process. They do more than disseminate facts; they also impact lives.

Wisdom

The "word of wisdom" refers to the revelation of the mind of God in doctrinal, redemptive areas (1 Cor. 2:6–7). This wisdom was not learned or acquired, but divinely imparted. Peter acknowledged that Paul wrote his epistles "according to the wisdom given to him" (2 Pet. 3:15). Paul asserted that Christ directly revealed redemptive truth to him (Gal. 1:11–12). Paul had instantaneous understanding of this imparted wisdom.

Some contemporaries claim they have the word of wisdom. They assert that God has revealed His mind to them concerning relevant issues, such as: Should we construct a new church building? Or, should we begin a television program? Or, there is someone in the audience who got a divorce last week. However, these contemporary claims and definitions do not agree with the biblical explanation of divinely revealed wisdom, necessary for the writing of Scriptures and the laying of the doctrinal foundation of the church.

Knowledge

The "word of knowledge" may have referred to the revelation of exhortations in practical areas of life. Directions concerning the roles of husbands, wives, parents, children, slaves, and slave owners (Eph. 5:22–6:9) may fall within the scope of the gift of knowledge. All believers should grow in spiritual knowledge through prayerful study (2 Pet. 3:18).

Family life counselors, such as James Dobson and Dennis Rainey, certainly have related the knowledge of the Scriptures to real-life problems. These leaders, however, have not been given divinely revealed knowledge beyond that given in the Scriptures.

Faith

All believers are justified by faith and should walk by faith. The gift of faith, however, was a Spirit-given capacity to attempt great tasks for God. It seems to be associated with outward demonstrations of God's power. Paul saw it as a faith that could "remove mountains" (1 Cor. 13:2).

Healings

The "gift of healings" is expressed in the plural, not the singular. It is not the gift of healing, but the gift of healings. This capacity was the ability to heal the sick of various physical problems: leprosy, lameness, palsy, and other afflictions that were beyond medical help. In cases of healing recorded in the Bible, people were restored to normal health immediately. Several apostles had the gift of healings. Peter and John, for example, healed a lame man (Acts 3:1–10), Peter healed a paralytic (9:32–35), and Paul delivered a demon-possessed slave girl from demonism (16:16–18), raised dead Eutychus back to life (20:7–12), and healed a sick official on the island of Malta and others on the island who were sick (28:7–8).

God can heal directly and indirectly. He can sovereignly remove physical afflictions from both the saved and the unsaved. He can graciously respond to the petition for healing uttered by the cry of intense faith. He can also heal through the expertise of the medical profession and the power of medicine. All healings, ultimately, are caused by His gracious mercy.

While God can and does heal, it is doubtful anyone has the gift of healings today. Many who have had the reputation of being faith healers, such as Jack Coe, Kathryn Kuhlman, and John Wimber, have themselves developed cancer and heart problems. They did not have the ability to heal themselves, nor did any others have the gift to heal them.

Miracles

The gift of working miracles involved remarkable power. Jesus performed miracles when He caused the wind over the Sea of Galilee to stop, when He multiplied bread and fish to feed the hungry, and when He raised the dead. Peter struck both Ananias and Sapphira dead (Acts 5:1–11), and Paul imposed blindness on Elymas (13:11). God authenticated His spokesmen, like Moses, Elijah, and the apostles, by miracles He performed through them (2 Cor. 12:12; Heb. 2:3–4).

The term *miracle* has been so misapplied that it has lost its distinctive biblical meaning. In a cartoon, Ziggy exclaimed, "I play golf religiously. If I make a shot, it's a miracle!" When a person walks away unhurt from a terrible car accident, he may call his deliverance a miracle. Biblical miracles, however, pointed their observers to the presence and activity of God. They created awe and wonder at the Lord's power. The onlookers knew that the miracle was not a freak accident of history.

Discernment

The gift of "discerning of spirits" was the ability to "discern the true from the false sources of supernatural revelation given in oral form."[9] Before the completion of the New Testament, God revealed truth through both writing and oral pronouncements. Satan, the master of delusion, used many false prophets and teachers in attempts to lead believers into moral and doctrinal error. Believers, possessing the gift of discernment, thus could distinguish between truth and error.

Today all believers should test truth-claims by the Word of God. We are instructed to "test all things; hold fast what is good" (1 Thess. 5:21). John appealed, "Beloved, do not believe every spirit, but test the spirits, whether they are of God; because many false prophets have gone out into the world" (1 John 4:1).

Bankers and government agents diligently study the detailed features of genuine paper money. Thus they can easily detect counterfeits. Likewise, as believers study the Scriptures we are better equipped to detect false teachings.

Speaking in Tongues

The gift of tongues was the Spirit-given ability to speak in foreign languages and dialects. The people with this gift spoke languages they had not spoken or learned before. The content of the speaking was the revelation of divine mysteries (1 Cor. 14:2). (This gift is discussed in chapter 13.)

Interpretation of Tongues

The gift of interpretation was the Spirit-given ability to provide translation of the tongues-utterance for others to understand what was said. [10] Because the interpreter did not naturally know the language or the meaning of the utterance, he or she needed this spiritual gift. (This gift is also discussed in chapter 13.)

Helps

The gift of helps is mentioned only once (1 Cor. 12:28). The Greek term *antilēmpsis* is based on the verb *antilambanomai,* which occurs three times (Luke 1:54; Acts 20:35; 1 Tim. 6:2) and is translated "helped," "support," and "benefited." The disadvantaged, Paul said, could be helped by income-producing labor, compassionate concern of others for them, and the willingness to give as Jesus directed (Acts 20:34–35). The gift thus may have centered on the deliverance of the needy through material means.

Administration

The gift of administration, *kybernēsis*, is mentioned only once (1 Cor. 12:28). A related noun, *kybernētēs*, is rendered "helmsman" (Acts 27:11) and "shipmaster" (Rev. 18:17). The captain of a sailing vessel guided the ship on its intended course. Thus a person with the gift of administration has the Spirit-given ability to guide the local church toward its divinely intended mission.

Ministry

While the gift of ministry is mentioned only twice (1 Cor. 12:7; 1 Pet. 4:11), the Greek term *diakonia* ("service" or "ministry") is very common. It is used of the ministry of Martha (Luke 10:40), the apostles (Acts 1:17, 25), Paul and Barnabas (Acts 12:25), saints in Ephesus (Eph. 4:12), Archippus (Col. 4:17), and Timothy (2 Tim. 4:5). The similar Greek word *diakonos* ("servant") refers to deacons (1 Tim. 3:8, 12), government officials (Rom. 13:4), Phoebe (16:1), Tychicus (Eph. 6:21), Epaphras (Col. 1:7), Timothy (1 Thess. 3:2), and Paul (Col. 1:23, 25).

The verb *diakoneō* is used of general serving, both in mundane and spiritual matters. It is also used of the function of deacons (1 Tim. 3:10, 13).

All believers should serve one another, even as Jesus served us (Matt. 20:28). God, however, has given a special gift of ministry to some. They are more concerned about serving others than meeting their own needs.

Exhortation

The gift of exhortation could also be called the gift of encouragement (Rom. 12:8). The Greek verb *parakaleō* literally means "to call beside." It is the same verb that depicts the Holy Spirit as the believers' Helper or Comforter.

This gifted person is able to relate to people and their needs, and to empathize with them. He can help people move from pessimism to optimism. He can encourage them as he applies the Scriptures to their difficulties.

Giving

All believers should give, but God has entrusted the gift of giving only to some (Rom. 12:8). A person with the spiritual gift of giving is marked by liberality, a freedom to give of one's resources, time, and energy.

Jesus distinguished between giving and the gift of giving when He observed the Jews at the treasury in the temple (Luke 21:1–4). The rich gave much, but the widow manifested the gift of giving when she gave all she had. Her giving was motivated by love, thanksgiving, and worship. She gave sacrificially.

Leadership

The Greek verb *proistēmi* ("to lead," Rom. 12:8) literally means "to stand before." The one who has the gift of leadership thus stands before other believers to guide them and to assist them in their spiritual development.

The verb is used to describe the work of elders (1 Thess. 5:12; 1 Tim. 5:17). One of the qualifications of the bishop-pastor-elder is that he rules well his own household (3:4, 5, 12).

He is no mere visionary, because he must lead "with diligence" (Rom. 12:8). His plans must be practical and attainable. He must give his full attention to the mission of the congregation.

Mercy

All believers have received mercy from God, and all should show mercy to others. However, some have received the gift of mercy (Rom. 12:8), the unusual ability to emphathize and to extend kindness and cheer to others. What they do and how they do it combine to bring hope and sunshine into the lives of others.

THEIR EXTENT

Are the gifts permanent or temporary? Should we expect to see these gifts operating today? Evangelicals hold one of two major positions on these questions. Some say all these gifts are for today, and others say some, not all, of the gifts are to be exercised today.

The View That All Gifts Are for Today

Pentecostalists, charismatics, and people in the so-called Third Wave movement all promote this view, sometimes called the noncessationist view. Donald Gee claimed, "There is nothing in Scripture, reason or experience to make us believe that the gifts are not for today—everyone of them."[11] These advocates present several arguments in support of their position.

Spiritual gifts continue until the second coming of Christ. Paul claimed that the gifts of prophecy, tongues, and knowledge would end when "that which is perfect has come" (1 Cor. 13:10). They identify "the perfect" with the second coming of Christ, the Millennium, or the eternal state. They claim that the gifts will function until we see Christ "face to face" (13:12). The Bible, however, never equates "the perfect" with the return of Christ. The Greek phrase *to teleion* ("the perfect") actually refers to the climax of a process, the movement from immaturity to maturity, whereas the coming of Christ is an instantaneous event (15:51–58; 1 Thess. 4:13–18).

Noncessationists point out that Paul wrote that he did not want the Corinthians to "come short" in the exercise of any gift, "eagerly waiting for the revelation of our Lord Jesus Christ" (1 Cor. 1:7). Proponents of this view assert that this verse means that believers will exercise all the spiritual gifts right up to the time Christ returns. This verse, however, is not a prediction. It is a description of their spiritual condition: They were blessed with gifts and they were waiting for Christ.

"Spiritual gifts are for the entire church." Noncessationists argue that since God gave gifts to believers to function as members in the body of Christ, present-day body-members must also be gifted.

However, as Ryrie correctly observed, "Actually, it is no argument to say that every gift must appear in every generation of the history of the church so that no generation will be slighted. If a gift is given once, it is given to the entire church. For instance, the gift of apostleship given to Saul of Tarsus is a gift to the entire church in all generations. We still profit today from that gift given once in the first century."[12]

"Spiritual gifts are signs of the gospel." In Mark's account of the Great Commission, Christ said, "And these signs will follow those who believe: In My name they will cast out demons; they will speak with new tongues; they will take up serpents; and if they drink anything deadly, it will by no means hurt them; they will lay hands on the sick, and they will recover" (16:17–18). Advocates of noncessationism claim that all five signs mentioned in this passage will continue so long as the gospel is being preached.

However, the authenticity of this passage has been disputed for centuries. The longer ending of Mark (16:9–20) is not found in most ancient manuscripts, as pointed out in most English study Bibles. Thus it is wise not to seek to prove or disprove any theological position from this passage.

In addition, these signs actually confirmed the oral proclamations of only the apostles: "And they went out and preached everywhere, the Lord working with them and confirming the word through the accompanying signs" (16:20). The signs could be seen only in that first generation of converts, saved under the direct ministries of the apostles. The five signs ceased when the apostles died.

The Third Wave movement claims that signs and wonders are necessary to confirm the power of the gospel to a pagan world, normally identified as Third-world countries marked by spiritism and superstition. If that position were true, then there would be no need for such signs in Christianized countries such as the United States. This claim is actually an argument against their position.

"Spiritual gifts can be gained by faith." Advocates claim that the gifts disappeared from church history because Christians failed to seek them by faith. Believers either lacked faith to obtain them or they did not believe the gifts were available to them. However, spiritual gifts are not given in response to prayer or faith. They are sovereignly given by the Spirit, "distributing to each one individually as He wills" (1 Cor. 12:11).

"God can do today what He did in the early church." Proponents of this view often point to Hebrews 13:8 for support of their position: "Jesus

Christ is the same yesterday, today, and forever." Of course, it is true that Jesus Christ is unchangeable in His divine personhood, for His essence and character are immutable. However, this passage says nothing about spiritual gifts; it doesn't even hint that the gifts are permanent. Furthermore, God's program does change. For example, Christ once told the apostles to preach only to Jews (Matt. 10:5–6), but He later charged them to preach to everyone (28:18–20).

Some noncessationists claim that since "the gifts and the calling of God are irrevocable" (Rom. 11:29), all the spiritual gifts must still be with us. No spiritual gifts, however, are mentioned in this verse. Paul was referring to the promises of salvation, given to both Israel and the church. He assured believers that God would complete His plan of redemption, beginning with election and concluding with ultimate glorification (8:28–39). God will never take back the gift of eternal life from a believer.

"Spiritual gifts are to be exercised in the latter rain." Pentecostals claim that the prophecy of Joel, quoted by Peter on the Day of Pentecost, has a double fulfillment (Joel 2:28–32; Acts 2:15–21). It was fulfilled first in the apostolic church of the first century, and it is being fulfilled for a second time in the contemporary church. They equate the "former rain" mentioned in Joel 2:23 with the outpouring of the Spirit in the early church and the "latter rain" in the same verse with the manifestations of the Spirit in the twentieth century.

However, these predictions in Joel were given to Israel, not to the church (2:23, 27; 3:1). The rains are literal rains, water from clouds, that will produce abundant crops in Israel. The early rain comes in the fall and the latter rain in the spring. The outpouring of the Spirit will happen when God intervenes on behalf of Israel at Christ's second coming to the earth at the end of the tribulation. The heavenly and earthly wonders mentioned in Joel 2:30–31 never occurred on the Day of Pentecost (Acts 2:19–20).

The View That Some Gifts Are for Today

Cessationists, including myself, believe that some spiritual gifts ceased to function during the first century, the time when the apostles ministered and the New Testament was written. Some of those gifts were *revelatory* gifts—gifts exercised when God revealed truth that became the normative basis of faith and practice. Those revelatory gifts included the gifts of apostle, prophet, wisdom, and knowledge.

Other temporary gifts were *sign or authenticating gifts.* God confirmed the revelation of truth through these gifts operating in the apostles, prophets, and their converts. Those gifts were faith, healings, miracles, discernment, tongues, and the interpretation of tongues.

The remaining gifts could be called *sustaining gifts.* God continues to give them in order for the church to sustain itself through the Holy Spirit and the Scriptures. These gifts are evangelist, pastor, teacher, helps, administration, serving, encouragement, giving, leadership, and mercy.

The following arguments demonstrate that the revelatory and the sign gifts ceased during the apostolic period.

God authenticated only the apostles and the prophets. In demonstrating the superiority of Christianity over Judaism, the author of the Book of Hebrews wrote, "How shall we escape if we neglect so great a salvation, which at the first began to be spoken by the Lord, and was confirmed to us by those who heard Him, God also bearing witness both with signs and wonders, with various miracles, and gifts of the Holy Spirit, according to His own will?" (Heb. 2:3–4). These verses point up a threefold sequence of revelation: the Lord, those who heard Him (the apostles), and "us" (including the author). God bore witness to the gospel message through confirming signs done by the apostles and observed by their followers.

Paul testified to the church at Corinth: "Truly the signs of an apostle were accomplished among you with all perseverance, in signs and wonders and mighty deeds" (2 Cor. 12:12). These phenomena were the signs of an apostle, not of an average believer.

Paul expressed the same truth to the church at Rome: "For I will not dare to speak of any of those things which Christ has not accomplished through me, in word and deed, to make the Gentiles obedient—in mighty signs and wonders, by the power of the Spirit of God, so that from Jerusalem and round about to Illyricum I have fully preached the gospel of Christ" (Rom. 15:18–19). God authenticated Paul's apostolic ministry to the Gentiles with signs and wonders. He exercised them as he preached in Gentile regions where the name of Christ was not known (15:20–21).

The foundation of the church was laid in the apostolic period. The church is "built on the foundation of the apostles and prophets, Jesus Christ Himself being the chief cornerstone" (Eph. 2:20). This "foundation" is the redemptive truth centered in the person of Jesus Christ and His atoning death and resurrection (1 Cor. 3:11; 15:1–4). The apostles and New Testament prophets laid the foundation as they evangelized others and wrote New Testament books. The foundation was completed when the last apostle died. Although the church has continued to grow through the centuries, the foundation has remained firm and constant. No new foundation can ever be built. The revelatory and sign gifts validated the foundation, the doctrinal basis for church belief and behavior. The purposes for those gifts ceased when the apostles and prophets completed their tasks.

Tongues-speaking was a sign to Israel. Paul wrote, "Therefore tongues are for a sign, not to those who believe but to unbelievers" (1 Cor. 14:22). Specifically he meant Jewish unbelievers. In the preceding verse he wrote, "In the law it is written: 'with men of other tongues and other lips I will speak to this people, and yet, for all that, they will not hear Me' says the Lord" (14:21). Israel was "this people" and "the men of other tongues and other lips" were the invading Assyrians (Isa. 28:11–21).

The church at Corinth met next door to the Jewish synagogue (Acts 18:7). When the Gentile believers spoke in tongues, it was a sign to the unbelieving Jews that God was about to judge Israel. The Romans destroyed Jerusalem, the temple, and the sacrificial system in A.D. 70. Thus the significance of the gift of tongues ended then.

Silence in later books. In the New Testament books written after 1 Corinthians, no mention is made of the revelatory and sign gifts. The qualifications of pastors and deacons do not include the sign gifts (1 Tim. 3:1–13; Titus 1:5–9). In their rebuke and correction of personal lifestyles and church problems, the biblical authors did not refer to these special gifts. Christ criticized the seven churches for errors of life and doctrine, but He did not discuss spiritual gifts (Rev. 2–3). The revelatory and sign gifts, described in the early life of the apostolic church, passed away in the first century as God's purpose for them was completed.

Decline in healings and miracles. God authenticated the apostles by giving them the ability to heal and to perform miracles. Their early ministries were constantly attested by supernatural powers: the healing of the lame man (Acts 3:1–10); the death judgment of Ananias and Sapphira (5:1–11); many unidentified signs and wonders (5:12); the healing of the paralyzed Aeneas (9:32–35); the raising of Dorcas from the dead (9:36–43); the release of Peter from prison by an angel (12:5–19); the imposition of blindness upon Elymas (13:6–13); the healing of a cripple in Lystra (14:8–10); the resuscitation of Paul from his stoning (14:19–20); the deliverance of the demon-possessed slave girl (16:16–24); the earthquake when Paul and Silas were in prison (16:25–26); and the unusual miraculous ministry at Ephesus (19:11–20).

The ministries of Stephen and Philip, under the authority of the apostles, were also marked by signs and wonders (6:8; 8:5–8).

However, miracles declined in frequency as their intended purpose was fulfilled. God delivered Peter from prison, but He allowed James to be martyred (12:1–19). In his later years, Paul experienced many beatings and imprisonments, but no angel came to deliver him (2 Cor. 11:23–27). He asked God three times to remove an affliction in his body, but God did not do so (12:7–10).

Paul encouraged Timothy, a man of God, to drink some medicinal wine for his intestinal distress and frequent infirmities (1 Tim. 5:23). Why did Paul not heal his beloved associate? Why did Timothy not heal himself? In subsequent correspondence Paul informed Timothy that he left his friend Trophimus "in Miletus sick" (2 Tim. 4:20). Again, why did Paul not heal him if the apostle still had the gift of healings? Apparently, it was the will of God for even the apostles to move from a miraculous to a nonmiraculous lifestyle.[13]

The sovereign purpose of God. God, of course, could do today what He did in early apostolic history. With God all things are possible, for He is omnipotent.

The issue regarding the sign gifts, however, is not His power; it is His purpose. Since God is sovereign, He can also choose not to do today what He did in the first century. He is under no obligation.

In fact, God has always acted in that fashion. He provided manna for forty years as Israel wandered in the wilderness, but that divine provision ceased after the nation entered the Promised Land.

Biblical predictions. No Bible verse predicted that the revelatory and sign gifts would end in the first century. Yet, at the same time, there is no verse that predicted they would continue to function beyond the apostolic period to the return of Christ. If such a verse existed, then the controversy would have never erupted.

In his discussion of spiritual gifts Paul did make this prediction: "Love never fails. But whether there are prophecies, they will fail; whether there are tongues, they will cease; whether there is knowledge, it will vanish away" (1 Cor. 13:8). The verse predicts the end of these three gifts of prophecy, tongues, and knowledge, but it does not give the time when they would end. Since the content of those gifts was divinely revealed truth, the content will continue throughout eternity. The mention of prophecy, tongues, and knowledge, therefore, points to the gift. The gifts would end, but not their content.

The verbs have significance. The verb *katargeō,* used twice, is translated "will fail" and "will vanish away." They are in the passive voice, indicating that the gifts of prophecy and knowledge would be rendered inoperative by someone or by something. The verb *pauō* is translated "will cease." It is in the Greek middle voice, which indicates that the gift of tongues would simply cease on its own. The suggestion of the three verbs is that the gift of tongues would cease before the other two gifts are rendered inoperative.

The coming of "that which is perfect" *(to teleion)* causes the gifts of prophecy and knowledge to end (13:9–10). "For we know in part and we prophesy in part, but when that which is perfect is come, the imperfect will disappear." Noncessationists believe that "the perfect" refers to the return of Christ, so they say the sign gifts continue until that future event.

Cessationists, on the other hand, interpret this prediction in two ways. Some believe the gifts of prophecy and knowledge will end when Christ returns, but tongues will cease before that event. Others, including myself, believe that "the perfect" refers to the completion of the foundation of the church, centered in the completion of the writing of the New Testament. The gifts of prophecy and knowledge ended with the writing of the Book of Revelation, whereas the gift of tongues ceased earlier, probably with the destruction of Jerusalem in A.D. 70.

No one can be absolutely dogmatic in his interpretation of this prediction. However, one's interpretation must be consistent with the teachings of other Scriptures.

IMPLICATIONS FOR US

First, we must distinguish between the gifts of the Spirit and the fruit of the Spirit. Gifts deal with our ability to do, whereas fruit manifests what we are. The essence of gifts is function, whereas the essence of fruit is character.

Second, we need to evaluate our personal interests and abilities. We need to look at our natural abilities, revealed in our IQ, musical aptitude, physical health, linguistic expertise, and other skills. We need to look at our acquired abilities, such as speaking, writing, and administering. What gives us joy? In what areas do we manifest enthusiasm?

Third, we need to take advantage of opportunities to speak, teach, witness, assist, encourage, and study.

Fourth, we need to listen to the counsel of those who are mature and spiritual.

Fifth, we must be faithful in our spiritual commitments—at home, work, and church. We learn the areas of our personal strengths and weaknesses by doing, by taking part, by observing others, and by honestly evaluating our skills.

Sixth, we must be submissive to the will of God and be willing to do anything for Him. We must realize that God has enabled us to work for Him.

Seventh, we must recognize that gifts must be developed through study, practice, and effort. For example, I believe God has given me the gift of pastor-teacher. When I was in a college speech class, I blanked out during a speech. I was nervous and forgot what I had memorized. I could have used that failure as an excuse not to go into the ministry. Instead, I worked harder, outlined better, and became more proficient in speaking and preaching.

CHAPTER THIRTEEN

Speaking in Tongues

The Old Testament nowhere describes the phenomenon of speaking in tongues. It is mentioned in only three New Testament books. It is at the center of the controversy between noncharismatic evangelicalism and the charismatic, Pentecostal position.

LANGUAGE

What was the nature of the biblical phenomenon? Did people speak in known foreign languages and dialects? Or did they speak in unknown ecstatic utterances? Or did they speak in both actual languages and ecstatic utterances?

Meaning

Basic to any discipline is a study of the usages and meanings of relevant words. This study is especially important to the understanding of the biblical phenomenon of speaking in tongues. The key term is *glōssa,* the basis for several English words that relate to the tongue. Sometimes tongues-speaking is called "glossolalia" (a combination of "tongue" and "speak").

Occurrences. The Greek word *glōssa* occurs fifty times in the New

Testament. It is used fifteen times of the tongue, the physical organ in the mouth (for example, Mark 7:33, 35). It is used once of the tongue of the intermediate body, the body a person has between death and resurrection (Luke 16:24). It is used figuratively of "cloven tongues like as of fire" (Acts 2:3), and it is used once of the content of speaking in contrast to actions (1 John 3:18).

The Book of Revelation uses *glōssa* seven times in connection with peoples, nations, and multitudes to describe ethnic groups that are denoted by their ability to speak foreign languages (for example, Rev. 5:9).

Twenty-five times *glōssa* describes the phenomenon of speaking in tongues (for example, Mark 16:17; Acts 2:4–11; 1 Cor. 12:10 [twice]).

Thus the biblical writers used *glōssa* to denote six separate ideas; and yet these are related, for they all deal with the basic entity of speech, including its organ, action, content, language, and results.

Phrases. There is no set pattern in which *glōssa* is used to describe the phenomenon. It is present in nine different Greek constructions. Once it is set forth as "new tongues" (Mark 16:17). It is also called "other tongues" (Acts 2:4). It appears once as a plural noun with the definite article (literally, the "tongues" 1 Cor. 14:22), and twice it is a plural noun without the definite article (literally, "tongues" 12:10; 13:8). It is also used to indicate "kinds of tongues" or "diversities of tongues" (12:10, 28).

Most often it is used in the plural with the verb *laleō* ("to speak"): "speak in tongues" (for example, Acts 2:4, 11). It is also used in the singular with *laleō* and is rendered "speak in a tongue" (1 Cor. 14:2, 4, 13, 19, 27). Once it is used with the verb "to pray" ("to pray in a tongue," 14:14), and once it is used in the phrase "to have a tongue" (14:26).

Biblical Accounts

Acts 2:1–11. When the Holy Spirit filled the disciples on the Day of Pentecost, they "began to speak with other tongues as the Spirit gave them utterance." What were these other "tongues"? The listeners, who were devout Jews "from every nation under heaven," were confused "because everyone [of the devout Jews] heard them [the apostles] speak in his own language." The Greek word for "language" is *dialektos,* normally transliterated "dialect."

The unsaved multitude marveled at the phenomenon and asked, "Look, are not all these who speak Galileans? And how is it that we hear, each in our own language *[dialektos]* in which we were born?" Later they said, "We hear them speaking in our own tongues *[glōssa]* the wonderful works of God."

Thus the passage uses *glōssa* twice (2:4, 11) and *dialektos* twice (2:6, 8) to denote what was spoken. Luke, the author of Acts, used both terms to describe the phenomenon (2:4, 6), and the multitude, in their own quoted words, also used both terms to describe what they heard (2:8, 11). The evidence is clear: The Holy Spirit enabled the apostles from Galilee to speak in foreign languages and dialects. They did not speak in unknown ecstatic utterances.

Luke actually listed the countries from which the multitude had come: "Parthians and Medes and Elamites, those dwelling in Mesopotamia, Judea and Cappodocia, Pontus and Asia, Phrygia and Pamphylia, Egypt and the parts of Libya adjoining Cyrene, visitors from Rome, both Jews and proselytes, Cretans and Arabs" (2:9–11). There can be no doubt that the foreign languages and dialects spoken in these geographical areas were those spoken by the apostles.

Acts 10:44–48. Peter evangelized the Roman centurion Cornelius, his family, and his friends. When they believed in Christ for the remission of sins, the Holy Spirit fell on them (10:43–44). Peter's companions were amazed that God had saved the Gentiles and had given the Holy Spirit to them (10:45). The outward evidence that Cornelius and his associates had received the Spirit was the phenomenon of speaking in tongues. "For they heard them speak with tongues and magnify God" (10:46).

This glossolalia, like that on the Day of Pentecost, was in foreign languages, as identified by three facts. First, Luke used the same words to describe the phenomenon as he did in the earlier account (2:4, 11; 10:46). The natural impression left with readers of the two records is that the same phenomenon occurred. Second, how could Peter and his companions know that Cornelius and his household were magnifying God unless they could understand what they were saying? Third, in Peter's report to the Jerusalem church he said that the Gentiles had received the "same gift" and that the Spirit "came on them as he had come on us at the beginning" (11:15, 17, NIV). This reference to the Day of Pentecost extends not only to the fact of receiving the Spirit, but also to the nature of tongues-speaking in foreign languages.

Acts 19:1–7. On his third missionary journey Paul guided twelve disciples of John the Baptist into faith in Christ. After he baptized them and laid hands upon them, "the Holy Spirit came upon them, and they spoke with tongues and prophesied" (19:6). Since Luke again used the same Greek words to describe the phenomenon as in the earlier two accounts, the twelve must have spoken in known languages. There is no indication that they spoke in ecstatic utterances.

1 Corinthians 12–14. Many advocates of tongues-speaking admit that the speaking in the Book of Acts was foreign languages. However, they also argue that tongues-speaking in 1 Corinthians permits speaking in both unknown ecstatic utterances and foreign languages. I disagree with their position. An intensive study of both Acts and 1 Corinthians reveals that the tongues-speaking was the same in essence, the divinely given ability to speak in a known foreign language. Eight facts in 1 Corinthians 12–14 need to be noted.

First, Paul designated the gift as "kinds of tongues" (12:10) and "varieties of tongues" (12:28). "Kinds" and "diversities" render the same Greek word *genē,* which can refer to a family, offspring, race, nation, kind, sort, or class. It always depicts things that are related to each other. For example, there are many "kinds" of fish, but they are all fish (Matt. 13:47). There are several "kinds" of demons, but they are still demons (17:21). Thus there are many "kinds" of languages or tongues in the world, but they are all known languages. These languages are all related in that they have a definite vocabulary and grammatical syntax. Paul could not have possibly combined known foreign languages with unknown ecstatic utterances under the same classification. They simply are not related.

Second, Paul always connected the gift of tongues to the gift of interpretation (Greek, *hermeneia*) of tongues (1 Cor. 12:10; 14:26, 28). In noncharismatic passages the word refers to an exposition of Old Testament Scripture (Luke 24:27) or to a translation from one known foreign language to another (John 1:39, 43; 9:7; Heb. 7:2). In both cases it was an attempt to make clear through translation or explanation what was said in a known language. These usages must govern the meaning of the gift of interpretation. The interpretation of tongues-speaking was necessary in order to clarify what was said to the listeners.

Third, Paul wrote about a hypothetical situation: "Though I speak with the tongues of men and of angels, but have not love, I have become sounding brass or a clanging cymbal" (1 Cor. 13:1). Some use this verse to divide the tongues phenomenon into known earthly languages ("of men") and unknown heavenly languages ("of angels"). However, the noun "tongues" is used just once with "men" and "angels." That grammatical fact shows that human and angelic languages can be grouped together. They have something in common. They are both languages, known and understood. Whenever men and angels talked to each other in biblical times, they conversed intelligently in known languages without the need for someone to interpret.

Fourth, the insertion of the adjective "unknown" in the King James Version (KJV) is most unfortunate (14:2, 4, 13, 14, 19, 27). The adjective is not in the Greek text, but it appears in italics in the English translation. The translators apparently added this explanatory word because they thought the Corinthian tongues phenomenon was unknown ecstatic utterances. The presence of the italicized "unknown" conveys the wrong impression. It should not be used as an argument for the position of ecstatic utterances.

Fifth, Paul wrote, "For he who speaks in a tongue does not speak to men but to God, for no one understands him; however, in the spirit he speaks mysteries" (14:2). In this instance, Paul was saying that no one present in the service could understand the language of the tongues-speaker. Knowing what language groups were present, God caused the person to speak in a foreign language not represented in the group. Thus the gift of interpretation was always necessary when the gift of tongues was employed in a local service.

Sixth, Paul quoted from the prophet Isaiah (14:21; Isa. 28:11–12). This prophecy dealt with the time when the Assyrians invaded Israel and Judah (2 Kings 17–18). The Assyrians spoke both Assyrian and Hebrew to the unbelieving Jews. Since the "other tongues" were definitely known foreign languages (1 Cor. 14:21), the "tongues" as a sign to unbelievers must also have been known foreign languages (14:22).

Seventh, Luke wrote Acts in about A.D. 60 after Paul composed 1 Corinthians in A.D. 57. Luke was an associate of Paul. He doubtless heard the teachings of Paul and read the writings of the apostle, including 1 Corinthians. In Acts 2, 10 and 19, Luke used the same terms, *glōssa* ("tongue") and *laleō* ("to speak"), that Paul used to describe the phenomenon. Therefore, since foreign languages were spoken in the instances reported in Acts, foreign languages must have been spoken in Corinth also. If that were not the case, then Luke should have used different terms to describe the phenomenon.

Eighth, speaking in foreign languages that were not learned would constitute a divine miracle. Speaking in gibberish or in unknown sounds could easily be done by either a Christian or an unsaved person. In fact, a student who once was deeply involved in Pentecostalism spoke in unknown utterances in my presence. I asked him to do so, and he repeated several syllables over and over. He testified that his tongues-speaking was learned and developed over many years. *Glossolalia,* in the Bible, however, was a miracle that people could not duplicate.

PURPOSES

Why did people speak in tongues in biblical times? Are those same purposes accepted by the modern advocates of tongues-speaking? If not, what are the purposes of tongues in the contemporary movement?

The Pentecostal and Charismatic Positions

There are differences of opinion within these two groups as to the purposes of tongues-speaking. Some are major, whereas most are minor. However, three key purposes are generally agreed on.

Sign of the baptism in the Holy Spirit. Pentecostals view speaking in tongues as the sign that one has received the baptism in the Holy Spirit.

David du Plessis asserted that the Pentecostal movement teaches that "all Christians should receive the baptism in the Holy Spirit as they did on the Day of Pentecost according to Acts 2:4, with the evidence of speaking with other tongues as the Spirit gives utterance."[1]

There is some debate in charismatic circles whether speaking in tongues is *the* sign or simply *a* sign of the baptism in the Holy Spirit. Laurence Christenson, a Lutheran charismatic, wrote, "Many people have received the baptism with the Holy Spirit as a definite experience and reality. In their life and ministry there has been the unmistakable evidence of increased power and effectiveness. Yet they have not spoken in tongues."[2] Christenson still believes, though, that tongues-speaking is the normative sign and that believers would have more power if they did speak in tongues.

Is it true that the baptism in the Holy Spirit, evidenced by the ability to speak in tongues, gives greater charismatic power in use of spiritual gifts? I believe the answer is no, for three reasons. First, as agreed earlier, the baptism in the Holy Spirit is not a postconversion experience to be sought by a believer. It rather occurs at the time of conversion and places a believer into the body of Christ. Second, tongues-speakers today are not speaking in foreign languages and dialects, the genuine nature of the biblical phenomenon (except in a few rare cases in which a person may have had some previous exposure to a foreign language). Third, there is no proof from the experiences of tongues-speakers that they are more effective in ministry than those who do not speak in tongues.

Edification of the church. Both Pentecostals and charismatics usually distinguish between the sign of tongues-speaking and the gift of tongues-speaking. As the sign of the baptism in the Holy Spirit, tongues-speaking basically occurs once in the life of a believer, as in the Book of Acts. But 1 Corinthians refers to the gift of tongues-speaking, a spiritual gift to only some believers.

I agree with their theologians that the purposes of tongues-speaking in Acts and 1 Corinthians differ, but I disagree over the exact nature of those purposes. In actual practice, those differences are blurred in their congregations. The gift was to be exercised one at a time, with a maximum of three, and always accompanied by interpretation (1 Cor. 14:27). But in actual practice today, those regulations are violated constantly. In addition, as noted earlier, people who claim to have the gift of tongues are not speaking in foreign languages.

Personal prayer. In the charismatic movement, devotional tongues-speaking for self-edification has emerged as the dominant purpose. Christenson wrote, "One speaks in tongues, for the most part, in his private devotions. This is by far its most important use and value."[3] Such tongues-speaking, according to charismatics, can be done publicly or privately, and never needs interpretation. According to this view all who have been baptized in the Holy Spirit can speak, sing, or pray in tongues any time they choose. They say they each have their own "prayer-tongue," a series of sounds they can utter without understanding. Christenson added, "Although one does not know what he is saying as he speaks in tongues, he does have a clear sense that he is praying to God."[4]

In my opinion charismatics have arbitrarily created a distinction between the gift of tongues for public edification and the devotional use of tongues for private edification, a distinction that is not in 1 Corinthians 12–14.

Their usage of a private utterance to trigger spiritual euphoria comes very close to the usage of mantras to induce trances through transcendental meditation. It can even open up a believer to the world of deceiving spirits.

We believers are to pray and to worship with our total being—body, soul, spirit, mind, emotions, will, and consciousness. To pray without understanding is not biblical.

The Dispensational Position

Sign of the coming of the Holy Spirit. The apostles spoke with tongues when the Holy Spirit filled them, even as Jesus Christ had promised (for example, John 7:38–39; Acts 1:5–8). Cornelius, his family, and his friends spoke in tongues when the Spirit came on them as they believed in Christ (10:43–46). The twelve disciples of John the Baptist spoke in tongues when Paul laid his hands on them (19:1–7).

In these three historical events God introduced the Holy Spirit to three distinct groups: the apostles who were Jews, the Gentiles, and the twelve disciples of John the Baptist who were Old Testament saints. On all other occasions when people received Christ as their Savior, they received the indwelling of the Holy Spirit without speaking in tongues.

Sign to Israel. Paul wrote, "Therefore tongues are for a sign, not to those who believe but to unbelievers" (1 Cor. 14:22). In the context of spiritual gifts the gift of tongues was a sign to unbelieving Jews (14:21), a sign that God would judge them for their unbelief. God judged them when the Assyrians conquered Israel (722 B.C.); and in the future God would judge Israel with the destruction of Jerusalem by the Romans (A.D. 70). Thus the purpose of the sign-gift of tongues-speaking ceased with the Roman conquest.

Channel for divine revelation. "For he who speaks in a tongue does not speak to men but to God, for no one understands him; however, in the spirit he speaks mysteries" (1 Cor. 14:2). A biblical mystery was a divine truth that had not been known in past ages, but was revealed in the New Testament era. Both the nature of the universal church and the rapture of the church were mysteries revealed to Paul (15:51–58; Eph. 3:1–6). In the early church God enabled tongues-speakers to praise God for new revealed truth. That mystery then became clear when a believer with the gift of interpretation gave the translation of the foreign language. This mystery, now revealed, became a part of the standard of faith.

Edification of the church. All spiritual gifts were given so that the entire church would be edified by their use in the local church (1 Cor. 12:7; 14:26). When a person spoke in tongues, he himself was edified at that moment (14:4). However, that value was not the divinely intended purpose. In order for the church to receive edification, an interpretation had to be given (14:5).

IMPLICATIONS FOR US

First, we must accept the miraculous nature of the biblical phenomenon of speaking in tongues. We must realize that God caused believers to speak in foreign languages for divinely intended purposes.

Second, we must also admit that God could cause a believer to speak in tongues today. We must not limit His sovereign power. At the same time, we must seek to understand His normative purpose for believers in the church age today.

Third, we must evaluate all personal testimonies of tongues-speaking in the light of the Scriptures. We must determine whether they are produced by self, Satan, or the Spirit of God. We need to determine whether these proponents have indeed spoken in foreign languages and dialects.

Fourth, we must develop spiritual vitality in our own times of prayer and praise. We must become examples of Spirit-caused enthusiasm. It is not right for us to criticize others for wrongful excesses if we are not growing in our own devotional lives.

Fifth, we must minister in love as we seek to edify others. We must merge character with conduct.

CHAPTER FOURTEEN

The Holy Spirit and the Future

Evangelicals hold one of three major views relating to the millennium and the return of Christ. Postmillennialism teaches that through spiritual and social influence on the world the church will bring in the kingdom, and Christ will return to rule over the Christianized world. In this system of interpretation the ministry of the Holy Spirit in the future will be the same as it is in the present.

Amillennialism teaches that Christ will come at some indefinite point in the future at which time everyone will be ushered into eternity. In this system the ministry of the Holy Spirit will continue until the eternal state begins.

Both postmillennialism and amillennialism deny that Christ will rule on earth for a literal one thousand years. To them there will be no defined seven-year period of worldwide tribulation before Christ returns to the earth. They also deny that Christ will rule on earth over national Israel and see no distinction between God's program for Israel and that for the church.

In contrast, dispensational premillennialists teach that there is a distinction between God's plan for Israel and His program for the church. We believe in the literal fulfillment of Daniel's seventieth week, commonly known as the Tribulation (Dan. 9:24–27). We affirm that Christ will return to the earth after that seven-year period and that He will reign from Jerusalem over redeemed Israel for a literal thousand years (Rev. 20:1–6). In this system the Holy Spirit will have a different ministry in the future than He has today.

AT THE RAPTURE

The Holy Spirit Will Complete the Formation of the Church

When Jesus Christ announced that He would build His church, He revealed a new program (Matt. 16:18). The church, the body of Christ, consists of saved Jews and saved Gentiles, made one in Christ through the baptism in the Holy Spirit (1 Cor. 12:13; Eph. 2:11–22). The foundation of the church is the death, resurrection, and ascension of Christ (Matt. 16:18–21; Eph. 1:20–23). From His ascended position Christ sent the Holy Spirit. Believers thus were first baptized in the Holy Spirit on the Day of Pentecost (Acts 2:1–4). Whenever a sinner in this church age believes in Jesus Christ for salvation, he is immediately baptized in the Holy Spirit into the body of Christ.

Jesus Christ will come someday to take the church to Himself (1 Thess. 4:13–18). When the last sinner is converted in this church age, the body of Christ will be completed, and the ministry of the baptism in the Holy Spirit will end at the Rapture. Although people will be saved after the Rapture, they will not become members of the body of Christ.

He Will Remove His Restraint of Sin

In his correspondence with new believers in Thessalonica, Paul discussed these topics of eschatology: the Rapture (1 Thess. 4:13–18), the Day of the Lord (5:1–11), the man of sin, also known as the Antichrist (2 Thess. 2:3–4), and the return of Christ to the earth (2:8).

When will the Antichrist manifest himself? Paul explained, "And now you know what is restraining, that he may be revealed in his own time. For the mystery of lawlessness is already at work; only He who now restrains will do so until He is taken out of the way. And then the lawless one will be revealed, whom the Lord will consume with the breath of His mouth and destroy with the brightness of His coming (2:6–8). Someone or something is restraining the revelation of this future satanic leader. He or it must be more powerful than the Antichrist or Satan. The only one who is more powerful is God. In what sense, however, will He be taken away?

The phrase "what is restraining" is the translation of *to katechon,* a verbal participle of neuter gender. The phrase "he who restrains" is *ho katechōn,* a verbal participle of the masculine gender. Apparently, both the work (neuter) and the person (masculine) of the restrainer is presented in this passage. In the Greek New Testament both masculine and neuter pronouns are used of the Holy Spirit. The word *pneuma* ("spirit") is in the neuter gender, but the Spirit is an eternal Person.

The Spirit thus is the Restrainer, and He does His work of restraining through the church. When the church is removed from the earth at the Rapture, then the presence of the Spirit in church-age believers will also be removed. He will leave earth even as He came to the earth.

The Holy Spirit was present on earth before He came to fulfill distinctive ministries on the Day of Pentecost. In the Old Testament era He convicted and regenerated sinners. After the Rapture He will have a ministry similar to that in the age before the church began; He will continue to convict and regenerate sinners.

IN THE TRIBULATION

The "Tribulation" refers to the entire seven-year period that will occur between the Rapture of the church and the second coming of Christ to the earth. It is a synonym for the seventieth week of Daniel, the climax of God's program for Israel (Dan. 9:24–27).

The Holy Spirit Will Save Both Jews and Gentiles

As noted above, the Holy Spirit convicted and regenerated sinners in the Old Testament era. The seven-year Tribulation period is the extension and climax of God's program for Israel which began in the old period (Dan. 9:24–27). Thus the Spirit will do in the future what He has done in the past.

In the Olivet Discourse, Christ described what would happen in the seven-year period just before His return to the earth (Matt. 24:25). In the parable of the sheep and the goats, the sheep represent the saved Gentiles of the Tribulation who will show kindness to the persecuted Jews (25:31–46). Modern Israelis would call them "the righteous Gentiles." In the parable of the virgins the five wise virgins symbolize the saved Jews who will be ready to meet the returning Christ (25:1–13).

In John's visions recorded in the Book of Revelation he saw 144,000 sealed servants of God, who were from the twelve tribes of Israel (Rev. 7:4–8). Through the ministry of the Spirit, God will save these Jews in the Tribulation period. John also saw "a great multitude which no one could number, of all nations, tribes, peoples, and tongues, standing before the throne and before the Lamb" (7:9). This description includes both Jews and Gentiles. They are the saved ones who will come out of the great tribulation, and [will have] washed their robes and made them white in the blood of the Lamb" (7:14). Because the Holy Spirit is God, He is omnipresent. So, even though He will leave the world in the Rapture, no longer indwelling the church, He will still be on earth, regenerating sinners as He did in prior ages.

He Will Energize God's Servants

No one can serve God out of his own energy. We are not sufficient in ourselves (2 Cor. 3:5). Thus the 144,000 Jewish servants in the Tribulation will serve by the power of the Spirit (Rev. 7:3–8).

God will also use two witnesses for a ministry of three and a half years (11:3–12). These anonymous witnesses will prophesy and perform miracles. In fact, they will do what Moses and Elijah once did: prevent rain from falling, turn water into blood, and smite the earth with plagues. Since Moses and Elijah were empowered by the Holy Spirit, it is reasonable to assume that the two witnesses will have the same power of the Spirit. The two witnesses are likened to two olive trees and two lampstands, an analogy used of the priest Joshua and the leader Zerubbabel, who guided the returning Jews to rebuild the temple (Zech. 4:1–14). These two Old Testament leaders were encouraged by these words: "This is the word of the LORD to Zerubbabel: 'Not by might, nor by power, but by My Spirit,' says the LORD of hosts" (Zech. 4:6). The two witnesses in the Tribulation will also minister by the power of the Spirit of God.

He Will Be Poured Out on Israel

Through the prophet Joel God said to Israel, "And it shall come to pass afterward that I will pour out My Spirit on all flesh; your sons and your daughters shall prophesy, your old men shall dream dreams, your young men shall see visions. And also on My menservants and on My maidservants I will pour out My Spirit in those days" (Joel 2:28–29). The phrase "all flesh" specifically included these groups within Israel: sons, daughters, old men, young men, male servants, and female servants.

The outpouring will be accompanied by "wonders in the heavens and in the earth: blood and fire and pillars of smoke, the sun shall be turned into darkness, and the moon into blood" (2:30–31).

Since Peter quoted this prophecy from Joel in his sermon on the Day of Pentecost, Pentecostals and charismatics claim that the prophecy was fulfilled on that day. However, as noted earlier, the visible phenomena did not occur then. There was an outpouring of the Spirit on the Day of Pentecost, but it simply manifested the power of the risen Messiah. In the future God will pour out the Spirit on Israel at the end of the Tribulation period when Christ returns.

He Will Prepare Israel for the Coming of Christ

Israel will enter the seven-year Tribulation, also known as "the time of Jacob's trouble" (Jer. 30:7), in an unsaved condition. In that difficult time, two-thirds of Israel will die (Zech. 13:8–9). Six million Jews died during the Nazi Holocaust (1939–1945), but even more will lose their lives at the hands of the Antichrist. Christ said it would be the worst period of persecution in the history of the world (Matt. 24:21).

Yet God will protect and save the surviving one-third (Jer. 30:7; Zech. 13:9). Israel will call on the name of the Lord and be saved (Joel 2:32; Zech. 13:9). Israel will be delivered when they see Christ returning to the earth (Rom. 11:26), and they will exclaim, "Blessed is He who comes in the name of the Lord!" (Matt. 23:39).

Christ told Nicodemus that a person had to be born of the Spirit in order to enter the kingdom of God (John 3:3–8). Thus Israelites will be born of the Spirit during the tribulation and at the return of Christ in order to enter the spiritual-political kingdom over which Christ will rule.

IN THE MILLENNIUM

The words "one thousand years" occur six times in the Scriptures (Rev. 20:2–9). The word *Millennium* is based on the Latin *mille* ("one thousand") and *annus* ("year"). Though the words "one thousand years" do not occur in the Old Testament, prophecies in the Old Testament do describe the millennial period. When Jesus Christ returns to the earth after the seventieth week of Daniel (Dan. 9:24–27), He will destroy the Antichrist and the wicked nations at the Battle of Armageddon (Rev. 19:11–21). He will then rule on the earth for one thousand years.

The Holy Spirit Will Energize the Reigning Christ

In a prophecy dealing with the blessings of the millennial kingdom, Isaiah wrote, "There shall come forth a Rod from the stem of Jesse, and a Branch shall grow out of his roots. The Spirit of the LORD shall rest upon Him, the Spirit of wisdom and understanding, the Spirit of counsel and might, the Spirit of knowledge and of the fear of the LORD" (Isa. 11:1–2). The Spirit of God came on Jesus at His baptism and remained on Him throughout His earthly ministry. The Spirit still remains on Him today and will continue to be on Him throughout His future earthly reign.

He Will Indwell Believers

God promised to make a New Covenant with Israel (Jer. 31:31–37; Ezek. 36:24–32), a covenant that will ultimately be fulfilled in the millennial kingdom. The blessings of that covenant include national restoration and unity in the Promised Land, the divine writing of God's law on the redeemed Israelites' minds and hearts, pure worship, forgiveness of sin, and material prosperity. In addition God promised, "I will give you a new heart and put a new spirit within you; I will take the heart of stone out of your flesh and give you a heart of flesh. I will put My Spirit within you and cause you to walk in My statutes, and you will keep My judgments and do them" (36:26–27). In the Millennium all believers will be permanently indwelt by the Holy Spirit, who will enable them to obey all of God's commands.

IMPLICATIONS FOR US

First, we must realize that a present task of the Holy Spirit is to complete the formation of the church. Believers are to be involved in that divine task by witnessing and evangelizing. Since the Rapture is imminent, we must be zealous in our attempts to win the lost.

Second, we must be holy channels through whom the Holy Spirit can restrain sin. We must be salt and light. We must not contribute to the moral decline of the world or the coldness of the church.

Third, we must pray for the peace of Jerusalem. We must love Israel, the covenant people of God. We must support the outreach of the gospel to the Jewish world.

CHAPTER FIFTEEN

A Final Word

Both pastors and lay leaders must have lives and ministries controlled by the Holy Spirit. Without dependence on Him, we are doomed to failure. Filled by Him, we can have spiritual success in the following areas.

First, we will have that conviction that God wants us to be leaders (Acts 20:28; 1 Cor. 12:7; Eph. 4:11; 1 Tim. 3:1). We will know that God has gifted us and has placed us into distinctive areas of ministry.

Second, our ministry will be centered in the Word of God (Acts 20:32; 1 Cor. 2:1–13; 2 Tim. 3:16–4:2). We will preach, teach, and share what the Holy Spirit directed the authors of Scripture to write. We will stress His Word, not our personal opinions.

Third, we will be people of integrity proclaiming the truth (2 Cor. 4:2–3). We will be aware of our human inadequacy and the sufficiency of the Spirit at the same time (3:5–6). We will work and pray that our ministries will result in others coming to Christ and becoming Christlike.

Fourth, we will desire to be blameless in all our relationships so "that our ministry may not be blamed (6:3).

Fifth, we will witness to the gospel of Jesus Christ with confidence and authority (John 15:26–27; 16:7–8; Acts 1:8; 4:8–13). We will not fear being rejected or persecuted by the unsaved.

Sixth, we will pursue holiness (2 Cor. 7:1; Gal. 5:16–23; Eph. 5:18–21; 1 Thess. 5:19), and not succumb to the temptations of sin.

Seventh, we will strive to maintain spiritual oneness in Christ (Eph. 2:11–22; 4:1–6). We will respect ecclesiastical differences, but we will stress our redemptive position in Christ and in the body of Christ, the church.

Eighth, we will promote peace in all relationships (Rom. 14:17; 15:13; Gal. 5:22), as ambassadors of reconciliation.

Ninth, we will be people of joy (Rom. 14:17; 15:13; Phil. 4:4), full of spiritual enthusiasm and optimism and rejoicing in our victory through Christ.

Tenth, we will be yielded to the Holy Spirit and to the authority of the Scriptures (Eph. 5:18; Col. 3:16). We will surrender our wills and ambitions to God in order to glorify Him through our Lord Jesus Christ.

It is my prayer and hope that we believers will become all God has planned for us—through the ministry of the Holy Spirit.

ENDNOTES

Chapter 1— The Personality of the Holy Spirit

1. Sinclair B. Ferguson, *The Holy Spirit* (Downers Grove, Ill.: InterVarsity, 1996), 12.

Chapter 2—The Deity of the Holy Spirit

1. Millard J. Erickson, *Christian Theology* (Grand Rapids: Baker, 1985), 3:857.
2. His role in our salvation will be presented in greater detail in later chapters.
3. Loraine Boettner, *Studies in Theology* (Philadelphia, N.J.: Presbyterian and Reformed, 1964), 109.
4. Ibid., 106–7.

Chapter 3—The Symbols of the Holy Spirit

1. For a full discussion of Jesus' many figures of speech, see Roy B. Zuck, *Teaching as Jesus Taught* (Grand Rapids: Baker, 1995), 183–202.

2. For more on the sealing of the Holy Spirit see Eldon Woodcock, "The Seal of the Holy Spirit," *Bibliotheca Sacra* 155 (April–June 1998): 139–63.

Chapter 4—The Ministry of the Holy Spirit in the Old Testament

1. Ferguson, *The Holy Spirit*, 21.
2. Merrill F. Unger, *Unger's Commentary on the Old Testament* (Chicago: Moody, 1981), 1:36.
3. John F. Walvoord, *The Holy Spirit*, 3d ed. (Findlay, Ohio: Dunham, 1958), 76.

Chapter 5—The Ministry of the Holy Spirit in Inspiration

1. Walvoord, *The Holy Spirit*, 58.
2. R. C. Sproul, *Explaining Inerrancy: A Commentary* (Oakland, Calif.: International Council on Biblical Inerrancy, 1980), 18.
3. Ibid., 16.
4. Ferguson, *The Holy Spirit*, 70.
5. Charles Hodge, *An Exposition of the First Epistle to the Corinthians* (reprint, Grand Rapids: Eerdmans, 1974), 40.

Chapter 7—The Ministry of the Holy Spirit in the Life of Christ

1. For a thorough discussion of the Incarnation and Jesus' virgin birth, see my book *The Virgin Birth: Doctrine of Deity* (Grand Rapids: Baker, 1981).
2. Walvoord, *The Holy Spirit*, 92.
3. Ibid., 101.
4. Ibid., 103.
5. For more on this subject see Robert P. Lightner, *Angels, Satan, and Demons*, Swindoll Leadership Library (Nashville: Word, 1998), 99–102.
6. "Interesting Facts about the Assemblies of God," *Pentecostal Evangel*, 16 September 1962, 12.

7. D. V. Hurst, "How to Receive the Baptism with the Holy Ghost," *Pentecostal Evangel,* 26 April 1964, 7–9.
8. Ferguson, *The Holy Spirit,* 37.
9. For more on the Holy Spirit's teaching ministry see Roy B. Zuck, *Spirit-Filled Teaching: The Power of the Holy Spirit in Your Ministry,* Swindoll Leadership Library (Nashville: Word, 1998), 11–47.
10. Walvoord, *The Holy Spirit,* 83.

Chapter 8—The Ministry of the Holy Spirit in the Book of Acts

1. Henry Alford, *The Greek Testament* (1894; reprint, Chicago: Moody, 1958), 2:13.
2. F. F. Bruce, *Commentary on the Book of Acts* (Grand Rapids: Eerdmans, 1954), 181. Also see "Tongues" in *Zondervan Pictorial Bible Dictionary,* ed. Merrill C. Tenney (Grand Rapids: Zondervan, n.d.), 859–60.
3. Carl Brumback, "*What Meaneth This?*" (Springfield, Mo.: Gospel, 1947), 214.
4. The word *deacon* comes from the Greek noun *diakonia* ("distribution") and verb *diakoneō* ("serve").

Chapter 9—The Baptism in the Holy Spirit

1. R. A. Torrey, *The Baptism with the Holy Spirit* (New York: Revell, 1897), 24.
2. Vinson Synan, *The Holiness-Pentecostal Movement* (Grand Rapids: Eerdmans, 1971).
3. Klaude Kendrick, *The Promise Fulfilled* (Springfield, Mo.: Gospel, 1961), 37.
4. David duPlessis, *The Spirit Bade Me Go* (Oakland, Calif.: By the author, n.d.), 9.
5. Ibid.
6. Howard Ervin, *These Are Not Drunken as Ye Suppose* (Plainfield, N.J.: Logos, n.d.), 46.
7. duPlessis, *The Spirit Bade Me Go,* 70 (italics his).

8. Laurence Christenson, *Speaking in Tongues* (Minneapolis: Bethany Fellowship, 1968), 55.

Chapter 10—The Indwelling and Filling of the Holy Spirit

1. Walvoord, *The Holy Spirit*, 155.
2. Andrew Reed, "Spirit Divine, Hear Our Prayer," in *The Hymnal* (Waco, Tex.: Word, 1986), 615.
3. Walvoord, *The Holy Spirit*, 189.
4. Andreas J. Kostenberger, "What Does It Mean to Be Filled with the Spirit?" *Journal of the Evangelical Theological Society* 40 (June 1997): 232.
5. Lewis Sperry Chafer, *Systematic Theology*, abridged, ed. John F. Walvoord (Wheaton, Ill.: Victor, 1988), 1:273.
6. William D. Longstaff, "Take Time to Be Holy," in *The Hymnal* (Waco, Tex.: Word, 1986), 441.
7. Stanley D. Toussaint, "The Filling of the Spirit," in *Basic Theology Applied*, ed. John R. Masters and Wesley R. Willis (Wheaton, Ill.: Victor, 1995), 213.
8. Ibid.

Chapter 11—The Holy Spirit and His Ministry In Believers

1. See my book *Salvation Is Forever* (Schaumburg, Ill.: Regular Baptist, 1989).
2. Ferguson, *The Holy Spirit*, 12.
3. *Apekdechomai*, "eagerly wait for," occurs seven times, in Romans 8:19, 23, 25; 1 Corinthians 1:7; Galatians 5:5; Philippians 3:20; and Hebrews 9:28.
4. See Renald E. Showers, *The New Nature* (Neptune, N.J.: Loizeaux, 1986).
5. Ibid., 41.
6. For an excellent book on the subject, see Zuck, *Spirit-Filled Teaching*.
7. Ibid., 110–11.

8. Ibid. 112. See also Roy B. Zuck, *Basic Bible Interpretation* (Wheaton, Ill.: Victor, 1991), 23–25.
9. Charles R. Swindoll, *Flying Closer to the Flame* (Dallas: Word, 1993), 42–50.

Chapter 12—The Gifts of the Holy Spirit

1. James L. Boyer, "The Office of the Prophet in New Testament Times," *Grace Journal* 1 (Spring 1960): 17.
2. Charles C. Ryrie, *The Holy Spirit* (Chicago: Moody, 1997), 125.
3. Ibid.
4. Ferguson, *The Holy Spirit*, 211.
5. Erickson, *Christian Theology*, 3:876.
6. See Zuck, *Spirit-Filled Teaching.*
7. Ryrie, *The Holy Spirit*, 124.
8. Walvoord, *The Holy Spirit*, 168.
9. Ibid., 188.
10. Donald Gee, *Concerning Spiritual Gifts* (Springfield, Mo.: Gospel, n.d.), 9.
11. Ryrie, *The Holy Spirit*, 127.
12. See Gary W. Derickson, "The Cessation of Healing Miracles in Paul's Ministry," *Bibliotheca Sacra* 155 (July–September 1998): 299–315.

Chapter 13—Speaking in Tongues

1. duPlessis, *The Spirit Bade Me Go*, 9.
2. Laurence Christenson, *Speaking in Tongues*, 55.
3. Ibid., 28.
4. Ibid.

BIBLIOGRAPHY

Edgar, Thomas R. *Satisfied by the Promise of the Spirit.* Grand Rapids: Kregel Resources, 1996.

Ferguson, Sinclair B. *The Holy Spirit.* Downers Grove, Ill.: InterVarsity Press, 1996.

Gromacki, Robert G. *The Modern Tongues Movement.* Phillipsburg, N.J.: Presbyterian and Reformed Publishing Co., 1967.

Laney, J. Carl. *God.* Swindoll Leadership Library. Nashville: Word Publishing, 1999.

MacArthur, John F., Jr. *Charismatic Chaos.* Grand Rapids: Zondervan Publishing House, 1992.

Ryrie, Charles C. *The Holy Spirit.* Chicago: Moody Press, 1997.

Showers, Renald E. *The New Nature.* Neptune, N.J.: Loizeaux Brothers, 1986.

Stott, John R. *The Baptism and Fullness of the Holy Spirit.* Downers Grove, Ill.: InterVarsity Press, 1971.

Swindoll, Charles R. *Flying Closer to the Flame.* Dallas: Word Publishing, 1993.

Synan, Vinson. *The Holiness-Pentecostal Movement.* Grand Rapids: Wm. B. Eerdmans Publishing Co., 1971.

Unger, Merrill F. *The Baptizing Work of the Holy Spirit.* Chicago: Scripture Press, 1953.

Walvoord, John F. *The Holy Spirit.* 3d ed. Findlay, Ohio: Dunham Publishing Co., 1958.

———. *The Holy Spirit at Work Today*. Chicago: Moody Press, 1973.

Zuck, Roy B. *Spirit-Filled Teaching: The Power of the Holy Spirit in Your Ministry.* Swindoll Leadership Library. Nashville: Word Publishing, 1998.

SCRIPTURE INDEX

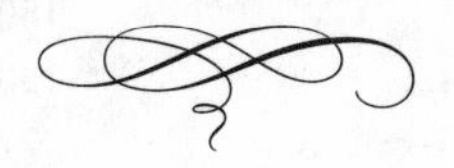

SUBJECT INDEX

The
Swindoll Leadership Library

Angels, Satan and Demons
Dr. Robert Lightner

The supernatural world gets a lot of attention these days in books, movies and television series, but what does the Bible say about these other-worldly beings? Dr. Robert Lightner answers these questions with an in-depth look at the world of the "invisible" as expressed in Scripture.

The Church
Dr. Ed Hayes

In this indispensable guide, Dr. Ed Hayes explores the labyrinths of the church, delving into her history, doctrines, rituals and resources to find out what it means to be the Body of Christ on earth. Both passionate and precise, this essential volume offers solid insights on worship, persecution, missions and morality: a bold call to unity and renewal.

Color Outside the Lines
Dr. Howard G. Hendricks

Just as the apostle Paul prodded early Christians "not to be conformed" to the world, Dr. Howard Hendricks vividly—and unexpectedly—extends that biblical theme and charges us to learn the art of living creatively, reflecting the image of the Creator rather than the culture.

Empowered Leaders
Dr. Hans Finzel

What is leadership really about? The rewards, excitement and exhilaration? Or the responsibilities, frustrations and exhausting nights? Dr. Hans Finzel takes readers on a journey into the lives of the Bible's great leaders, unearthing powerful principles for effective leadership in any situation.

End Times

Dr. John F. Walvoord

Long regarded as one of the top prophecy experts, Dr. John F. Walvoord now explores world events in light of biblical prophecy. By examining all of the prophetic passages in the Bible, Walvoord clearly explains the mystery behind confusing verses and conflicting viewpoints. This is the definitive work on prophecy for Bible students.

The Forgotten Blessing

Dr. Henry Holloman

For many Christians, the gift of God's grace is central to their faith. But another gift—sanctification—is often overlooked. *The Forgotten Blessing* clarifies this essential doctrine, showing us what it means to be set apart, and how the process of sanctification can forever change our relationship with God.

God

Dr. J. Carl Laney

With tenacity and clarity, Dr. J. Carl Laney makes it plain: it's not enough to know *about* God. We can know *God* better. This book presents a practical path to life-changing encounters with the goodness, greatness and glory of our Creator.

The Holy Spirit

Dr. Robert Gromacki

In *The Holy Spirit,* Dr. Robert Gromacki examines the personality, deity, symbols and gifts of the Holy Spirit, while recapping the ministry of the Spirit throughout the Old Testament, the Gospel Era, the life of Christ, the Book of Acts and the lives of believers.

HUMANITY AND SIN

Dr. Robert A. Pyne

Sin may seem like an outdated concept these days, but its consequences remain as destructive as ever. Dr. Robert A. Pyne takes a close look at humankind through the pages of Scripture and the lens of modern culture. As never before, readers will understand sin's overarching effect on creation and our world today.

IMMANUEL

Dr. John A. Witmer

Dr. John A. Witmer presents the almighty Son of God as a living, breathing, incarnate man. He shows us a full picture of the Christ in four distinct phases: the Son of God before He became man, the divine suffering man on Earth, the glorified and ascended Christ, and the reigning King today.

A LIFE OF PRAYER

Dr. Paul Cedar

Dr. Paul Cedar explores prayer through three primary concepts, showing us how to consider, cultivate and continue a lifestyle of prayer. This volume helps readers recognize the unlimited potential and the awesome purpose of prayer.

MINISTERING TO TODAY'S ADULTS

Dr. Kenn Gangel

After 40 years of research and experience, Dr. Kenn Gangel knows what it takes to reach adults. In an easy-to-grasp, easy-to-apply style, Gangel offers proven systematic strategies for building dynamic adult ministries.

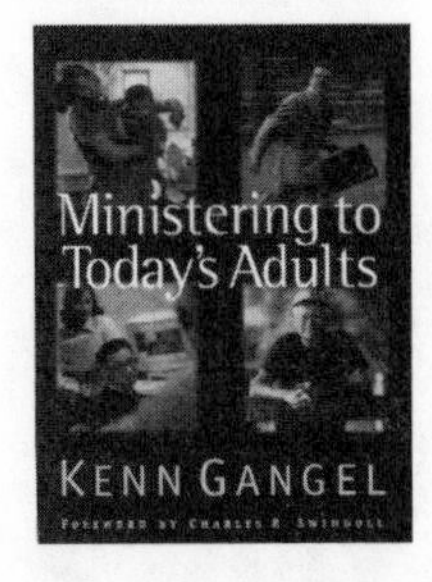

Moral Dilemmas

J. Kerby Anderson

Should biblically informed Christians be for or against capital punishment? How should we as Christians view abortion, euthanasia, genetic engineering, divorce, and technology? In this comprehensive, cutting-edge book, J. Kerby Anderson challenges us to thoughtfully analyze the dividing issues facing our age, while equipping believers to maneuver through the ethical and moral land mines of our times.

Spirit-Filled Teaching

Dr. Roy B. Zuck

Whether you teach a small Sunday school class or a standing-room-only crowd at a major university, the process of teaching can be demanding and draining. This lively book brings a new understanding of the Holy Spirit's essential role in teaching.

Tale of the Tardy Oxcart and 1501 Other Stories

Dr. Charles R. Swindoll

In this rich volume, you'll have access to resourcing Dr. Charles Swindoll's favorite anecdotes on prayer or quotations for grief. In *The Tale of the Tardy Oxcart,* thousands of illustrations are arranged by subjects alphabetically for quick-and-easy access. A perfect resource for all pastors and speakers.

Women and the Church

Dr. Lucy Mabery-Foster

Women and the Church provides an overview of the historical, biblical and cultural perspectives on the unique roles and gifts women bring to the church, while exploring what it takes to minister to women today. Important insight for any leader seeking to understand how to more effectively minister to women and build women's ministries in the local church.